PAPERS ON LEXICOGRAPHY AND DICTIONARIES

Perspectives in Lexicography: Asia and beyond

New and selected papers from the Fourth ASIALEX
International Conference, National University of Singapore, 2005

Editors
Vincent B.Y. Ooi · Anne Pakir · Ismail S. Talib · Peter K.W. Tan

KDICTIONARIES

PAPERS ON LEXICOGRAPHY AND DICTIONARIES • 1

Series Editor: Ilan J. Kernerman

Perspectives in Lexicography: Asia and beyond

Editors: Vincent B.Y. Ooi • Anne Pakir • Ismail S. Talib • Peter K.W. Tan

ISBN: 978-965-90207-1-3

Published in Tel Aviv.

© 2009 K DICTIONARIES LTD All rights reserved.

No part of this publication may be reproduced, stored in a retrieval system, or transmitted, in any form or by any means, without the prior permission in writing of K Dictionaries Ltd.

Graphic Design: Studio Orna Cohen

http://kdictionaries.com

Contents

Introduction • *Vincent B.Y. Ooi*   7

Asian perspectives

Lexical concerns about neologism in Chinese lexicography • *Yihua Zhang*   9

A survey of pragmatic information in bilingual English-Chinese learners' dictionaries • *Saihong Li*   25

Grammatical class, tags and lemmas: A corpus-based study of the Malay lexicon • *Gerry Knowles and Zuraidah Mohd Don*   39

Analysing *sorrow* and *grief*: A contrastive-semantic perspective • *Ruihua Zhang*   51

Lexical innovations in the multimodal Corpus of Asian Magazine Advertising • *Andrew Moody and Azirah Hashim*   69

Pedagogical perspectives

EFL dictionaries on the Web: Students' appraisal and issues in the Cambridge, Longman, and Oxford dictionaries • *Shigeru Yamada*   87

The potential of learner corpora for pedagogical lexicography • *Yukio Tono*   105

A trilingual dictionary for learners of Cantonese, English and Putonghua • *Jacqueline Lam, Lan Li and Tom McArthur*   117

Electronic dictionaries in the classroom • *Shinya Ozawa and James Ronald*   129

The benefits of CD-ROM dictionaries in teaching • *Monika Szirmai*   139

Dictionary use strategies by EFL learners in Taiwan • *Da-Fu Huang*   149

English learners' dictionaries: An undervalued resource • *Julia Miller*   161

Multiple word class entries in advanced learner's dictionaries of English • *Sadayuki Nakane*   173

Representation of word combinations in illustrative examples in English learners' dictionaries • *Hai Xu*   183

Not quite first language, not quite second language either: Dictionary entries for learners caught in between • *Peter K.W. Tan*   193

General perspectives

Interlingual lexicography, with special reference to research priorities
• *R.R.K. Hartmann*   203

Internet-based communication and the ecology of dictionaries
• *Wengao Gong*   213

Relational network notation and the intelligent Web
• *Jonathan J. Webster and Ian C. Chow*   225

Putting the corpus into the dictionary • *Adam Kilgarriff*   239

Towards a multimodal dictionary of narration • *Ismail S. Talib*   249

References   259

Index   281

Editors and Contributors   287

Introduction

This volume contains a balanced selection of revised papers from the 4th ASIALEX (Asian Association for Lexicography) Conference, held in Singapore from 1-3 June, 2005, as well as new ones, that comprise three complementary strands or perspectives: Asian, Pedagogical, and General.

In practice, all three strands are often present and reinforce one another in most of the papers found in this volume. Such is the nature of multi-disciplinary knowledge, that a paper classified under a particular strand can arguably be said to belong to another. The 'Asian' strand reflects an engagement with an Asian culture, such as Chinese or Malay, and the attendant interaction between English and the Asian language in question. The 'Pedagogy' strand focuses on the strategies that the dictionary can provide learners in order to increase their linguistic competence, and shows that lexicography has direct and practical relevance to the wider community of users. Finally, the 'General' strand contains methodologies and sources of data for studying the lexicon, and a number of papers take cognizance of the fact that we live in a world in which the computer is often indispensable to everyone.

The chapters in this volume, collectively embracing all the three strands, affirm the view that the lexicon is the central repository of language and its study leads to an indispensable connection between the lexicon and other levels of linguistics: phonetics, phonology, morphology, syntax, semantics, pragmatics and discourse.

We wish you an enjoyable read, which is made possible only because the international contributors to this volume have been patient with us by running through their drafts time and again in the course of this two-year project. It has not been easy to assemble a volume in which different academic practices are often in tension (including the more "correct" way to cite a dictionary). The common bibliography of over twenty pages invites an acquaintance of not-so-familiar dictionaries and the vast scholarly citations on which the volume stands.

It remains for us to thank the following: Associate Professor Robbie Goh, Head of the Department of English Language and Literature, National University of Singapore, for his support of this book project; the Asia Research Institute at the National University of Singapore, for their indispensable support that enabled the ASIALEX 2005 Conference to take place at the time; our part-time student assistants, Bai Shuping and Yvonne Lo, for their hard work on the volume; and, not least, Ilan Kernerman, who is indefatigable in his promotion of all matters lexicographic in nature.

Vincent B.Y. Ooi (for the editors)

Lexical concerns about neologism in Chinese lexicography

Yihua Zhang
Guangdong University of Foreign Studies
bilex@mail.gdufs.edu.cn

1. Introduction

In the last decade, both globalization and the Internet have brought about lots of changes in the Chinese language: new words (terms) and new expressions can be found in large numbers in every communication medium. Especially with the coming of the cyberage, the rate of spread of new words has increased tremendously. Along with other communication media, not only do thousands of new words from all domains in the Chinese-based Internet come about annually but approximately 1200 to 1500 of them also become 'fixed'. Within a short span of 20 years, the Chinese language has accumulated a large quantity of new words including loan words and lettered words, so that the Chinese writing style seems to have experienced a great change. Let us look at the following examples:

> **APEC**记者招待会后，我约了**STV**的记者和一群**MBA**、**MPA**研究生朋友，讨论中国加入**WTO**后**IT**业对**GDP**的影响。读**MBA**的张小姐本来想去**.COM**当**CEO**，但觉得**IT**业风险大，转而想去**Nike**公司。读**MPA**的李先生却认为加入**WTO**后政府职能将大有改变。随后大家相约关掉**BP**机，也不上**Internet**的**QQ**和**BBS**聊天，而是去了**KTV**唱卡拉**OK**......
> (The People's Daily, 20 April 2005)

This is a piece of news report quoted by a professor to criticize the abuse of lettered words in Chinese newspapers. Even if this report were translated to English without the acronyms being explained, native English speakers can not quite understand the passage. Such a phenomenon is rather common. When I randomly picked two official newspapers from my bookshelf and went through them quickly, the following lettered words leapt to my eyes:

(1) Guang Ming Daily (31 March 2005): NEC, CMMI, Erwin Neher, DNA, RNA, HOTHEAD, HDTV, CDT, LCD, TFT, GDP, TCL, MP3, IT, PC, CD, DVD, PRGR, COMBO, CNGI, DRW, CD-ROM, DVD-ROM, PSV,

IPv, Show NET, QQ, PDA, CPU, XL, VOIP, RFID; the mixed lettered words: 'U盘', 'E考通', 'T计划', etc.

(2) Nan Fang Daily (26 March 2005): 3+X, KTF, KT, MPL, ARD, CPI, ST, CCTV, GDTY, OTC, NBA, CBA, initialized economy, pay-per-click, Google, Monster.com, COTTON US, CD; the mixed lettered words: X光, B超, A股, B股, AA制, 卡拉OK, IT行 业, J.K罗琳.

The above-cited lettered words involve general names, technical terms as well as commodity names, company names, people names, trademarks, etc. In addition to these, there are lots of other borrowed words. It goes even further on the Web; when you browse a Chinese website at random, you can see many foreign words mixed with Chinese characters.

2. Distribution characteristics of new words

The new terms involve mainly content words: most of them are nouns and verbs, and no function words have been found. As for word-formation, compound words (including acronyms and initialisms) are by far more numerous than simple words. According to the *Electronic Dictionary of Contemporary Chinese Neologisms*, the distribution of new words is as follows:

Table 1

Items	Dist. number	Percent	Items	Dist. number	Percent	Items	Dist. number	Percent
daily life	13502	34.93	social field	9693	25.07	economics	2970	7.68
politics	2899	7.50	culture	2094	5.42	science/technology	1608	4.16
education	1405	1.51	agriculture	814	2.11	sanitation	794	2.05
military	715	1.85	sports	582	1.51	law	520	1.35
business	520	1.35	industry	410	1.06			

To our surprise, the most important portion of new words falls within everyday life and the social field instead of within business and industry; this suggests that new words do have influence upon our life. Related studies indicate that the population distribution is regular; the number of users is inversely proportional to their ages, but directly proportional to their knowledge. Netizens take the most active part in creation and use of neologisms.

3. Different attitudes towards neologisms

Since dictionaries hold the ultimate authority in their users' mind, lexicographers and linguists are very careful about new concepts and their definitions. In the past ten years, three to five academic conferences have been held annually with respect to Chinese lexicography, and neologism is always one of the main topics for discussion. I remember that, in conferences of the early 1990s, speaking of the inclusion of neologism in dictionaries, the voice of disagreement was far louder than that of agreement with regard to lettered words and overseas Chinese words.

It was believed that lettered words were an abuse of loanwords and such words would profane the purity of the Chinese language. Some scholars, with a wait-and-see attitude, thought that time would prove whether these neologisms were here to stay. With the popularity of the loan words in daily life, those who voiced disapproval became fewer in number by the late 1990s. What remained was a concern about how to standardize the new words and guide their use in dictionary-making, especially about the exotic loanwords and lettered words.

In the new century, exotic loanwords and lettered words have become a common occurrence in the Chinese media as mentioned at the beginning of the chapter. There has been a deluge of these. How should dictionaries confront all such problems? When CHINALEX (the Chinese Association for Lexicography) held an academic conference in Chengdu at the end of September 2002, the main topic focused exclusively on new words and expressions, as well as on the compilation of dictionaries of neologism. The dominant opinion focused on *how* instead of *whether* such special lexicons should be dealt with in dictionaries. While lexicographers hold a positive view of neologism, there exist different voices in social and cultural circles. In order to solve this problem, the Language Application Administration of the Ministry of Education has initiated a 'Web Questionnaire Survey on the Hotspot Issue of Language Application' in order to solicit social opinions about neologism, lettered words, cyber-language, etc.

In 2004, however, a so-called 'Chinese Defence Campaign' was launched through the Chinese media. Shi Fang, a journalist at the People's Daily Online, published an article entitled 'Pidgin English should be Eliminated, and Loan Words should be Standardized'[1]. Liu Hanjun wrote an article published in the China Daily (20 April 2004), 'Do Respect Our Mother Tongue', in which he even cited 'La Derrière Classe' (The Last Lesson) by Alphonse Daudet, so as to stimulate people's cherishment of our own language. Also, in his article 'Safeguard Our Mother Tongue'[2], Lin Zhipo pointed out that the harm to the Chinese language proceeds from three aspects: (a) inadequate selection of entry-words for dictionaries; (b) Hong Kong and Taiwan dialects; and (c) pidgin English. In 2005, some high officials even submitted a written statement to the Ministry of Education raising an objection to the abuse of lettered words.

However, most scholars hold rather favourable views of such neologisms. Wang Huidi, from the Chinese Language Society of HK, expressed his view in response to the above arguments. In an article put out on the Huayuqiao website[3], he said that the occurrence of lettered words in Mandarin was a progressive development that showed the Chinese people have self-confidence in their mother tongue. As for the overuse of such words, guidance is better than prohibition. In reality, an appropriate use of lettered words may enrich

Chinese expressions. For example, 'MP3' is widely used, but who knows its Chinese name? Some Chinese scholars are willing to develop a national standard for 'LINUX system' so to compete with Microsoft, but is there any ordinary person who knows the name for LINUX in Chinese? Everybody knows B超 (B-ultrosonography), IP电话 (IP phone), IC卡 (IC card). Even farmers in China use IP电话 for chatting, B超 for medical diagnosis, and IC卡 for shopping. Yet seldom would they question what the Chinese equivalents 'B', 'IP' and 'IC' are. Another example is 'NBA match', where the Chinese equivalent 美国全国篮球联赛赛场 (US National Basketball Association Match) is neither cognitively economical nor acceptable to the audiences.

4. Research on neologism and dictionaries of neologism

The development of neologism has always been the concern of lexicographers. According to the statistics of the 'Index database of academic papers on Chinese lexicography in the 20th Century', there were only forty-five papers related to neologism from 1900 to 1993; the statistics based on the data of CNKI show that the number of articles about neology published from 1994 to the present has greatly increased.

Table 2

Items	1994–1999		2000 up to the present	
neologism	number	annual average	number	annual average
related to neologism	496	82.6	1537	196.6
neologism as topic	226	37.6	741	92.6
lettered words				
related to neologism	7	1.16	335	41.8
neologism as topic	6	1	120	15
borrowed words				
related to borrowed words	212	35	542	67.7
borrowed words as topic	128	21	227	28.4
total	**1075**	**179.1**	**3502**	**437.7**

Table 2 shows that the number of research papers on new words, lettered words and borrowed words in the Chinese language has augmented tremendously, especially for papers on lettered words (where there is an increase of at least fifteen times). This, from one aspect, proves that there is an increase in the numbers of borrowed and lettered words in the Chinese language, a phenomenon that has increasingly drawn the attention of scholars.

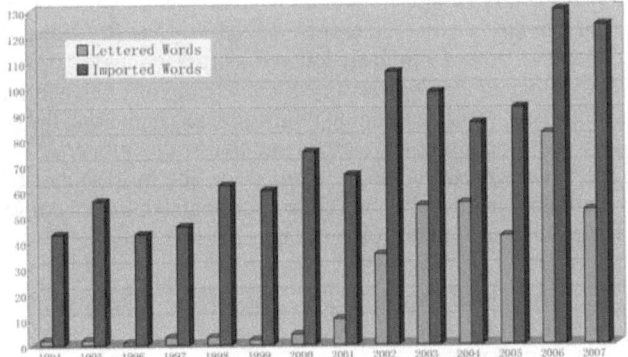

Figure 1 An aspect of development of imported words and lettered words

In April 2004, the First International Conference on Chinese Lexicology was held in Wuhan University. Many lexicographers attended this conference and one of the most important topics was Chinese neologism. Many scholars participated in the discussion. Sun Maosong, from Tsinghua University, jointly with other scholars, launched a special research project on the formation of modern Chinese lettered words. They concluded that seven types of components contributed to their formation in about a dozen ways. Zhou Hongbo, senior editor of the Commercial Press, put forward the idea that dictionaries of neologism are urgently needed so as to inform the public of the well-formed new words and provide the necessary guidance for their use. Kang Shingyong undertook a systematic study of Chinese neologisms based on a special corpus, including: (1) family trend of word formation; (2) overall situation of new word family; (3) configuration of new word family; (4) syntactic features of new word family; and (5) motivation for new word 'familization'. Guo Xi provided a general principle to set a standard for lettered words' use, that is: being scientific, compatible and flexible. He also suggested that lettered words should be pronounced on the basis of IPA, and be written in accordance with the orthography of the Chinese Pinyin and the Romanization (Pinyin) of Chinese, in an attempt to normalize the use of lettered words.

The achievements in neologism research naturally find their place in the dictionary. Since 1987, about forty-seven Chinese dictionaries of neologism, including those of lettered words, have been published. In terms of the selection of entry words, some of the above dictionaries mainly include the words formed since the early 20th century, while many others are limited to a rather small range of vocabulary (e.g. those extracted from a certain style of text; others include only several hundred words). But those published in the 21st century take more care about newly coined words. For example, the *Xinhua Dictionary of Neologisms* (by Zhou Hongbo) includes exclusively the words coined since the 1990s. The *Comprehensive Dictionary of Neologisms* (by Kang Shiyong) includes the words (many of which are lettered words) that have appeared since 1978. The *Dictionary of Neologisms* (by Shen Mengying) has two parts. The first part includes new words beginning with Chinese characters; the other part includes new words beginning with letters and the Arabic numerals.

In 2002, the *Contemporary Chinese Dictionary*, the most authoritative and well-styled dictionary in China, published a revised and enlarged edition which included a large number of new words, such as the following:

三个代表 ('The Three Represents'); 一国两制 ('One country, two systems'); 纳米技术 ('nanotechnology'); 蓝牙 ('bluetooth'); 宽带 ('broadband'); 克隆 ('clone'); 大盘 ('large cap'); 建仓 ('open a position'); 补仓 ('cover short position'); 套牢 ('hung up'); 前卫 ('very modern'); 非礼 ('incivility'); and lettered-words like CEO, CFO, CGO, CIO, COO, CTO, and so on.

As for improving the dictionary of neologism, and in order to standardize Chinese neologisms that include borrowed words and lettered words, we should investigate the constituent parts, phonetic rules and family trend of neologism. The research on the mechanism and the motivation for word-formation has turned out to be an effective way to carry out such an investigation.

5. Motivation of lexical composition of neologism

The motivation for word-formation refers to the ways in which new things, events and phenomena are designated a certain linguistic expression. It illustrates the relationship between the sign and its denotatum, such that the meaning of a word can be ascertained from the sum of the meanings of its constituents. The motivation can be based either on linguistic form and its concept or on social and cultural background. The former is micro-motivation while the latter is macro-motivation. The recognition of motivation for neologism is a key in the selection of dictionary entry-words and lexicographical definitions, especially for bilingual dictionary translation. According to theoretical models of cognitive linguistics, such as mental space (Fauconnier 1985, 1998) and conceptual integration (Turner et al. 1995, 1998, Turner 1996, Coulson 1997), the representations of language can be illustrated by image schema. The recognition of the composition of linguistic expression and its image schema is the main way to the comprehension and representation of meaning.

The following discussion will examine the mechanism of word-formation from the perspective of linguistic and conceptual schema, as well as cross-space mapping and conceptual blending, so as to bring to light the micro-motivation of words, including composition, abbreviation, metaphorization, sound imitation, borrowing, and calque formation. It must not be forgotten that, since new technology and new concepts relatively originate from English-speaking countries, the motivation for Chinese neologism usually bears the influence of English word-formation.

5.1. Metaphorization and its motivation of word-formation

Metaphorization is very influential on the development of language; it affects directly linguistic activities, including the way of thinking, the creative power of the mind and the formation of concept. George Lakoff carried out a broad analysis of metaphors in the 1980s, and two fundamental conclusions can be made from his analysis: (a) all language is metaphorical, and (b) all metaphors are ultimately based on our bodily experience. Thus, metaphorization is a conventional cognitive module of a language community. Making use of certain relations between the source and target domain, a metaphor can represent semantic information in a vivid and figurative way.

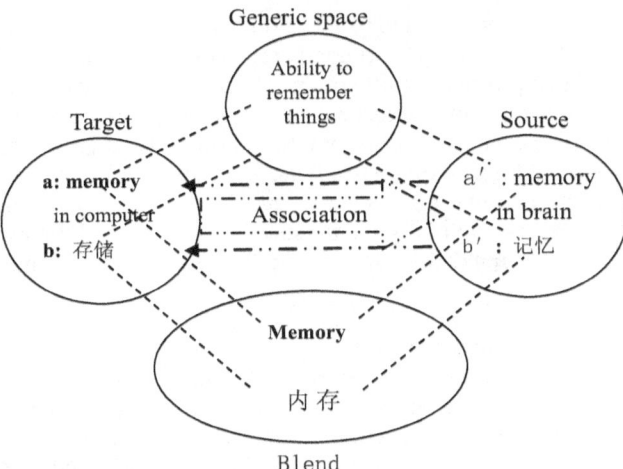

Figure 2 Blending of metaphoric concepts

From the point of view of the morphological structures of specialized words, metaphors are realized through implicit comparison without comparative words. It is only the partial projection and mapping of structural schema between the tenor and the vehicle. For example, in the evolution of Informatics terms, inventors usually name a new concept after a well-known term and create the new one by means of conceptual mapping. There are two cognitive bases for metaphor: similarity-based metaphoric mapping and relevant experience-based metaphoric mapping. The neologisms in the following table are coined by similarity.

Table 3

Sign	Tenor	Vehicle	Similarity
mouse/鼠标	hand-operated device for the control of the cursor on a PC screen	a small furry animal	Form and action
window/视窗	operating environments for PC	a space of glass in the wall	Structure
memory/内存	part of a computer that retains information	a property of the human mind	Function: process information
explorer/搜索器	Microsoft's popular Web browser	someone travelling through unknown area to find out about it	Character: seek knowledge of unfamiliar regions
package/软件包	stored collection of written programs of a computer	things wrapped in paper or a box	Function: collect things
virus/病毒	a self-replicating program that spreads and destroys data	a very small living thing that causes infectious illnesses	Nature: infectious and harmful

Metaphors not only apply to noun-formation but also to verb-formation. For example, 炒鱿鱼 (chǎo yóuyú) originally refers to 'cooking a dish': the squid curls up when being cooked. And now it is used figuratively to describe the scene of 'a man, who is fired, rolls up his quilt and prepares for departure'. 跌眼镜 (diē yǎnjìng), which comes from dialect, literally refers to a man who is so surprised that his pair of glasses falls, and it metaphorically means that an event goes beyond one's expectation, and is extremely astonishing. This overstatement expresses vividly the manner of surprise. And the expression 令人大跌眼镜 (lìngrén dàdiē yǎnjìng) is often found in various media.

5.2. Composition and its motivation

Composition means that two or more simple conceptual schemas (input space) are projected into blending space through cross space mapping, completion and elaboration processes so as to construct new terms. The denotatum of the composed concepts is simple, and readers can easily capture the whole meaning immediately in light of its compositional motivation. In the process of conceptual integration, both conceptual metaphorization and language schema take effect. For example, the compound 'spaceship' is precisely the product of the conceptual mapping between 'underwater vehicle' and 'space vehicle' and also of the structural projection from the 'space' and 'ship' into the blend space. The compound words listed in the following table all fall into this category.

Table 4

spaceship	⇐	space + ship	⇒	航天 [hángtiān] + 飞船 [fēichuán]
hypertext	⇐	hyper + text	⇒	超 [chāo] + 文本 [wénběn]
Internet	⇐	inter + net	⇒	互联 [hùlián] + 网 [wǎng]
Internet Explorer	⇐	Internet + Explorer	⇒	英特网 [Yīngtèwǎng] + 浏览器 [liúlǎn qì]
electronic commerce	⇐	electronic + commerce	⇒	电子 [diànzǐ] + 商务 [shīngwù]

The composition shows a strong tendency to form words as a family. For instance, 'webaholics' were initially called 网虫 (net worm) in Chinese, and then other words were derived to form a 'word family', for example 准网虫 (quasi-worm: green hand on the Internet), 爬虫 (reptile worm: webaholic at primary level), 小虫 (small worm: webaholic at an intermediate level), 大虫 (big worm: webaholic at advanced level), 飞虫 (flying worm: webaholic at high level), and so on. So do the lettered words. Let us see the compound words based on such words:

(1) Compound words based on RNA (ribonucleic acid/核糖核酸): RNA干涉 (RNA interference), RNA杂交 (RNA hybridization), RNA复制酶 (RNA replicas), etc.
(2) Compound words based on DNA (deoxyribonucleic acid/脱氧核糖核酸): DNA排序 (DNA sequence), DNA基因图 (DNA images), DNA基因图谱测定 (DNA profiling), DNA亲子鉴定 (DNA paternity testing), DNA计算机 (DNA computers), etc.

In the above examples, the lettered words RNA and DNA function as 'affixes', as many new words and terms are formed with them and are used widely in Chinese language communication.

5.3. Abbreviation and its motivation

Abbreviation conforms to cognitive economy; it can reduce a group of long string terms to a short expression. English abbreviated words constitute the main source of Chinese lettered words. Abbreviations are regularly formed in the following ways:

(3) Initialisms: BBS (bulletin board system/电子公告牌), GPRS (General Packet Radio Service/通用分组无线业务), IE (Internet Explorer/英特网浏览器), etc.
(4) Acronyms: CEPA (Mainland and Hong Kong Closer Economic Partnership Arrangement/内地与香港更紧密经贸安排), APEC (Asia Pacific Economic Cooperation/亚太经济合作会议), OPEC (Organization of Petroleum Exporting Countries/石油输出国组织), etc.
(5) Clipping: It refers to a coinage by clipping the head or the end, or both,

of a long word, e.g. phone = telephone (电话), demo = demonstration (示范), bus = omnibus (公汽), flu = influenza (流感), etc.

(6) Blending: It aims to blend two or more clipped words so as to coin a new term, e.g. telex/电传 = teleprinter + exchange; taikonaut/宇航员 = taikong + astronaut; netizen/网民 = net + citizen, etc.

The above shortened words are introduced from English, while Chinese people themselves coined a lot of abbreviations in the Chinese language as well. For example:

(7) Abbreviations of Chinese character: 春晚 (春节联欢晚会: Chinese New Year's Day Party), 春运 (春节期间的交通运输: Passenger Transport around Spring Festival), 边贸 (边境贸易: Border Trade), 节育 (节制生育: Birth Control), 消协 (消费者权益保护协会: Customer's Right Protection Association), etc.

(8) Abbreviations of Chinese character Pinyin: GB: GuóBiāo (国标: National Standard), RMB: RénMín Bì (人民币: Chinese People's Currency), HSK: HànYǔ Shuǐpíng KǎoShì (汉语水平考试：Chinese Language Evaluation Test), 3F 现象: Fúzào, Fúqiǎn, Fúkuā Phenomena. This kind of abbreviation is prevalent in cyber language. For example: MM: mèimei (妹妹: younger sister); JJ: jiějie (姐姐: elder sister); GG: gēge (哥哥: elder brother); DD: dìdi（弟弟: younger brother); PLMM: piàoliang mèimei (漂亮妹妹: pretty girl); WAN: wǒ àini (我爱你: I love you); etc.

(9) Common English abbreviations for Chinese Netizens: IC: I see; IDK: I don't know; TKS: Thanks; TYVM: Thank you very much; CU: See you; CUL: See you later; BRB: Be right back; ROTFL: rolling on the floor laughing; GTG: got to go.

5.4. Sound imitation and its motivation

Sound imitation consists of using certain signs or words to supersede other words with similar pronunciation so as to attract attention by novelty. Sound imitation, mainly used in cyber-language, includes these two aspects:

5.4.1. *Expression of numeral sound imitation.* This refers to those expressions composed of numerals, which can be classified into different groups by the initial number. Among them, a majority of the expressions are initiated by the number 5.

Table 5

514 无意思 [wú yìsì]	Nonsense	51930我依旧想你 [wǒ yī jiù xiǎngnǐ]	I miss you as before
5376我生气了 [wǒ shēngqì le]	I am angry	5366 我想聊聊 [wǒ xǎng liáoliáo]	I want to have a chat
584我发誓 [wǒ fāshì]	I swear	51095我要你娶我 [wǒ yāonǐ qǔwǒ]	I want you to marry me

5.4.2. *Expression of sound imitation in Pinyin.* These expressions are adopted by netizens to show their personalities. For example: 共眠 [gòngmián] (sleep together) refers to 共勉 (encourage each other); 幽香 [yōuxiāng] (subtle aroma) refers to 邮箱 (mail box); 竹叶 [zhúyè] (bamboo leaves) refers to 主页 (homepage); 酷鸡 [kùjī] (cool chicken) refers to 酷机 (cool computer); 温酒屋 [wēnjiǔwū] (warm pub) refers to Win95 (Windows95); 温酒吧 [wēnjiǔbā] (warm bar) refers to Win98 (Windows98); etc. There are also some offbeat expressions, e.g. 瘟都死 [wēndōusǐ] (All die of the plague) stands for Windows; 瘟酒吧 [wēnjiǔbā] (a bar spreading plagues) stands for Win98. These two expressions show that the young men of our time seek verbal stimulation by uttering a malediction against themselves.

5.5. Calque translation and its motivation

Calque, originally a French term, is now used to refer to a new word coined after an existing word in the same language or another language. The former is called intralanguage calque, and the latter interlanguage calque. These calques are an important source for Chinese neologism.

5.5.1. *Intralanguage calque.* When scientists try to name a new thing or a new concept, they usually abstract the semantic features from it and find out its conceptual prototype through cognitive association, and then look for a linguistic sign conceptually relevant within the prototypic category. If such a term exists, they can change one or two morphemes so as to coin a new word representing this new thing or concept. This kind of word-formation is called intralanguage calque. In the development of modern language, calque is one of the major ways to produce new words. For example, 的士 [díshì] is originated from the Cantonese calque after the English word taxi, which initially refers to 'car for hire'. However, with the emergence of other motor vehicles for hire, for example, motorbikes, minibuses, trucks and flatbed cart, the words 面的 (minibus for hire), 摩的 (motor-cycle for hire), 货的 (truck for hire), and 板的 (flatbed cart for hire) are then calqued on the basis of the prototype 的士 (taxi); while the original 的士, which is now called 轿的 for distinction, has become a generic word of this category, and 的, that is originally a functional expression in Chinese, has acquired the sense of 'vehicle for hire'. Words formed in such a way have strong family cohesion. For example, the word 酷 transliterated from 'cool' is widely adopted in Chinese communication, and lots of new expressions are coined on the basis of 酷: we have 酷哥 (cool boys) for males, 酷姐 (cool girls) for females, 酷文 (cool articles) for writing, 酷装 (cool suit) for clothing, and many others such as 酷站 (cool website), 酷脚 (cool feet), 酷臀 (cool hips), 酷臂 (cool arms), 酷手 (cool hands), 酷腿 (cool legs), 酷胸 (cool bosom), 酷毙 (cool to die/very cool), 酷机 (cool computer), 酷语 (cool expression), etc. This 'infectiousness' is naturally the consequence of such production of calques.

5.5.2. *Interlanguage calque.* The interlanguage calque is a kind of translation that consists of projecting the source language spaces into those of the target language. The Chinese neologisms or technical terms are modelled after certain foreign words in meaning or in morphological structure, or both — the signifiant and signifié of the source words are preserved. This is in fact a cross space and cross language mapping of expressional schemas and concepts, and it aims to coin new terms for new concepts in the target language, while being modelled after the structural patterns of the source language.

5.5.2.1. *Morphological calque.* As Chinese and English differ considerably in terms of morphological structures, it is very difficult to find a Chinese word that is similar to that of English at the level of morphology. When a certain English expressional form is to be introduced into the Chinese language, it is often reduced to a transplantation, where it aims to project the source lexical form directly into the target language: Chinese. For example, such words as NBA, CEPA, DNA, APEC, CFO, etc. are directly used in Chinese, and are then called lettered words. The motivation for these transplantations is cognitive economy, that is, compared with their Chinese counterparts, the transplanted forms are much simpler. Lettered words mainly come from English abbreviations (see 5.3), or high frequency words.

Note that lettered words usually co-occur with Chinese translations, but the former are relatively far more economical in cognitive processing, and are easier to pronounce, and as such they are more frequently used than their Chinese equivalents. The following is a contrastive analysis of frequency between the two. The data was obtained by searching simplified Chinese webpages with Baidu Search Engine4 at the time.

Table 6

lettered words	frequency	Chinese equivalents	frequency	ratio		
MPEG	14,900,000	电影专家组系统	4	3725000	:	1
MSN	62,700,000	微软实时通讯软件	55	1140000	:	1
CEPA	1,100,000	内地与香港更紧密经贸安排	621	177139	:	1
NBA	55,700,000	美国篮球协会	36,200	1538.6	:	1
CBA	15,600,000	中国篮球协会	133,000	117.3	:	1
GPS	49,400,000	全球卫星定位系统	529,000	93.3	:	1
WTO	16,700,000	世界贸易组织	2,780,000	6.0	:	1
GDP	20,400,000	国内生产总值	4,700,000	4.3	:	1
CEO	35,200,000	首席执行官	8,830,000	4.0	:	1
DNA鉴定	399,000	脱氧核糖核酸鉴定	180	2216.7	:	1
3G	48,200,000	第三代移动通信（系统）	192,000	251.0	:	1
IC卡	8,310,000	集成电路卡	75,200	110.5	:	1
ATM机	2,240,000	自动柜员机	441,000	5.0	:	1

From the above data we can conclude that the ratio of occurrence frequency between the lettered words and their Chinese equivalents is closely related to cognitive economy and their 'memorizability'. Such simple words with fewer letters as MPEG, NBA, CEPA, IC卡, 3G and DNA are easier to utter and memorize, while their Chinese counterparts are complicated and hard to remember due to their lengthy components and indistinct lexical features. Thus, the Chinese translations are seldom used. Yet other Chinese translations with relatively distinct lexical features like 世界贸易组织 (WTO), 首席执行官 (WTO), 国内生产总值 (GDP) and 自动柜员机 (ATM 机) are less complicated and easier to understand. So their occurrence frequency is comparatively higher than the others. (See Table 6.)

An investigation was made on the basis of the Monitor Corpus of Chinese Language Resources by a group of Chinese scholars in 2006. The result shows that 'lettered words' account for 9% of the total lexical tokens, and they are no longer in occasional occurrence in Chinese language, but instead a constituent part of Chinese vocabulary, e.g. VS, NBA, GDP, AC, IT, MP3, QQ, AMD, DVD, CEO, etc. have entered the list of the 5,000 most frequently used words of the Chinese language. (Li Mingyu 2006: 38-40)

5.5.2.2. *Phonological calque.* This is a product of language schema blending, in which the sound of a source language is projected directly into the blending space to form a new Chinese word, that is, the pronunciation of the word is directly represented in the form of Chinese Pinyin with its concept being transplanted totally or mostly to Chinese language. Therefore, sound is the key motivation for this kind of word formation. Due to lexical domestication, the pronunciation of calques may differ somewhat from that of the source language. For example: 卡通 [kǎtōng]: cartoon; 特氟隆 [Tèfúlóng]: Teflon; 厄尔尼诺 (è'ěrnínuò): El Nino; 拉尼娜 [lānínà]: La Nina; 克隆 [kèlóng]: clone; etc.

5.5.2.3. *Semantic calque.* The conceptual mapping between corresponding expressions, i.e. a new meaning is to be projected from a foreign expression onto a corresponding Chinese word. Let us take the IT domain for example. By imitating the English words notebook and engine, the Chinese counterparts 笔记本 and 引擎 have respectively acquired new meanings: a small flat computer and a searching tool. In the same way, the Chinese words 鼠 and 窗 are now used to refer respectively to 'hand-operated device for PC' (鼠标) and 'operating environments for PC' (视窗) after their English counterparts.

5.5.2.4. *Phono-semantic calque.* This refers to the cross language mapping between expressional schema and conceptual schema, where not only the pronunciation of the source language is mapped, but the concept is also conveyed. Phono-semantic calques can be divided into the following types according to their formal structure:

(a) The source language is the name of a product, whereas the target language, based on transliteration, will use Chinese morphemes to represent both the quality and function of the product. In this way, not only is the phonetic feature of the source language retained, but the meaning is also expressed. Let us take the medical expressions for example: 眠尔通 [Mián'ěrtōng]: Milton; 带尔眠 [Dài'ěrmián]: Dakmane; and 酣乐欣 [Hānlèxīn]: Halcion. From the Chinese terms, we can easily infer that they are sleeping tablets. More examples are: 息斯敏 [Xīsīmǐn]: Hismanal; 鼻可灵 [Bíkělíng]: Beconase; 利肝灵 [Lìgānlíng]: ligalon: and 伟哥 [Wěigē]: Viagra. Their Chinese equivalents clearly show the functions of these medical products. This is also true for calques for some pesticide brands, such as 速灭杀丁 [Sùmiè shādīng]: Sumissadin; 禾大壮 [Hédàzhuàng]: Ordran; 灭草特 [Miècǎotè]: Machette.
(b) The source words are nouns, their calques in the target language can rebuild the sounds and meanings of their corresponding source words. For example, the word *cool* is calqued as 酷 [kù], and both the pronunciation and the meaning (fashionable and attractive) of the source word are vividly portrayed through the conceptual mapping and blending. The same goes for words like 黑客 [hēikè]: hacker; 红客 [hóngkè]: hongker; 朋客 [péngkè]: pank; 基因 [jīyīn]: gene, and so on. Such translated expressions are an excellent combination of paraphrase and transliteration. They are the top-grade as in the interlanguage calques.
(c) The source language usually occurs as a single word, and the target language has to generalize its conceptual meaning based on transliteration. For example, from the word *ballet*, we get 芭蕾舞 [bālěiwǔ]. In this expression, 芭蕾 carries the sound of the source word, and 舞 expresses its concept. Here are some similar examples: 桑拿浴 [sāngnáyù]: sauna; 华尔兹舞 [huá'ěrzīwu]: waltz; 高尔夫球 [gāo'ěrfūqiú]: golf; and so on.
(d) The source word is a compound word, and the target language is to use an expression to convey both its phonetic and meaningful features. For example, the word *miniskirt* is calqued as 迷你裙 [mínǐ qún]. The first two characters 迷你 express both the sound and an 'emergent' meaning (Fauconnier 2001), and the third character 裙 summarizes the referent content of the source language. According to rules of phono-semantic calques, we have coined new Chinese words: 蹦级跳 [bèngjítiào], 霹雳舞 [pīlìwǔ], 迷你光盘 [mínǐ guāngpán] and 因特网 [Yīngtèwǎng] respectively from the English words: *bungee jumping, break dance, minidisk* and *Internet*.

5.5.2.5. *Morpho-semantic calque.* Some languages may make use of a certain letter or a 'shaping word' to designate a shaped thing, as the mere referential concept is insufficient to convey the whole meaning of such expressions, and it is preferable to adopt an image mapping to calque a word representing the similar shape, so as to make up for the insufficiency of paraphrases. That is the morpho-semantic calque. There are two kinds of examples:

(a) 丁字尺: **T**-square; 工字钢: **I**-steel; 工字梁: **H**-beam; 丁字接头: **T**-junction; K形坡口: **double-V** groove.
(b) 环形圈: **O**-ing; 三角皮带: **V**-belt; 交叉支撑: **X**-brace; 叉形曲线: **Y**-curve.

In group (a), it is evident that each pair of the boldface words (both in English and Chinese) are similar in shape, while in group (b), the Chinese characters are simply a description of the shapes of the objects as represented by the shapes of the English letters.

5.5.2.6. *Phono-morphological calque.* In the English language, some terms may contain special codes or hieroglyphs. When those terms are translated into Chinese, this special sign should be retained in order to convey the special information. This is the phono-morphological calque. Note the pairs of equivalents below:

X射线 [àikèsī shèxiàn]: X-ray; Y射线 [gāmǎ shèxiàn]: Y-ray; V形管 [wēixíng guǎn]: V-shaped tube; T恤衫 [tǐùxu shān]: T-shirt; IP电话 [āipī diànhuà]: IP phone; V形轴封 [wēixíng zhóufēng]: V-packing; E型弯头 [yī xíng wāngtóu]: E bend; H型网络 [aī qěxíng wǎngluò]: H-network; X形支撑 [àikèsī xíng zhī chī ng]: X support; etc.

Evidently, the phono-morphological calques not only partially retain the expressional form of the source language, but also convey the distinctive conceptual features. (Note: the Chinese character 形 [xíng] means *the form/shape* in English.)

6. Conclusion

The study on the major dictionaries of neologism and relevant materials has revealed that borrowed words have attracted much interest of Chinese linguists and lexicographers because their exotic features have important effect on Chinese expressions. The neologism occurrence is a process of conventionalization, which is neither created artificially nor left unchecked. The coinage of a new word or expression must conform to the basic requirements such as rational structure, well specified meaning and unsubstitutability. For this purpose, contrived instruction for the use of neologism is a necessity. One of the most efficient tools for instruction is the dictionary of neologism, which plays a significant role in formalization, standardization and utilization of new words and expressions. The studies on the motivation or mechanism of word-formation of neologism with a cognitive approach prove to be an important theoretic evidence for the selection of entry words and lexical definition for the dictionary compilation. In the meantime, the motivation provides an effective guidance for the construction of new words and expressions and for the translation of bilingual dictionaries.

Notes

1. http://www.people.com.cn/GB/wenhua/27296/2543319.html
2. http://www.people.com.cn/GB/guandian/1035/2773586.html
3. http://huayuqiao.org/articles/yuwenjianshetongxun/7901.htm
4. http://www.baidu.com

A survey of pragmatic information in bilingual English-Chinese learners' dictionaries

Saihong Li
University of Copenhagen
saihong@hum.ku.dk

1. Introduction

Most recent developments in semantics and pragmatics are widely used in lexicographical studies today (Béjoint 1990; Svensén 1993; Thomas 1995; Cock 2002; Pruvost 2004; Cowie 2004). However, John Sinclair (1985:135) claims that this development has to work to 'fit into the established lexicographic formats' or 'into the whole conceptual background of lexicography'. At the same time, the discipline of lexicography influences linguistic theories, especially those concerning language use (Atkins 1998; Hartmann 1996). The study of lexical meaning in dictionaries should be ruled by semantics and governed by pragmatic principles.

Pragmatics, a relatively new area of linguistics, is 'meaning in interaction' (Thomas 1995:22). It describes how people use language and the relationship between language and human life. Pragmatics foreshadows many of the issues which are of major importance to lexicography today. As far as we know, a dictionary of a living language can never be complete. Language is 'mobile and liable to change[1]; thus, to record the reality of the basic characteristics of language is becoming the main goal of a lexicographer's work. Semantic and pragmatic information are added to give life to language varieties in dictionaries in order to achieve this goal. Due to the great difference between the conventions and cultures of languages, learners' dictionaries, especially bilingual ones, need to provide users with pragmatic information so that learners can better understand another language. Some sentences may be grammatically correct, but pragmatically improper. A word has no meaning unless it is placed in context; the illustrative phrases and sentences bring the word to life (Cowie 1995:294). If the first aim of dictionary work is 'to exhibit the actual variety of usage' (Murray 1888:x) and 'to capture meaning potentials rather than meaning' (Hanks 1994:24), then the integrated pragmatic information is one of the most important components of dictionaries. In the past, 'dictionary compilers have paid little attention to the pragmatic aspect of communication, merely giving unsystematic indications via Usage Labels' (Hartmann 1998:111).

Pragmatic perspectives on pedagogical lexicography at the macro-level normally provide extra intercultural information, on the avoidance of language errors and societal cultural information. Pragmatic information can be integrated into definitions, exemplifications, translation equivalents and other information regarding usages, registers, frequencies, currency, styles, and status. In the absence of a fully-developed and coherent committed theory of pragmatics for lexicography in this study, a series of tentative categories are advanced, together with some illustrations of their application.

Based on my understanding of Verschueren's 'pragmatic perspective', 'theory of adaptation' and linguistic meaning theory, this study has the following assumptions:

1. The two levels of linguistic meaning: semantic and pragmatic meaning is well integrated into learners' dictionaries for advanced learners' bilingual dictionaries;
2. Lexicographers' perspectives meet users' expectations in pragmatic information.

2. Bilingual dictionaries: problems

The main problems in bilingual dictionaries, in my opinion, are twofold. First, language anisomorphism and second, there is meaning discrimination by lexicographers. It is widely known that 'languages are not isomorphic' (Zgusta 1971 cited in Pedersen 1988:121), and language anisomorphism influences and shapes the modality, meaning and forms of pragmatic information in bilingual dictionaries. Meaning discrimination is already very tricky in monolingual dictionaries, let alone in bilingual dictionaries. Both language anisomorphism and meaning discrimination are concepts of great significance in bilingual learners' dictionaries and two major problems that lexicographers have to deal with.

2.1. Language anisomorphism

The anisomorphism between languages increases exponentially as the number of languages which are treated in a dictionary increases. Consequently, very small sets of lexical items from the various languages are incorporated in these dictionaries. (Sterkenburg 2003:80)

Isomorphism comes from a term in mathematics for 'an exact correspondence between both the elements of two sets and the relations defined by operations on these elements' and now it is used by linguistics, indicating 'a set of oppositions in one language [that] could at an abstract level correspond to, or be 'isomorphic wit', one in another, only the forms by which they are realized being different' (Matthews 2007). Hartmann defines anisomorphism as 'a mismatch between a pair of languages due to their semantic, grammatical and cultural differences' (Hartmann 1987:6). Anisomorphism was first addressed by Zgusta (1971) in a lexicography study. Zgusta claimed that the fundamental difficulty of bilingual dictionaries is 'caused by the anisomorphism of languages and by other differences between languages' (Zgusta 1971:294). The anisomorphism of languages has been widely studied by both linguists and lexicographers from Boas, Sapir and Whorf, to Hjelmslev, Lyons and Zgusta. Language anisomorphism is one of the major barriers in bilingual dictionaries, especially for translation equivalents. It can be extended into different levels, such as the cultural, linguistic, componential and extra-linguistic level. Cultural anisomorphism accounts for the differences that emerge when cultural groups are compared and it is normally difficult to find a translation equivalent in the target language. Therefore, the best possible solutions for cultural anisomorphism are 'literal translation or transliteration followed by pragmatic and cultural explanations' (Yong and Peng 2007:140). 'Trojan Horse', for example, will be very difficult for the Chinese learner to understand, if the dictionary gives only the literal translation as '特洛伊木马' or transliteration as '颠覆分子'. It is very useful for the learner to have the origin of the idioms as it is in OALD: '源自神话古希腊人为了潜入敌城特洛伊而藏进空心的木马中' (a person or thing that is used to deceive an enemy in order to achieve a secret purpose ORIGIN: From the myth in which the Greeks hid inside a hollow wooden statue of a horse in order to enter the city of their enemies, Troy) (OALD 1891). However, a study of the four tested dictionaries shows that MECD and MFECD have no origin information but only translation equivalents. Linguistic anisomorphism refers to the asymmetries between form and content in languages and is 'based on the arbitrary nature of languages, with the logical consequence of a different division of semantic fields, a different distribution of grammatical categories or of compulsory and optional features' (González-Jover 2006:215-234). Explanatory and descriptive equivalents at the level of paradigmatic and syntagmatic relations are normally given for the linguistic anisomorphism.

2.2 Meaning discrimination

The best way to handle meaning discrimination in any given dictionary should be determined by the kind of use of the dictionary is intended… Various arrangements are possible, the determining factors being for whom the dictionary is intended and for what use or uses it is intended. (Iannucci 1967:204)

Meaning discrimination also refers to sense discrimination. In Hartmann's definition, meaning discrimination includes 'the division inside a dictionary entry of distinct senses of a word or phrase. Each sub-sense may be marked not only with a sense number, but by additional means' and in a bilingual dictionary, 'each of these senses may have a different translation equivalent, so clear meaning distinction is essential' (Hartmann 1998:125). Meaning discrimination is necessary when the source language word is polysemous. In 1957, Iannucci studied meaning discrimination in bilingual dictionaries. According to his study, meaning discrimination is 'handled very inadequately and inconsistently' in many bilingual dictionaries. Iannucci suggests that meaning discrimination is primarily in the source language, and therefore, it should be placed before the target words. He further suggests that mono-directional bilingual dictionaries should provide 'meaning discrimination only in the native-foreign side' and 'the foreign-native side can omit meaning discrimination altogether' (Iannucci 1957:272-281). In 1977, Al-Kasimi once again stressed the importance of meaning discrimination for a bilingual dictionary. Al-Kasimi strongly recommended that a bilingual dictionary should 'provide meaning discriminations which enable the user to select the appropriate equivalents or the proper sense of an equivalent' (1977:68). Al-Kasimi (1977:72) further suggested that 'briefer discriminations, such as context words, are preferable because space is an essential practical and economic consideration in lexicography'. Meaning discrimination should be provided both 'systematically' and 'consistently' (Iannucci 1957; Al-Kasimi 1977). By definition, polysemous words have several senses, and each sense may have a different translation equivalent. It is very important for a learners' bilingual dictionary to provide meaning discriminations. 'The accumulation of equivalents in an active (=expression) dictionary, without any meaning discriminating glosses, is one of the deadly sins of lexicography, but accumulation is possible in a passive (=comprehension) dictionary' (Kromann et al. 1984:210). Meaning discrimination can be achieved in a dictionary by punctuation; definitions; synonyms, illustrative examples; part of speech; usage labels; context words or phrases.

3. Pragmatic information from the user's perspective

The main purpose of the study is to find how pragmatic information is provided from the user's perspective; therefore, proficiency test combined with questionnaires and interviews are used for the empirical study. The tests and questionnaires were conducted with 480 undergraduate students from Dalian Maritime University and Henan Technology University. Each group had 120 participants and every person took the same test, which consisted of 10 multiple choice questions; 10 'culture words' translation questions; 10 matching questions for 'usage labels' and 10 sentences tested 'politeness principles' followed by evaluation questionnaires. The maximum correctness score is 40. The participants were allotted 45 minutes for the tests and questionnaires. The 480 persons were divided into four groups. Each group was given a copy of one of the above mentioned dictionaries. Short interviews were given after the test. Group 1 was provided with a copy of LDOCE, Group 2 with a copy of OALD, Group 3 with MECD, and Group 4 with MFCED. Not surprisingly, most of the participants had no idea about pragmatic information in learners' dictionaries. In order to carry out the tests and the questionnaires, I first explained what pragmatic information was and where and how to find it in a dictionary. Interviews with 18 volunteers were carried out to get feedback on participants' understanding of test and questionnaires.

4. Data analysis and discussion of results

The survey that has been carried out among users indicates that the maximum score of all the questions is 40. The mean score of correctness for the four groups is 22; the average mean score for each group and standard deviation can be seen in Table 1.

For Group 1 with LDOCE, the mean score is 27.2, with a standard deviation of 5.16. 80% of the participants were satisfied with the usage information. However, they were not really satisfied with the translation equivalents, 'deteriorate 使(shǐ) 恶(è)化(huà)' being a case in point. They could not find the right answers by looking up the translation equivalents. 80% of the participants gave the right answers to the tested cultural words.

In Group 2 with OALD, 90% of the participants had no problems finding the right answers for multiple choice questions and all agreed that the usage information provided was very useful. In this group, the mean score of correctness is 26.8, with a standard deviation of 4.31. 80% of the participants gave the right answers to the tested cultural words in this group too.

The participants in Group 3 with MECD had no problem finding right answers for multiple choice questions. All participants agreed that the usage information was very useful. 17.3 of the answers are correct. Many participants could not find the right answers according to the translation equivalents given. Only 40 % of the participants provided the right answers for the tested cultural words.

Group 4 with MFECD are not happy with the translation equivalents. 16.7 of the answers are correct. 30% of the participants had the right answers to the cultural words. All the participants in this group agreed that the usage notes are very helpful for synonyms or easily confused words. However, many participants could not find all the answers for the questions from the given dictionaries.

Table 1 Comparisons of mean score of correct answers

Group	Number of cases	Mean	Std. Deviation	Std. Error	95% Confidence Interval for Mean		Mini-mum	Maxi-mum
					Lower Bound	Upper Bound		
Group 1 with LDOCE	120	27.2	5.15967	1.63163	23.509	30.891	16	34
Group 2 with OALD	120	26.8	4.31535	1.36463	23.713	29.887	20	35
Group 3 with MECD	120	27.3	5.22919	1.65362	13.5593	21.0407	10	24
Group 4 with MFECD	120	16.7	5.45792	1.72595	12.7956	20.6044	8	24
Total	120	22	7.02377	1.11056	19.7537	24.2463	8	35

The table also shows that there is no significant difference between Group 1 and 2, nor between group 3 and 4; however, there is a significant difference between group 1 and 2 on the one hand, and group 3 and 4 on the other hand. This suggests that bilingualized dictionaries are more practical than monolingual dictionaries for Chinese learners of English. The statistics also suggests a general tendency of the participants' evaluations on pragmatic information in the tested dictionaries.

4.1. Results of pragmatic information of avoiding common language errors

The pedagogical dictionaries should help the learner to be aware of, and if possible avoid, common sources of error in the language he is attempting to acquire (Jain 1981:275).

Warning about language errors for second language learners could come in the form of examples of any kinds of improper use of words, phrases or sentences in certain contexts; they are also called pragmatic errors. However, 'the concept of language errors is a fuzzy one' (Brians): language errors can be reflected as semantic, syntactic, grammatical and pragmatic errors. Due to the big differences between both languages and cultures, it is not surprising that Chinese learners of English can make errors in speaking, writing and misunderstanding of the concepts or context meaning. Therefore, providing extra pragmatic information to help the users to avoid the language errors is most important; pragmatic information should be systematically included into bilingual learners' dictionaries. Both my own 14-year teaching experience and the analysis results of the examinations at Dalian Maritime University show that the types of language errors for Chinese learners of English can be at word level, phrase level, sentence level or discourse level.

1. Avoidance of language errors at word level: Some common language errors at word level are quite normal for Chinese learners of English. Chinese learners of English are mostly exposed to the Chinese language environment. Media, such as TV, are mostly in Chinese. Unlike the Danes, who watch English movies with Danish subtitles, most Chinese only watch Chinese movies or foreign movies that have been dubbed, and they read only Chinese newspapers. At the university, the teaching materials and instructions are almost always in Chinese. Therefore, words, phrases or sentences that the students learn in class are relatively separated from real language contexts. Consequently, dictionaries become one of the first learning materials for new words or phrases. In 2002, Year 2 non-English major students were asked to make up some sentences with given words. A large percentage of students made mistakes with 'deteriorate' and 'intimate'. The two words were learned during the semester, and most students learned the meaning and usage by looking them up in the dictionaries or by consulting the teachers. Over 75% of the students made a mistake with 'intimate' and over 64.5% of students made a mistake with 'deteriorate'. For example, 'I have lots

of intimate friends in my class' or 'My parents are also my intimate friends'. Most students take 'intimate friend' as a synonym of 'close friend, good friend', without knowing that 'intimate' can also mean a friend with whom one has sexual relations. A look at the dictionary will show the reason why students make mistakes like that. MECD, for example, supplies only one example as 'intimate friend', and near translation equivalents as '亲密的，密切的 (close)'; therefore, it is not a surprise that the students use the above sentences after looking the words up in the dictionary.
2. Language errors at phrasal level: Language errors at phrasal level are mostly the improper use of idioms or collocations, e.g. talk **on** the weather.
3. Language errors at sentence level and discourse level: language errors at sentence or discourse level are mainly due to the cultural difference between two languages, such as expressions for thanks, criticism etc., which are given as politeness principles in LDOCE and MECD, for example, the conversation between the two persons:
Tom: 'You look great today'.
Chinese girl: 'No, no (or where, where)'. (It is considered polite to say 'no, or not so good' in China and Japan etc.)

Information to help users with common language errors in dictionaries can be realized in many ways, such as brackets with short notes on usage, examples to give context information on usage, and usage notes or language notes within the entry, or as a separate study page in the front or back matter of a dictionary.

Test 1 Multiple choice in this study is mainly designed to test some common errors made by Chinese learners of English and how the information is provided in the tested dictionaries. Table 2 shows Chinese users' evaluation of some common language errors in the tested dictionaries.

It is interesting to see that the result indicates very high positive evaluation trends, even though some of the participants did not give the right answers to the questions. As Table 2 shows, OALD has 73.2% positive evaluation, LDOCE has 75.7% positive evaluation; MECD has 73.6% positive evaluation and MFECD has 71.4% positive evaluation. The results also demonstrate that positive or negative evaluations may have nothing to do with the right or wrong answers. This shows one of the limitations in this research, that evaluations of a dictionary may involve many factors, such as personal preference for a particular dictionary; skills in using a dictionary etc.

Table 2 Evaluations of avoiding common language errors

		OALD	LDOCE	MECD	MFECD
Positive	very useful	32.70%	34.40%	25.40%	34.20%
	useful	40.50%	41.30%	48.20%	37.20%
	not sure	14.00%	12.30%	16.70%	13.70%
Negative	not useful	8.00%	6.00%	5.40%	7.40%
	not at all useful	4.80%	6.00%	4.20%	7.50%

4.2. Results of cultural information

Certain lexical meanings and meaning relations in a language are rooted in cultural factors. Meaning in such cases will not be conveyed through paraphrase in a simple controlled vocabulary and the specification of selection restrictions. (Jain 1981:281)

Culture refers to 'that complex whole which includes knowledge, belief, art, morals, law, custom, and any other capabilities and habits acquired by man as a member of society' (Tylor 1871:1). For example, the colour 'red' in Chinese stands for 'happiness, good luck, popular' and it is a very positive word, but 'red' normally stands for danger and blood in the West. 'White' in the Chinese culture stands for 'pure, clean' and it also has more positive connotations; the word 'black' is connected with dirty and death and it has more negative than positive connotations. If you take the metro in Copenhagen, you will see many people wear black jackets, but if you take the metro in Beijing, you will see all kinds of colours. This mean that in Europe black has nothing to do with negative connotations as it does in China. A bilingual dictionary, which aims at providing 'help to someone who understands one language but not the other' (Landau 1984:7), plays an important role in cross-cultural communication by breaking through cultural as well as linguistic barriers. As we know, 'most of the vocabulary is culture-specific' (Tomaszczyk 1983: 43) and 'our understanding of a foreign vocabulary is distorted if we force it into the concepts of our own language and world view' (Snell-Hornby 1986: 215). Therefore, the bilingual dictionary should also aim to help 'clarify alien concepts against their own cultural background' (ibid:216) and 'carry out pragmatic functions in the real world' (Jain 1981:283). For the Chinese, being old is good and old people are respected, so the phrase 'old Li', for example, has positive connotations of an experienced and mature person, even when he may be only in his twenties or thirties. Old people in China will not easily get offended by hearing the word 'old', let alone the young ones. However, in Denmark as in other western countries, 'old' implies something useless and hopeless; it has nothing to do with respect. In China, it is natural to ask a person's age, even though you meet each other for the first time; however, it is normally impolite to ask a person's age, especially ladies', in the western countries.

A survey of pragmatic information 33

> **cream 'tea** *noun* (*BrE*) a special meal eaten in the afternoon, consisting of tea with SCONES, jam and thick cream
> （下午进用的）奶油茶点

'Cream tea', for example, is tested in Test 2. OALD receives the highest percentage of positive evaluations and MFECD has the highest negative evaluations. Among the four dictionaries, only OALD provides direct information about 'cream tea' and translation equivalents. However, 'cream tea' is not provided directly in LDOCE, MECD and MFECD. The results indicate that cultural words or expressions are not always included in the learners' dictionaries, even though those words are among the most difficult words for learners.

Bilingual dictionaries are recommended for Chinese users who will need more cultural, social and cross-linguistic information. Those in Group 1 using LDOCE are able to find 80 % of the words and are satisfied with the information provided. However, for 10% of the words, they are not sure of the answers, and for another 10% of the words, they could not get any answers from the dictionary.

Those in Group 2 using OALD were able to find 78% of the correct answers from the dictionary and they considered the information to be presented clearly. The correct answers they got in this group are 86%. Two participants agreed that they just guessed the answers instead of finding the answers in the dictionaries. They could not find 20% of the total number of tested words in the dictionary.

For those in Group 3 using MECD, they could not find answers in the dictionary for 30% of the total number of words, and they could find the correct answer for 61%. For 50% of the words the participant could not figure out the meaning from the equivalents given by the dictionary. According to the 60 participants in Group 3, only 20% of the translation equivalents are helpful in finding the answers.

Those in Group 4 using MFECD are able to find 70% of the tested words from the dictionary. The participants claimed that there were over 30% of the tested words that they could find but could not help them to give the answers from the information given in the dictionary. The correct answers in this group are 59%.

4.3. Results of usage labels

Regardless of the increasing debates on stylistic labels, all participants were happy with the usage labels given in the dictionary for Test 3 and commented that they were very useful. They were all satisfied with the usage notes in OALD, LDOCE and MECD and agreed that those were very useful. The users were also very satisfied with the frequency of occurrence information presented in the LDOCE pertaining to common errors made in spoken and written English. MFECD has few usage notes; however, it has a lot of collocations, phrasal information in a separate column, which is very suitable for Chinese learners.

Over 200 participants agreed that some of the labels were ambivalent, such as 'derogative' and 'taboo'. The users also claimed that it was very difficult to recognize the usage labels, due to the fact that each dictionary had its own way of indicating usage labels. They agreed that the usage labels in LDOCE were the most inconvenient to use and remember. All of the participants were happy with the usage labels in OALD. They think that OALD is easy to read and use. MECD has most information on usage labels. MFECD has only general information on usage labels, and it does not have much information on what kinds of usage labels are used in the dictionaries.

4.4. Results of pragmatic information in politeness

Test 4 is an open question. The participants are asked to write down how to use an expression of politeness such as criticism and praise, invitation and offers, requests and tentativeness, addressing people from the information given in current learners' dictionaries. The result of the survey suggests that politeness expressions concerning apologies, criticism and praise are similar to Chinese. Therefore, it is not really necessary to include these in bilingual English-Chinese dictionaries. Everyone agreed that politeness principles in addressing people, invitations, offers, politeness, requests, tentativeness and gratitude are very useful; the information on 'thank you', whose equivalents in Chinese are seldom used for small things, is beneficial. LDOCE, OALD and MECD provide such politeness expressions either in the language note or on the study page, or they indicate them in their definitions; however, MFECD has no information on politeness usage at all.

4.5. Results of context information

> Meaning is something contextual with respect to language and the world, and is also something active toward other meanings and the world. When a word meaning consists of an inherent lexical meaning which has a core and a periphery, the peripheral, Figurative or motivated meaning is the part of the lexical meaning that is especially subject to contextual modulation. (Sterkenburg 2003:291)

Pragmatics is the study of language use in context. 'Lexical choices in text' and 'many word meanings' make it difficult to 'pinpoint out of the contexts in which they normally occur' (Béjoint 2001:211 and 217). Hence, it is very important to bring the concept of context into a bilingual learners' dictionary. The contextual features in pedagogical dictionaries have been well represented by COBUILD dictionary. Context includes both linguistic context and situational context. Linguistic context refers to the language surrounding the phrase in question. Situational context, on the other hand, refers to every non-linguistic factor that affects the meaning of a phrase. As it is well-known, it is impossible to identify the particular meanings of a polysemic word without a context. In dictionaries, both the linguistic context and situational context can be integrated thoroughly. The meaning of a word can be realized in its usage and analyzed on the basis of its usage. The context can also be understood as a form of realization of a concrete meaning, which is potentially included in the word. Nowadays, many learners' dictionaries, such as OALD, LDOCE, CALD and MEDAL, also incorporate contextual features with their analytical, descriptive definitions. The statistic analysis of the sample tested words in bilingual English Chinese dictionaries shows that 19.7% of words or phrases have contextual definitions. Context information is also used for some pragmatic-featured words, such as 'by the way', 'actually', 'I mean', or politeness principles, some indexical words and some other functional words. Context information can be represented through definitions, exemplifications and usage notes.

In this study, some pragmatic expressions, such as 'by the way', 'I mean', and 'actually' were used to evaluate the participants' satisfaction with contextual information in Test 2. The results can be seen in Table 3.

Table 3 Evaluations of contextual information

		OALD	LDOCE	MECD	MFECD
Positive	very useful	44.43%	45.50%	29.63%	51.33%
	useful	28.53%	37.57%	33.30%	27.53%
	not sure	12.17%	7.37%	16.40%	11.63%
Negative	not useful	7.10%	3.20%	0%	1.60%
	not at all useful	10.03%	7.40%	20.60%	8.43%

The results show that the percentages of positive evaluations on both 'very useful' and 'useful' are over 71%. The results indicate that there is a very high degree of satisfaction from the dictionary users. Furthermore, the results also suggest that the users are very satisfied with sentence or contextual definitions.

5. Conclusion

The analysis from the user's perspective shows that pragmatic information has received great attention from lexicographers today. However, there is still room for lexicographers to investigate how to cater to different groups of users, especially for bilingual learners' dictionaries. Usage labels such as style labels and attitude labels still remain a big challenge. It would be easier for users if lexicographers could be committed to employ an agreed set of abbreviations and labels. It is true that every dictionary intends to be unique; however, being unique should be focused more on giving different kinds of usage information for different users, instead of being unique or just idiosyncratic in its use of abbreviations and labels. In terms of utilizing parallel corpora in making a bilingual/bilingualized dictionary, the results show that the two bilingualized dictionaries, LDOCE and OALD, are corpus-based; however, the two bilingual dictionaries, MECD and MFECD, are not based on corpora.

The present study also demonstrates the strong and weak points of the four tested dictionaries. LDOCE has 20 unique language notes to indicate the pragmatic usage of expressions, such as addressing peoples, apologies and so on. It also has 400 usage notes to suggest the difference of usage concerning some common language errors. The dictionary has 83,000 definitions with only 2,000 words as defining vocabulary, and has 80,000 examples, more than 20 pages of colour illusions and more than 1,000 other kinds of illustrations. Many participants said that LDOCE is a good learners' dictionary with much pragmatic information that is suited to learning and word recognition. LDOCE received the highest percentage of positive evaluations among the six tested dictionaries. However, the dictionary is designed by native speakers of English and the target group of users is made of second language learners of English; at this early stage, therefore, it offers no help as to how to avoid common errors.

The first edition of OALD was published in 1948 with A.S. Hornby as editor. In 2005, it published its 7th edition with Sally Wehmeier as the chief editor. OALD released its 7th edition in 2005. The present research is based on the 5th edition published in 1995, which was translated and published in China in 2004. The dictionary has 90,000 examples, 40 study pages and 1,700 illustrations to indicate language usage. OALD uses 3,000 definition words. It has 'new usage notes, word-family boxes, topic and study pages show links between vocabulary items and, together with the user-friendly help notes, give invaluable guidance on usage' (Sally Wehmeier:xv). OALD also has a short-cut function to 'help the user pinpoint the meaning they are looking for' (ibid). OALD does not have as much pragmatic information as LDOCE, but focuses more on the grammatical, syntactic and semantic meaning of a word. In this study, OALD receives the second highest positive evaluations, which is 0.1% higher than MFECD. According to the participants, OALD seems to lack more pragmatic information for Chinese learners, for example, politeness principles. Besides, it is hard for users without receiving any instructions to figure out the syntactic function of a transitive or intransitive verb by looking up the abbreviations. However, if the user can grasp the usage of abbreviations for the grammatical and syntactical function, OALD is a very powerful tool to learn both grammatical and pragmatic usage of a word.

MFECD and MECD are two bilingual dictionaries selected for this study. MFECD[1] claims to have 12 innovations that are suited to intermediate or advanced learners of English. These innovations are: (1) collocations to help users to make sentences and writing (2) different sentence patterns to help users with different writing styles (3) verb pattern drills to help users to imitate (4) marking separate collocations, e.g. go...into... (5)

giving POS (part of speech) to idioms (6) building-up vocabulary columns (7) illustrations (8) showing usage of spoken and written language etc. The dictionary is multifunctional, because it has many illustrations, usage notes and cultural notes. According to the evaluations from the Chinese participants, MFECD receives the third most positive evaluations. However, the content of the dictionary seems to be diverged. Some of the pragmatic functions are obvious to learners of Chinese but much of the information is superfluous and redundant.

MECD is a good example of being simple, brief and clear. The dictionary has 489 usage notes and 200 illustrations. Similar to LDOCE, MECD also gives pragmatic information on politeness principles of speech act verbs, such as addressing peoples and apologies. However, these politeness principles are given within the entry after the definitions, examples and translation equivalents. However, it is a pity that MECD only cites politeness principles from LDOCE without adding any comments to pinpoint to the Chinese learners about the difference. It is hard to conclude which ways of giving politeness principles is better: separate pages like LDOCE or within the entries. Some interviewees prefer the previous one, some prefer the later one. Maybe due to the size, MECD receives the lowest positive evaluations among the four tested English-Chinese dictionaries.

The study also shows that the lexicographer's expectations and the user's linguistic needs in the learning and cognition process have not quite matched fully. Therefore, pedagogical lexicography in the near future should add more pragmatic information in bilingual dictionaries.

Notes

1. This is the English translation of L2 innovations on page III in MFECD. Due to constraints of space, some of the innovations are not listed here – further information can be found in MFECD.

Grammatical class, tags and lemmas: A corpus-based study of the Malay lexicon

Gerry Knowles
Lancaster University
g.knowles@lancaster.ac.uk

Zuraidah Mohd Don
University of Malaya
zuraida@um.edu.my

1. Introduction

This chapter raises the question of the role of word class in automatic text processing. The conventional 'parts of speech' are generally treated as though they existed in their own right; but we shall argue that they conflate at least two quite different kinds of classification. The unwritten rule that members of the same lemma belong to the same 'part of speech' may be practically useful in the analysis of some languages – especially English and other Indo-European languages – but leads to a confusion between the class of the lemma and the class of individual lexical items.

An important point raised by Azhar M. Simin (1968) is that empirical data is essential for the description of Malay grammar. This is a point which we take for granted and which we develop further in our corpus-based approach. In this respect we are not doing something entirely new but rather using computer technology to update long-standing practice in linguistics generally, and in Malay grammatical analysis in particular.

The work reported here was undertaken on the MALEX project, which takes a systematic approach to the structure of Malay, using corpus data so far amounting to some three million words (see Knowles and Zuraidah 2006). The first stage was to design a grammatical tagset for Malay, and it quickly revealed that Malay grammatical classes do not operate like English 'parts of speech'. The complexity of Malay syntax makes it inappropriate to talk of 'ambiguity' in tagging, and an alternative approach had to be devised. Work on the tagset required an analysis of the morphology, which in turn raised the question of the status of the Malay lemma. Malay lemmas are so structured that it is not possible to claim that their members all belong to the same grammatical class. The classification of Malay lemmas raises fundamental theoretical issues quite different in nature from those involved in tagging individual lexical items. As far as we are aware, these issues have not hitherto been addressed in corpus linguistics. However, they have major practical consequences not only for text processing but also for lexicography, since assigning a class to dictionary headwords is not the same as assigning a class to words grouped under the headword. At the time of writing, the database contains some 27,000 lemmatised lexical items extracted from the corpus, and work is underway on the classification of over 7,000 lemmas.

1.1. Grammatical class in Malay

The starting point for the study of grammatical class in Malay is the morphology (Abdullah 1974; Mahmood 1995). For example, the affixes *peng-*, *pe-*, *per-* and *-an* form nouns irrespective of the class of the lemma to which they belong. Words with the prefix *di-* are passive verbs which can be followed by an agent phrase introduced by the preposition *oleh*. Words containing the suffix *-kan* are with very few exceptions transitive verbs, and the exceptions form an arbitrary set of words and do not constitute an otherwise motivated subclass of lemmas. In other cases, however, words of a morphological class belong to several grammatical classes, and words of the same grammatical class belong to several different morphological classes. For example, the prefix *ter-* forms a superlative when added to an adjective, and an agentless passive when added to a transitive verb. Simplex forms can belong to any grammatical class, and there is no automatic method of assigning them to their grammatical class. Using a conventional relational database, a lexical entry has to therefore contain information on both morphological class and grammatical class.

Given the grammatical class of a word, we can predict the kinds of syntactic environment in which it will occur in texts, and also the restrictions on its occurrence. If we examine words in detail, we might also find occurrences and restrictions or other idiosyncratic ('idiomatic') behaviour which are not predictable from the general class label. There are also words, typically frequent words such as *sudah*, *lepas* and *lalu* (words that describe something that happened in the past), which behave in such highly idiosyncratic ways that any grammatical class label can at best account for only part of their distribution in texts. In designing a tagset based on grammatical class, we aim to maximise the predictability, so that the parser can handle the greatest possible amount of data with the simplest possible set of rules. The parser still has the task of tracking idiosyncratic word behaviour, and is subject to diminishing returns, for a large amount of programming and processing is devoted to the last few percent of the data.

At the beginning of the project we were very careful to use Malay terms for Malay grammatical classes, e.g. *kata nama* 'noun' or *kata kerja* 'verb'. This is because a *kata kerja* does not have the same properties or distribution as an English verb, and so logically has a different definition. As work progressed, and the relationship between Malay and English classes was better understood, it became possible to use English terms for Malay without confusion, *mutatis mutandis*. However, an important outcome of this approach was that words that never really fitted into the system of parts of speech emerged as interesting classes in their own right.

For example, the list is in origin an ordinary syntactic structure with co-ordinated items, e.g. *Ali dan Zalina minum kopi* ('Ali and Zalina drink coffee') or *Ali minum teh dan Zalina minum kopi* ('Ali drinks tea and Zalina drinks coffee'). Words such as *and* and *or* are opaquely classed as coordinating conjunctions, while there are no satisfactory terms for other words which construct lists, including *too*, *also*, and *either*. The list is, however, an extremely useful logical structure, and in recent decades it has been given an increasingly important status in structured documents. In order to process modern texts (in any language) we need to process lists, and it would be perverse to force list organisers into a system of conventional 'parts of speech'

The traditional domain of syntax is the grammatical sentence, but there are a number of words and morphemes which are found in sentences but which operate at discourse level. For instance, discourse level clitics such as the questioning *-kah* and the 'emphatic' *-lah* can be ignored by the parser at the syntactic level because they relate to such things as speech acts and so-called 'emphasis'. Sentence level criteria do not necessarily apply at discourse level. In English, for example, *enter* is indisputably a verb, and *entrance* is indisputably a noun. In Malay, *masuk* can be used as an invitation to enter a room, or as a sign at the entrance to a carpark: and to ask whether it is a 'verb' or a 'noun' is to miss the point that it is not necessarily either. Words of this kind do not have grammatical class as a fixed property, but take on grammatical class when they enter into a syntactic structure.

2. Grammatical class and syntax

In order to establish well motivated grammatical classes, we have to find a link between sets of words in the lexicon and the syntactic patterns in which we find them in the texts. If we had a list of grammatical classes, then using our corpus we could identify the syntactic patterns with which they were associated. Conversely, if we knew what the syntactic patterns were, we could identify the classes of word associated with them. Our problem is that we have to identify the grammatical classes and the syntactic patterns at the same time. We could of course examine the distribution of individual words, but that would give us information about collocations, not grammatical class, and would require a huge corpus in any case.

As grammatical analysis proceeds and more detailed analyses are made, classes have to be subdivided into subclasses. For example, nouns of time, such as *malam* ('night') and *minggu* ('week'), emerged as a subclass of nouns with special properties, including the property that when they head noun phrases they tend to function as adverbial expressions (e.g. *malam ini* ('this night'), *minggu lepas* ('last week')). These are now marked in the lexicon so that the parser can deal with them together as a group. Subclasses can sometimes be subdivided again, and in extreme cases we get down to singleton classes with just one member. A number of frequent words, including *telah*, *sudah*, *lepas* and *lalu*, are highly idiosyncratic in their syntactic behaviour, and belong to singleton classes. The only way to deal with such words is to study their distribution in a concordance, and to write individual program modules to track their behaviour.

It is conventional to think of syntactic structures as providing a number of structural positions or 'slots' into which words can be fitted. A grammatical rule of the form
NP = Determiner + Adjective + Noun
and the corresponding rule for Malay
NP = Noun + Adjective + Determiner
imply that there is a special adjective slot which is filled by adjectives. However innocuous this might appear, there are obvious logical dangers in using the same term for the slot and its filler, for these are related as container and contents. Using terms loosely, we might say that 'adjectives' precede 'nouns' in English and follow them in Malay without concern for whether we are talking about slots or fillers. But this kind of logical slippage causes serious problems when we attempt to automate our analytic procedures, particularly for a language like Malay for which grammatical classes have not yet been ascertained.

The Malay rule (ignoring the determiner) generates such phrases as *rumah besar* ('big house'), *pintu hijau* ('green door'), and *kampung baru* ('new village'). However, in corpus texts the noun + adjective sequence is only one of a set, and is not even the most frequent type. Alongside the *pintu hijau* ('green door') type we have the far more common noun + noun *pintu rumah* ('house door'), and there is also noun + simplex verb *pintu masuk* ('entrance door'), and noun + relative clause *pintu yang hijau* ('the door which is green'). Viewing syntax from parts of speech gives us a distorted view, and we have to examine syntactic positions in their own right. In more general terms, what we have here is the familiar head + modifier construction. The head is normally a noun, and there are several possible fillers for the modifier slot, one of which is an adjective. The use of an adjective as a modifier is one prototype for this construction, but only one amongst several.

In fitting words into syntactic slots, we are interfacing two different kinds of linguistic organisation, syntax and lexis. From a syntactic point of view we can ask what kind of expressions can fit the noun modifier slot, and we find that adjectives, amongst others, can do so. From a lexical point of view we can ask what kind of syntactic slots adjectives can fit into. The noun modifier slot is of course one, and the predicator slot is another, for example, *pintu ini hijau* ('this door is green'). An important property of Malay adjectives is that they fill the predicator slot without the help of a copula verb. A third slot is the predicator modifier position, as in a sentence such as *nasi ini sedap benar* ('this rice is truly delicious'). Both *sedap* ('delicious') and *benar* ('true') are lexically adjectives, the first filling the predicator slot and the second the modifier slot. If we fail to make and maintain a rigorous logical distinction between slots and fillers, we can argue endlessly whether *sedap* is a verb or an adjective, and whether *benar* is an adjective or an adverb. The chronic confusion over 'adverbs' in Malay is a direct consequence of the failure to make the logical distinction between slots and fillers.

3. Syntactic drift

Derivational morphology apparently converts words from one grammatical class to another. For example, the English suffix *-ness* turns the adjective *good* into the noun *goodness*, and similarly the Malay circumfix *ke-..-an* converts the adjective *adil* ('just') into the noun *keadilan* ('justice'). It would be more precise to say that *-ness* and *ke-..-an* enable adjectives to fit into slots normally reserved for nouns. In other cases, words that belong to one class can be used without modification in slots associated with some other class, so that the English verbs *walk* and *talk* can fill head noun slots, and the nouns *bottle*, *chair* and *table* can be used to fill the predicator slot. In some cases the conversion is regular, so that it can be regarded as part of the grammar of the language, while in others it applies only to particular lexical items, for example, the adjective *deep* drifts idiosyncratically into the head noun slot in the poetic phrase *the deep* 'the ocean'.

We use the term 'syntactic drift' (Knowles et al. 2003) to refer to the use of words in syntactic slots away from their 'home' slot without morphological marking. Drift has been long understood by Malay scholars, including Western scholars working on Malay. For example:

'Malay words change their function according to context. Be prepared for this, and do not attempt to force the language into a set mould. It will escape.' (Lewis 1947: xvii)

In the conventional grammatical tagging of English texts, drift is treated as a kind of 'ambiguity', so that words like *walk* and *bottle* are regarded as ambiguously nouns or verbs; and such ambiguities have to be resolved before the task of syntactic parsing can begin. There will be a large number of these 'ambiguities' in an English text, but not enough to cast doubt on the general procedure. If we approach Malay texts in this way, we find 'ambiguity' so systematic and general that it becomes obvious that this is the wrong way of going about the task of solving the problem.

The extent of syntactic drift in Malay is immediately apparent from a cursory examination of the grammar of texts. Here it is possible to give only some brief indications. We are essentially tracing the occurrence of members of lemmas in different syntactic slots, and since morphological marking restricts the slots which a word can fill, we are particularly concerned with the simplex form. Consider again the case of *masuk* ('enter'), which is normally regarded as a verb, which means that it fills the predicator slot. It can also fit the noun modifier slot, as in *pintu masuk*, in which case it feels more like a 'noun'. However, it cannot fill the head noun slot, for to do that it must take the *ke-..-an* circumfix, thus *kemasukan*. Words relating to feelings, such as *cinta*, *benci*, and *hormat*, can also be thought of as verbs, but when they are considered out of any syntactic context, whether they are 'noun' or 'verbs' is again irrelevant. Unlike *masuk*, these words can drift into the head noun slot, as in the phrase *hormatnya kepada ibunya* 'his respect for his mother'. 'State' words such as *besar* 'big' or *hijau* 'green' pattern rather like *masuk*, normally occurring as predicators, such as *kereta saya hijau* ('my car is green') or *kereta yang hijau* ('car which is green'). They can drift into the noun modifier slot, such as *kereta hijau itu* ('that green car'), but cannot fill the head noun slot. And as already noted, a number of adjectives fill the predicator modifier slot. If we were to take an English view of Malay we might assume that the normal use of an 'adjective' like *hijau* is in the attributive position after the noun, and we would treat the use of an 'adjective' as a predicator without a copula verb as an oddity of the language, and regard as an unrelated fact the use of some 'adjectives' as 'adverbs'. By tracing syntactic drift, we find that adjectives pattern as a subset of verbs, and have their own patterns of distribution. In this way the intrinsic patterns of the language begin to emerge.

The recognition of drift has important consequences for the design of tagger and parser. In tagging English, many words may be given multiple tags in the lexicon, and the 'ambiguities' are resolved by the tagger so that the correct tag is sent to the parser for any instance of the word in the text. But if the parser is designed to follow syntactic drift, then patterns of drift can be predicted from a single tag in the lexicon, and so tagging in the lexicon can be simplified considerably. We do need some way of tracking the behaviour of idiosyncratic words, but these will have to be specified individually anyway by the parser. For example, *pukul* ('strike') is essentially a verb, but occurs idiosyncratically in time expressions such as *pukul tiga* ('three o'clock'), and so the parser will have to look for the specific item *pukul* in time expressions. If the ambiguity of this word is handled systematically by the parser, there is no point in storing the same information redundantly in the lexicon.

4. Lemma classification in Malay

The lemma is a set of lexical items (Knowles et al. 2004). For example, the English lemma WALK contains the members *walk*, *walks*, *walked* and *walking*. If all members of the lemma are held to belong by definition to the same part of speech (as is standard practice for English), then the lemma has the same class as any of its members. But if members belong to several different classes, it is not clear which of these, if any, the whole lemma should belong to. The standard approach for English leads to a number of awkward conclusions, for instance that corresponding to words like *walk* and *bottle* are two completely different lemmas, one a noun and the other a verb. But *walk* is like many verbs that can be used unmodified as nouns, and *bottle* is like a number of nouns referring to containers which can be used as verbs meaning 'put into a <container>'. If we trace English words back through the derivational morphology, we get back to a simplex form with which we can perhaps determine the class of the lemma.

In the same way, the Malay verb *membotolkan* ('bottle') can be traced back to the noun *botol*. As in English, we take for granted that the class of the lemma is connected with the simplex form rather than with morphologically complex forms. Here we encounter a problem, for the simplex form in Malay can be highly idiosyncratic in its behaviour. For example, the verb *berjalan* ('walk') is a member of the lemma JALAN, but the simplex form *jalan* is typically used to mean 'street, road'. Another more general problem is that the simplex forms of many of the lemmas we might wish to class as verbs can only be used as verbs if they are imperative.

In reality, this approach to the classification of lemmas is unlikely ever to work. We defined grammatical class above in terms of the syntactic distribution of words: given the class of a word we can predict the syntactic slots it is allowed to fill. The lemma, by contrast, is a lexical concept, and given the class of a lemma we can predict its membership (within limits) and the grammatical class of its members. For example, the lemma BESAR has the members *besar* ('big'), which is an adjective, and *membesarkan* ('increase'), which is a verb; and in the case of the lemma TULIS ('write'), the form *menulis* is a verb while *penulis* ('writer') is a noun. Reduplication affects grammatical class in different ways, making a kind of plural in the case of nouns, such as *buku-buku* ('books'), but having different interpretations in *awak-awak*, *apa-apa* and *tiba-tiba* ('suddenly'). The prefix *ke-* forms ordinals when added to numbers, such as *kedua* ('second') or *ketiga* ('third'), but forms a noun *ketua* ('head') from *tua* ('old'). Words formed with the prefix *ber-* are typically verbs, but the subclass of verb depends on the lemma class, as in the case of *bertanya* ('ask'), *beristeri* ('have a wife') and *berdua* ('be in a twosome'). We can use patterns of this kind to identify lemma classes and subclasses. So although it might appeal to common sense to suggest that the lemma WALK feels like a verb and BOTTLE like a noun, it is quite inappropriate to use grammatical class as labels for lemmas.

In classifying lemmas, the first distinction to be made is between those that relate to concepts, and those which do not. This distinction is better known as that between 'content' words and 'function' words. Content lemmas divide into those denoting states of affairs and those denoting participants in states of affairs. Lemmas relating to participant roles are those typically thought of as 'nouns'. States of affairs divide further into dynamic and static, roughly corresponding to verbs and adjectives respectively.

Lemmas denoting states of affairs are more commonly referred to as predicates, while those denoting participant roles are referred to as arguments.[1] For predicates the lexical entry needs to include the number and type of argument, such as MINUM ('drink'), which typically has an associated animate drinker, and a liquid which is drunk. These properties are inherited by members of the lemma, such as in the phrase *minuman sejuk* ('a cold drink') the drink is still a liquid to be drunk by an implied drinker. Predicates usually pattern syntactically as verbs or adjectives, while arguments pattern as nouns, such as in *Ali minum kopi* ('Ali drinks coffee'), *minum* is a verb, while *Ali* and *kopi* are nouns. Grammatical class is a predictable property not of the lemma itself, but of the members of a lemma when used in a syntactic context.

5. Semantic tagging

In distinguishing predicates, arguments, and function words, we have made a rough typological classification of lemmas. A more interesting task is to classify them according to their meaning. This can be done in a number of ways, of which the most accessible involves the use of some kind of thesaurus, which roughly groups words according to their meaning. By using appropriate labels for word groups, it is possible to devise a set of semantic tags to label the words of a text, such as *hijau* ('green'), which can be tagged as a colour term.

One of the difficulties of this approach is that words can be grouped in many different ways, and some words belong to several groups. As in the case of grammatical tagging, some words are easy to classify, while others are extremely difficult. Colour terms, for example, are straight forward, whereas *puasa* ('fast, not eat') or *amuk* ('[run] amok') have complex meanings and can therefore be treated in different ways. Semantic classification cannot be left to the judgement of the person who happens to undertake the task, and clearly has to be based on some firm semantic evidence.

6. Ontology

The concept of an ontology was developed in the last quarter of the twentieth century, but disappeared almost without trace in the 1990s, and then re-emerged at the beginning of the present century as a key concept in knowledge representation (e.g. Sowa 2000). An ontology goes beyond a thesaurus in making explicit the relationships among meaningful items. At the heart of an ontology is a taxonomy in which classes are formally related in different ways but most importantly by the 'is a' relation. For example, a mouse is a rodent, which is a mammal, which in turn is a vertebrate. If an object is classed as a mouse, then using propositional logic we can infer that it is also a mammal and a vertebrate. More interestingly, we can make inferences that enable us to interpret 'the mouse gave birth to baby mice', because we know that giving birth is a property of mammals; and similarly we can interpret 'the mouse's neck was broken' because we know that vertebrates have necks containing bones that can be broken. In the ontology, the taxonomy is enriched by rules that enable inferences to be drawn.

The subset of lemmas in a given language corresponding to concepts belongs to an ontology. The taxonomy is constructed using the noun-like arguments, as in the mouse example above. Predicates, by contrast, are properties of classes in the taxonomy. For example, *run* is a property of all land animals, while *die* is a property of all living things. Similarly, *taciturn* and *talkative* can be attributed only to human beings, while *old* can be attributed to any living thing, and *green* to any object or physical substance.

There is an important connection between the taxonomy and the properties of its classes. If we possess the complete taxonomy, it is possible to link properties to the appropriate class; and conversely, if we know the class to which each property relates, we can infer the structure of the taxonomy. The problem is that (as before) we have to work them out together. This work is currently underway, and while it is too early to publish the results, some interesting problems have already emerged.

To begin with, the structure of the taxonomy is a lattice rather than a tree. The difference is that in a tree, each class is a subclass of only one higher class, whereas in a lattice a class may be a subclass of more than one higher class. The examples above show that the taxonomy has to include mammals, land animals and vertebrates. Mammals are a subclass of vertebrates, but part of the class of vertebrates forms a subclass of land animals, while the remainder form a subclass of sea animals. This means that, for example, a horse inherits some of its properties as a land animal, and other properties as a mammal. At a higher level, land animals and sea animals are subclasses of animal. This is a simple example, but it illustrates some of the complexity of the relationships among lemmas.

It would be very convenient if it were possible to set up a single ontology to model the structure of human knowledge, but the second problem is that this is alas not the case. In practice there is a large set of possible ontologies, even for an area such as medicine, and the experience of constructing ontologies shows that their structure depends on the purpose for which they are designed. Ontologies are normally thought of as existing outside language, and belong to some area of expert knowledge, such as medicine, law or biology. However, since the kind of ontology outlined here traces relationships between the lemmas of a particular language, it is clearly a structure that belongs within language. Fortunately, there is no need to argue in favour of one view at the expense of the other, for both types of ontology clearly coexist. For example, *heart attack* is an everyday expression that belongs to a traditional linguistic ontology, and it corresponds to *myocardial infarction*, which belongs in an expert medical ontology. The linguistic ontology reflects the way the outside world is traditionally encoded in language, while the expert ontology represents an attempt to represent the outside world directly and independently of language.

7. Conclusion

A clear distinction has been drawn in this chapter between grammatical class and lemma class. From grammatical class we can predict the syntactic positions which a word can fill. The lemma class relates a lemma to other lemmas in the lexicon, and from the class of a lemma we can to a certain extent predict its membership, and the meaning and grammatical class of its members. The motivation for setting up classes is that they can be used to make useful predictions in the processing of texts; and the motivation for distinguishing grammatical class and lemma class is that they lead to different sets of predictions.

The distinction has a number of practical applications. First, regarding conventional applications of linguistic theory, it has applications in Malay lexicography. In a dictionary, such as Kamus Dewan, it is appropriate to specify the grammatical class of individual lexical words, so that *menulis* ('to write') can be labelled a verb, and *penulis* ('writer') a noun, on the condition that traditional 'parts-of-speech' are redefined in a corresponding grammar in a manner suitable for Malay, and in terms of the syntactic positions words of different classes can fill. On the other hand, it would be totally inappropriate to use the term 'verb' to label the headword TULIS, which roughly corresponds to the lemma. In the case of modern speech and language technology, the distinction is fundamental, and the long delay in developing technologies for Malay is due in no small measure to the lack of solutions to problems of this kind.

Text processing starts with the data, and as the text is processed – normalised, grammatically tagged, parsed, and semantically tagged – the labels applied to the text become increasingly abstract. The output of this endeavour is expertly annotated data. Extremely valuable as it is, this does not amount to a theory of how language works. However, given data which is annotated in sufficient detail and with sufficient accuracy, we can work out the different components of language, and how they work together as a system. This is known to engineers as 'reverse engineering'. The engineer typically creates a set of components which work together as a system; in linguistic analysis we reverse the process because we begin with a set of components that works together as a system, and we have to find out what those components are and how they work.

The important difference is that in linguistic research we adopt a viewpoint inside language, and if we deal with meaning at all, we look from within language to meaning outside language. The engineer, by contrast, stands outside language, and looks into language to understand how things are encoded. While we are finding out how the language works, we have to take an inside-out perspective; but when we understand the workings of the language system, we use it as a component in language-based applications, and at this stage an outside-in perspective is more appropriate. Twentieth century linguistics was largely concerned with the workings of the language system; in the present century we can look forward to using the language system as a component in the investigation of larger scale problems.

Notes

1. On this there is a huge literature emanating from the work of Fillmore (1968), including work on 'valence' or 'valency' (e.g. Allerton (1973)). We are moving here in a slightly different direction, because predicates and their arguments are included in a working system.

Analysing *sorrow* and *grief*: A contrastive-semantic perspective

Ruihua Zhang
National University of Singapore
ruihuaz@gmail.com

1. Introduction

The emotional lexicons of different languages vary remarkably, which reveals considerable differences between ideas and beliefs about emotions and between cultural models of emotions. Analysis of the emotional lexicon of a certain language helps reveal the concepts available to its speakers through which they categorize the emotions they witness or experience. Where they are lexicalized in a single word, the presence of a word implies the existence of the concept it expresses. Language-specific sets of emotion words might overlap across languages. The comparison of the emotion lexicon of a language with that of another language can therefore suggest similarities and differences in the conceptualization of emotion.

This chapter examines two emotion-denoting English words, *sorrow* and *grief*, and their Chinese equivalents relying on concordance lines, with a focus on identifying what elements are common to both languages and what elements are specific to English or Chinese. By comparing and contrasting the meanings of these emotion terms, their emotive content is revealed and cultural difference of emotion between English and Chinese is highlighted.

2. *Sorrow* and *grief*

Sorrow and *grief* are two common emotion-denoting terms in English, which are usually viewed as synonyms. In the sentence 'His fervent soul was full of sorrow for the world and its sinfulness', it seems to be possible that *grief* can be substituted for *sorrow*. However, most native speakers of English would agree that in these two sentences 'Grief gave way to a guilt that gnawed at him' and 'A magic harp music made its listeners forget sorrow', *grief* cannot be replaced by *sorrow*, and vice versa (Teubert 2000). So, in a strict sense, they cannot be regarded as synonyms. Native speakers of English may understand their meanings, but they are less competent in describing them. To determine what emotion concepts they are associated with respectively, I turned to two dictionaries, the 1987 COBUILD and the 1998 *New Oxford Dictionary of English* (NODE). There I found the following entries:

COBUILD
sorrow
- a feeling of deep sadness or regret, or caused by the death of someone you love or because of your sympathy for the sufferings of someone else
- a sorrow is an event or situation that causes deep sadness

grief
- extreme sadness
- a grief is something unpleasant that happens which causes someone great sadness or unhappiness

NODE
sorrow
- a feeling of deep distress caused by loss, disappointment, or other misfortune suffered by oneself or others
- an event or circumstance that causes such a feeling

grief
- deep or intense sorrow, especially caused by someone's death

According to COBUILD and NODE, it seems obvious that sadness is the hypernym of *sorrow* and *grief*, and that *grief* is a more intense feeling of sadness than *sorrow*, though both of them can be caused by someone's death. But do they differ only in intensity? To explore their semantic differences, I went to WordNet, an online dictionary:

sorrow
- **S1:** (n) sorrow (an emotion of great sadness associated with loss or bereavement) 'he tried to express his sorrow at her loss'
- **S2:** (n) sorrow, regret, rue, ruefulness (sadness associated with some wrong done or some disappointment) 'he drank to drown his sorrows'
- **S3:** (n) grief, sorrow (something that causes great unhappiness) 'her death was a great grief to John'
- **S4:** (n) sadness, sorrow, sorrowfulness (the state of being sad) 'she tired of his perpetual sadness'

grief
- **S1:** (n) grief, heartache, heartbreak, brokenheartedness (intense sorrow caused by loss of a loved one (especially by death))
- **S2:** (n) grief, sorrow (something that causes great unhappiness) 'her death was a great grief to John'

A comparison of the four senses of *sorrow* (n) above with its two senses of NODE and COBUILD reveals that WordNet senses 1, 2 and 4 are combined into sense 1 of NODE/COBUILD. WordNet sense 3 corresponds to sense 2 of NODE/COBUILD. The breakdown of one sense into three senses can be explained by Sinclair's 'Thespian' approach (1996). Words like *sorrow* may be said to have a prototypical meaning (Lakoff and Johnson 1999), but lexicographers find difficult to provide a plausible definition that can capture all the features (Teubert 2000). A close inspection of the definitions above

Analysing *sorrow* and *grief*: A contrastive-semantic perspective 53

shows that the senses of *sorrow* are closely related, basically referring to a sad feeling or an event/situation that can cause such a feeling. The same is true of *grief*. However, we are still not told how to distinguish them from each other; why in the sentences we mentioned earlier they can not be substituted for each other. It might be helpful to draw on corpus data if we want to have a full understanding of their semantic components and differentiate them from each other.

Since the senses of *sorrow* as a noun are all associated with the same emotion concept, I simply searched for *sorrow*/NOUN (inclusive of its plural form) in the Bank of English (containing about 450 million words). By the same token, I looked at *grief* and its plural form *griefs*. 9033 hits for *grief(s)* and 3615 hits for *sorrow(s)* were found in the large corpus. Their collocates are shown below (looking-up only gives the 50 most frequent collocates with the node word), with grammatical words and some insignificant words omitted:

Table 1 Most frequent collocates of *grief* and *sorrow*

	GRIEF(S)	SORROW(S)
Emotions	anger (281), pain (170), grief (106), fear (95), guilt (90), sorrow (58), joy (52), rage (52), sadness (49), mourning (46), despair (45)	anger (151), joy* (170), pain (101), grief (65), fear (48), love (48), regret (38), guilt (28), rage (28), despair (27), happiness (25), sadness (19)
Others	stricken (367), loss (270), cause* (185), death (187), family (164), share* (149), shock (118), mother (96), outpouring (82), tears (57), suffering (55), overcome (53)	drown*(228), death (65), loss (58), heart (43), suffering (40), tears (37), eyes (35), shock (30)

* inclusive of possible inflectional forms

It is not surprising that the most frequent collocate of *grief* is *stricken* (367), which comes from the prefabricated phrase – *grief stricken*. The high co-occurring frequency of *shock* (118) might imply that the trigger of the grief feeling may well be an unexpected event, leading to a sudden violent disturbance of the mind or emotions. We might assume that one's initial response to an immediate cause, a recent loss, often the death of a close person, would be numbness and disbelief as one would feel it hard to accept the extremely unpleasant fact. Then it may develop into a mixture of feelings, with grief mingled with other emotional responses such as anger/rage, pain, fear, guilt or despair (as found in its collocates) when s/he is more aware of the situation. The complexities of feelings that can be invoked in grief-contexts are clearly exhibited in the following examples from the corpus:

(1) Instead, the families had to spend a long night of fear, worry, grief and total despair.

(2) They arrange to leave Lahardane in the hands of Henry and Bridget,

their housekeepers. But Lucy, with a passion for her home and the landscape around her, runs away. Torn by guilt and grief, her parents wait for news. When none comes they assume that they have driven Lucy to suicide and leave.

(3) Then she broke down in tears again and buried her head in Maggie's shoulder. Banks took a deep breath. Claire's pain and guilt and grief were so real they broke over him in waves and made his breath catch in his chest.

It appears that common discussions of various feelings together in the discourse (if we regard the Bank of English as a discourse) may also have helped contribute to the high frequencies of emotion words in its collocates, as exemplified below:

(4) It is not enough just to recognize what society has done to us which leads us to feel shame, guilt, hate, grief, pride, envy and fear.

From the statistics in the table, it can be argued that the principal determinant of grief is loss (270), which is well in line with psychological findings. The loss may be temporary (separation) or permanent (death), real or imagined, physical or psychological. The loss of a loved person often results in the experience of grief; losing a loved one also means the loss of strong bonds of friendship, companionship or love, etc. (Izard 1991). From a psychological perspective, people who experience grief may come to blame themselves for the loss (*guilt*, 90); *anger* (281), *fear* (95) and *despair* (45) may also occur as a result of blaming someone else for the separation or as a result of feeling left alone or deserted (Izard 1977).

149 occurrences of the word *share* or its other inflectional form in its contexts might suggest that grief is an intense emotion elicited by a misfortune over which the individual has no control, but it may be overcome (53) by sharing it with others. For example, at a time of death, a family comes together to mourn, and although it is death that brings about this closeness, there is a keen sense of affectionate ties with other members of the family. This sense of belonging is an extremely important part of a person's psychological roots. Shared grief over the loss of a loved one can thus reunite a family and facilitate cohesiveness (Izard 1991). Grief is inherently adaptive for the individual since it enables her or him to 'work through' or overcome the loss (Izard 1991).

The word *outpouring* (82) in its collocates may indicate that grief is a sudden and strong feeling which is usually expressed publicly. Outpouring of grief provides 'some relief and a sense of release' (Wellenkamp 1988:495). Expressions of grief can also serve a communicative function, eliciting empathy and strengthening bonds among all those who are bereaved; they may convey to others the message that the bereaved person is a loving and caring individual via public mourning (46) rituals (Izard 1977).

The fact that *joy* collocates frequently with *grief* is, on the one hand, due to frequent discussions of various feelings (negative or positive) together in

the discourse, as pointed out earlier, and on the other hand, due to the use of patterns such as *joy and grief* (or *grief and joy*), as exemplified below:
(5) Effects of Alcohol Ever since Stone Age people became intoxicated from drinking the liquid oozing from fruit left too long in a warm place, alcohol has been bringing both joy and grief to humankind.

The same explanations can account for sorrow's frequent co-occurrence with positive emotion words, such as love, joy(s), happiness, etc.

So far, the discussion has focused on *grief* as a feeling. The following examples illustrate what is a *grief* in its WordNet sense 2 (something that causes great unhappiness), which only accounts for a tiny percentage of the total instances:
(6) ...the love of money forces our thoughts in other directions. Consequently right in our own day, unless I am much mistaken, some of your books have disappeared, I fear beyond recovery. It is a great grief to me, a great disgrace to this generation, a great wrong done to posterity. The shame of failing to cultivate our own talents, thereby depriving the future of the fruits that they might have...
(7) Although it had been known that Grant was in failing health, his death on May 13, 1902, in the midst of his work, at a crisis in Queen's affairs, came to the university not only as a grief and a loss, but as a grave blow.

Grief is conceived of as an emotion prototypically linked with death, so the death of someone who is special to a particular group might come as a grief as shown in Example 7. However, it can also be extended to other situations where one will suffer to a similar degree as consequence of other intolerably unpleasant events. The desertion of books and pursuit of money in Example 6 is a good illustrative example of such events.

A glimpse of *sorrow*'s collocates will show that it might also be caused by the loss of something or the death of someone. But from the absence of words such as *family, mother* in its 50 most frequent collocates, it is reasonable to assume that, typically, it means something quite different. Like grief, sorrow is also highly related to a range of other negative emotional responses, such as rage, pain, fear, guilt and despair, as found in its collocates. As pointed out earlier, the emotional responses towards an unpleasant event or situation might be complex. The reactions may go through several phases: the first response would be the awareness of the loss; then one might think about the cause, the circumstance or the change it may bring about, etc.; and finally the emotion would be transformed into a combination of sorrow with rage, fear, guilt, despair or anger, or some (or all) of them, depending on the associations invoked by the given event. So it is hardly surprising to find that *sorrow* and *anger* often co-exist:
(8) ...is that 300 people died in the bombing of the building where they took shelter, the building the US says was a military communications bunker. Wertheimer: Reaction in the Arab world is both sorrow and

anger. Jordan and Tunisia have declared days of mourning.
The fixed phrase 'more in sorrow than in anger' may explain partly why *sorrow* co-occurs most frequently with *anger* (151). Here are some typical examples from the corpus:

(9) I must say that, like the solid citizen who took Julia Somerville's boyfriend's nudie snaps of her daughter to the police, I was all for contacting the boys in blue here. All I can say, more in sorrow than in anger, is what a strange picture of the British adult is emerging here: the women using innocent babes for sensual gratification, and the men beating their tiny daughters on the bare...

(10) Now, when she complains about the damp, the council says, 'You used to complain because you were four in a room in a mixed hostel, but now you can close the door behind you!' She says this more in sorrow than in anger. 'Even animals in the zoo, they treat them nicely. Who am I, what can I say, what can I do? Nothing. I am nothing, I count for nothing...'

It is clear that if you deal with something more in sorrow than in anger, you probably mean that you have considered the whole matter carefully and come to the conclusion that you are very sad or disappointed rather than angry about it. In Example 9, the speaker is extremely disappointed because he knows clearly what that terrible picture might suggest, and in Example 10, the speaker is very sad because she is aware how unimportant she is in other people's eye. Such conclusions require more thinking about what has happened. From the discussion above, it follows that sorrow is not an emotional response as simple as anger or grief. It involves a deeper thinking about everything around what has happened rather than a simple perceptual or emotional reaction. It is a more advanced and rational emotion involving 'higher' thought processes, as compared with anger or grief.

Table 1 shows that *regret* (38) occurs quite frequently with *sorrow*, but not *grief*. Their co-occurrence mainly comes from the phrase 'sorrow and regret', as illustrated below:

(11) Details from the files are not yet available. Yeltsin expressed sorrow and regret over the incident and extended his condolences to the families of those who were killed.

(12) '...I wish to offer today a formal apology to the people of Samoa for the injustices arising from New Zealand's administration of Samoa in its earlier years, and to express sorrow and regret for those injustices,' she said.

Here regret refers to a painful state 'aroused by circumstances beyond one's control or power to repair' (Santangelo 2003:392). It is the element of regret that makes the difference between sorrow and grief. Sorrow implies that the experiencer considers the situation as uncontrollable and thus is not likely to attempt to do something about it. In other words, it is the awareness of powerlessness that is salient for sorrow. It suggests a degree of resignation ('I can't do anything about it'); it implies a 'semi-accepting', or 'semi-resigned' attitude towards what has happened (Wierzbicka 1999:66). The pain comes not only from the irreparable loss, but also from what one has obtained from a rational analysis of the whole matter. This explains why people will be more in sorrow than in anger, as discussed earlier, when they clearly know that the outbursts of anger will not help.

The following examples illustrate what a sorrow in the WordNet sense 3 (something that causes great unhappiness) could be (like *grief*, this sense of *sorrow* only accounts for a tiny percent of the total instances in the corpus):

(13) Wertheimer: What does Magic Johnson's resignation mean to you, to the commission? What is the loss? <p> Rogers: Oh, it – it's the – it – of course, it's – it's a sorrow to all of us. It's a loss of a fine human being, a very articulate force.

(14) You and I have been associated together for fourteen years – in name at least – and I had hoped for closer association in the future so that it is a very real sorrow for me to have the association end. And I can't help but ask why.

(15) I noticed that she had aged more than the years warranted. She had lost her husband and then there had been the death of her daughter-in-law, Lucian's wife. That must have been a sorrow to her.

(16) 'But her father died just before the wedding, which was a great sorrow to Ruth after the long separation from him.'

(17) …read to me and told me tales up to about my second year in elementary school, I think I would have been between four and seven. At that age, I had not yet known anything you could call a great sorrow. For that reason no doubt, when I learnt that in the end the little snail had stopped bemoaning his lot, I simply thought, 'oh, good'. That was all. I gave no special thought to the whole matter…

Examples 13-16 show that a sorrow could be someone's resignation leading to 'the loss of a fine human being, a very articulate force', or the ending of a former association, or the loss of one's husband and daughter-in-law, or the death of one's father. It would seem that sorrow and grief talk about the emotional reactions towards someone's death at different stages. Grief implies 'poignant suffering for an immediate cause, a recent loss' (Santangelo 2003:389). 'Sorrow may have its roots in the past, but the stress is on the on-going, long-term state' (Wierzbicka 1999:66). So it is likely that one still feels sorrow, which is less intense than grief, after even several years of the death of a close person. Example 17 seems to suggest that a young child does not know what a sorrow is because s/he never gives a special thought to a sad matter due to the cognitive constraints.

The most typical collocate of *sorrow* is *drown* (228). This can be explained by the idiomatic expression 'drown one's sorrows'. WordNet sense 2 uses the example 'he drank to drown his sorrows' to illustrate its meaning 'sadness associated with some wrong done or some disappointment'. Let us look at more examples from the corpus:

(18) An embassy employee who was present said: 'We were slightly depressed when the first England goal went in, but then we decided we might as well drown our sorrows and forget it.'

(19) The Locust Room is his first novel since The Mercy Boys, an exploration of maleness which had a cast of characters who drank in the same pub in a vain attempt to drown their sorrows.

(20) Don't drink alone. If you use liquor at all, drink on social occasions only. If you use it to drown your sorrows and wash away your frustrations, liquor will use you – roughly.

As shown in the examples above, the phrase basically means one drinks a lot of alcohol in order to forget his/her problem, which could be some disappointment in Example 18, frustrations in Example 20 or something else. A *vain attempt* in Example 19 seems to show that it is not so easy, as they like, to forget the problems they are aware of by getting drunk. 'In the case of grief and grieving the experience intentionally focuses on the painful subject ('I want to think about this'), whereas in the case of sorrow there is rather, an inability to forget ('I can't not think about this')' (Wierzbicka 1999:67). Sorrow is a long-term suffering which cannot be forgotten easily because there is always a conflict between the consciousness of powerlessness and the reluctance to accept the unpleasant reality. Compared with grief, sorrow 'is a longer lasting, deeper, but less intense, more introverted than extraverted, more individual than communal, more voluntary than ritualized, more personal than culturally mediated feeling' (Teubert 2000:166).

To find out whether this distinction is shared by Chinese, we need to explore the Chinese lexicon of sadness by examining their equivalents in Chinese texts.

3. Chinese equivalents of *sorrow* and *grief*

Parallel corpora are repositories of the practice of translators. 'The community of translators from language A to language B and vice versa know a lot more about translation equivalence than can be found in any of the bilingual dictionaries for these languages' (Teubert & Cermakova 2004:123). Translators often do not rely on bilingual dictionaries and 'have to acquire a competence that is the result of experience and interaction with other members of the bilingual discourse community of which they are a part' (p. 155). So parallel corpora could be a reliable resource to analyse and contrast meaning which is believed to be fuzzy and vague. Besides, cross-linguistic studies on emotions can produce more accurate descriptions of the meanings of emotion words and more generally, ways to describe emotions.

Emotions do not arise and are not expressed in vacuums. They are phenomena constructed within social contexts. The conceptualization of the individual vs. society is, I believe, mostly formed in narration. 'No inquiry into the emotions (affections) can afford to overlook poetry and narrative, since the writers of such works are more perceptive than anyone else on these matters' (Qian 1998:84). Novels seem to be a good choice for the exploration of emotion words as novels are believed to be the best embodiment of life-experience. As such, I went to an English-Chinese parallel corpus of fiction, which comprises 1,597,627 English words and 2,090,694 Chinese characters. The results (only the 4 most frequently occurring Chinese equivalents are chosen to avoid the possible complexity) are shown as follows:

Table 2 The 4 most frequently occurring Chinese equivalents for *sorrow* and *grief*

English words/ Chinese equivalents	*sorrow* 91 hits	*grief* 72 hits
beishang	27	23
you/chou**	9	—*
shangxin	9	10
nanguo	6	—*
beiai	—*	8
beitong	—*	7

* less frequent in the parallel corpus
** indicating a group of words denoting you/chou (worry) concept

On the basis of the selection criterion (the 4 most frequent), I found 5 Chinese equivalents of *sorrow* and *grief*: *beishang, shangxin, nanguo, beiai* and *beitong*, excluding *you/chou* which is not a proper equivalent because it is realized by different Chinese words. The reason why I list it here is that quite often sorrow is associated with this concept, though I am not going to discuss it in this study, otherwise it will lead us away from the core of the sadness topic. Before investigating further, I looked for their definitions in the most authoritative Chinese dictionary, Xiandai Hanyu Cidian (XHC): Bilingual edition.

Table 3 Definitions according to Xiandai Hanyu Cidian

Categories /Words	Chinese definition	English definition
beishang	shangxin; nanguo	sad: sorrowful; mournful
beitong	shangxin	sorrowful: grieved
beiai	shangxin	sad: sorrow: grief
shangxin	Youyu zaoshou bu ruyi de shiqing er xinli tongku: (suffering mentally due to an unfortunate experience)	sad: grieved: broken-hearted
nanguo	The same as nanshou–shangxin; bu tongkuai)	feel sad; feel bad

From the definitions given above, it seems impossible to identify the differences within the sadness group. What I can find is that *shangxin* is the commonest Chinese word to describe a sad feeling. Literally, it means the heart is hurt, which is reminiscent of the English *heart-broken*. In Chinese, some descriptions of the inner sensations of sadness are expressed by the same words that are used to denote physical pain. It is a typical example of component metaphorical lexicalization by Packard (2000), in which one or both of the individual word components take on a metaphorical meaning, while the overall meaning of the word continues to be a compositional sum of the meanings of its metaphorical parts. *Shang* and *xin* here have taken on metaphorical meanings, though their relationship remains the same, resulting in *shangxin* acquiring the meaning of a sad feeling. But what does *shangxin* exactly mean? The dictionary says:

(21) *youyu zaoshou bu ruyi de shiqing er xinli tongku*:
because undergo not as wished ASSOC thing CONJ heart pain
'suffering mentally due to an unfortunate experience'

Tongku is found in the definition for *shangxin*. Then what does *tongku* mean? Its definition (XHC 2002) is as follows:

(22) *shenti huo jingshen gandao feichang nanshou*
body or mind feel very uncomfortable
'feeling very uncomfortable physically or spiritually'

Another word *nanshou* is introduced, and fortunately, its definition is also given in the table:

(23) *Shangxin; bu tongkuai shangxin*
not happily relieved of a burden/overjoyed

It seems that we will never get out of the circle of cross-explanation if we restrict ourselves to dictionaries. An alternative approach to exploring their semantic components is to resort to a monolingual corpus of Chinese.

3.1. *Shangxin* and *nanguo*

3.1.1. *Shangxin*. In a modern Chinese corpus composed of 10,610,000 Chinese characters compiled by Xiamen University, I found 293 hits of *shangxin* (27.6 per million). Using ParaConc (since no other suitable software available can provide collocates within the span of 4 left to 4 right), I found *ku* (41), *luolei* (5), *kuqi* (2), and *si* (6) in its collocates. Among these, *ku* (cry), *luolei* (falling tears), and *kuqi* (weep) all have to do with producing tears, usually when you are unhappy, hurt or very sad. *Si* (death) could be a cause for *shangxin* since it is also closely related to tears. From the biological reactions such as *ku* to what has happened, we can infer that *shangxin* is prototypically a transient emotion since you cannot continue crying for a long time, but a typical Chinese phrase shows that *shangxin* could last long:

(24) *zhengri yi lei xi mian*
all day long with tears wash face
'so sad that the face is always covered with tears (possibly for even several months)'

You may feel *shangxin* when you are reading a sad story, when you think of a sad past event, or because your dog died, because you have been cheated by one of the persons you trusted most, because the person you have been loving dearly fell in love with one of your best friends, because you are ignored by your teachers at school, because, if you are young, other pupils have been picked up by their parents and you know no one will come to collect you, because your parents divorced without considering what you might feel, or because you have heard one of your close relatives or friends has died recently, etc. It may be argued that *shangxin* can be elicited by anything which will make you produce tears or over which you want to since there is an old Chinese saying:

(25) *naner you lei bu qing tan*
fine man has tears not lightly shed
'A real man won't shed tears lightly'.

3.1.2. *Nanguo*. Another similar term to describe sadness is *nanguo*. The internal structure of this disyllabic lexeme is 'the adjective prefix *nan*+*guo*' difficult+live. Similar examples of this structure are:

nande difficult+get 'hard to come by'
nanchi difficult+eat 'taste bad'
nanshuo difficult+say 'difficult to say'

A common feature of this group of words is simple and less formal. I found 304 hits of *nanguo* (28.65 per million) in the Chinese corpus. Its typical collocates are *xinli* (30) and *xinzhong* (2), which both mean in the heart. As mentioned earlier, the behaviour of the heart has a lot to do with a person's emotional state. If you feel *nanguo*, your heart will feel uncomfortable. It is interesting that I did not find any word which is associated with *ku* in its collocates. In fact, there is a frequently used phrase in Chinese:

(26) *nanguo de dou xiang ku nanguo*
ASSOC even want cry/weep
'so sad that one wants to cry/weep'

Obviously, *nanguo* is a less intense feeling than *shangxin*, but it does not mean you will never *ku* when you are *nanguo*. Usually, it is a feeling lasting not very long, but someone may feel *nanguo* for a long time if his or her parent or even a beloved pet died.

You may feel *nanguo* because your daughter (suppose you have one) says she is leaving for another country but you want her to stay with you, because your little child is not well-behaved, or because the teacher says your son has no talent for college, because you failed in an exam or an interview, or when you are listening to your friend's sad story, etc.

3.2. *Beitong*, *beiai* and *beishang*

Before going on to analyse the other 3 Chinese emotion terms starting with *bei*/*beitong*, *beiai*, and *beishang*, let us take a look at the Chinese system of lexicon. Modern Chinese words (polysyllabic *ci*) evolved from old Chinese characters (monosyllabic *zi*). In old Chinese, each single character (*zi*) has its own self-contained semantic meaning, such as *bei, ai, tong, shang,* etc.

The vast majority of modern Chinese words come from the combination of two or more old characters and have developed their new denotations and connotations over time, but there are still close links between the meanings of old character components and the modern words, especially in some conventionalized phrases and idioms. Yip (2000) gives a detailed account of the structure of Chinese lexicon. He proposes that although 'Chinese is not a language totally deprived of morphological derivations, it is perhaps far less morphologically prone than a language such as English. Generally speaking, instead of being composed of 'base+affix', a Chinese *di-* (or poly)syllabic lexeme will, in the majority of cases, assume the look of a compound, that is, with the two (or more) constituent monomys contracting a kind of quasi-syntactic relationship with each other, which makes it possible to analyse the internal composition of a Chinese word in syntactic terms' (p. 90). One of the syntactic structures found in disyllabic lexemes is juxtapositional type (juxtaposer+juxtaposed/juxtaposed+juxtaposer), in which the combination of two monomys of similar orientation and syntactic category forms a word. The primary motivation behind adopting a juxtapositional structure is perhaps to conform to the overall disyllabification tendency of the modern lexicon. In such a set, 'the distinctive feature of a juxtaposer is actually its juxtapositional capacity. It is the monomy that finds a wider distribution and occurs more frequently in a group of similar juxtapositions. This is particularly true for adjectives. In a semantically related set of disyllabic adjectives, the juxtaposer is usually the one which occurs more frequently or enjoys greater combinatory power and therefore defines and charts the general semantic orientation of the set, whereas the juxtaposed is the one which tends to make more minute differentiations of meaning within the same general semantic orientation set down by the juxtaposer or determine the syntagmatic potentiality of the resultant combination' (p. 95).

In the case of the *bei* set, obviously, *bei* is the juxtaposer, which sets the tone for the whole set, and the other three monomys are the juxtaposed, fine-tuning the meaning of the juxtaposer. In order to distinguish all the emotion-describing monomys in question, I turned to two Chinese dictionaries. The results are given in Table 4:

Table 4 Definitions from *Ci Hai* (*A Grand Dictionary of Chinese*)

Dictionary/ Character	Xiandai Hanyu Cidian	Ci Hai
悲 bei	悲伤 beishang	悲哀、伤心 beiai; shangxin: 'bei xi jiaoji'
哀 ai	悲伤 beishang; 悲痛 beitong; 悼念 daonian	悲伤 beishang 'you furen ku yu mu zhe er ai'
伤 shang	悲伤 beishang	忧思、哀悼 yousi; aidao
痛 tong	悲伤 beishang	悲伤、苦恼 beishang; ku'nao

It is plain that not much can be expected from these superficial and perfunctory explanations. However, a careful examination of the definitions and examples available reveals that *bei* implies a basic sadness quality since Chinese has:

(27)   bei xi jiaoji bei
       joy intermingle
       'have mixed feelings/feel grief and joy intermingled'

ai, prototypically, has to do with death situations, since *daonian* means 'mourn, grieve over'. The following is a quote from an old article:

(28)   you furen ku yu mu zhe er ai
       there's woman cry PREP tomb SUF COMJ ai
       'There was a woman grieving in front of a tomb'

It seems that *ai* is a typical emotion for a person to cry at a tombstone. *Shang*, apart from the *aidao* (mourning or grieving) element, has a pessimistic thinking (*yousi*) and a missing quality implied in it.

To come back to the modern Chinese emotion terms in our focus, I will try to tease out the semantic differences between them. The discussion will start with *beitong*.

3.2.1. *Beitong.* Let us continue the quest by repeating the same process. Only 4 hits of *ku* and 5 hits of *wenxun* (hearing the news) were found in its collocates because only 82 hits of *beitong* (7.7 per million) were found in the whole corpus, but its basic semantic components can still be captured from the concordance lines. 53 of 82 hits of *beitong* are definitely caused by the death of someone and the causes of the rest need to be examined further in wider contexts. Unfortunately, the search in the Chinese corpus can only be done online and all we can get from the Internet for each hit is one complete sentence containing the node word. It is interesting that a 4-character idiom, *beitong yujue*, occurs 12 times of the 82 hits of *beitong*:

(29)   beitong yu jue beitong
       on the point of stopping breathing
       'so beitong as to come to the end of life'

From this fixed phrase, it can be inferred how sad *beitong* is. There is a similar but non-idiomatic phrase *shangxin yujue*, 4 hits of which were found in the corpus, but there is no such a term as *nanguoyujue* in Chinese. From the discussion so far, it is reasonable to assume that *shangxin* is a generic term to denote a sad feeling, and *beitong* is a more intense feeling than *shangxin*, prototypically invoked by the death of a close person. From its collocates *ku* (cry/weep) and *wenxun*, we can argue that *beitong* is an overwhelming and transient emotion erupting like a volcano, invoked by something unexpected and extremely unpleasant you are unwilling to face or find hard to accept. It usually co-occurs with some biological reactions (tears or loss of appetite, etc.) It may come suddenly and fade away over time. It is more extroverted than introverted, more individual than communal, more voluntary than ritualized, more personal than culturally mediated. It is similar to sorrow in terms of the latter three dimensions, but to grief in terms of extroversion, intensity and length.

3.2.2. *Beiai.* 160 hits of *beiai* (15 per million) were found in the Chinese corpus. Interestingly, I found quite a few hits of:

(30) *shengli* (victory) *de beiai*
(31) *Minzu* (nation) *de beiai*
(32) *Rensheng* (life) *de beiai*
(33) *Renlei* (humans) *de beiai*
(34) *Renshi* (the human world) *de beiai*
(35) *Wei ziji gandao beiai*
 For self feel *beiai*

According to the corpus, a young girl who is not good-looking may be shrouded in *beiai* if she finds no boy who notices her existence at all. If we feel *beiai* for ourselves, we are fully aware what we did or what has happened to us is really not something worth being proud of or something which should be encouraged, but something which will turn out to be the opposite. It is a *beiai* thing if a young girl abandons herself to despair, if a nation does not give some serious thought to its history, if people think love is worth nothing compared with money, if a person cheats his or her own mother, if the movie industry is only seeking commercial profits without thinking about the negative influence it may have on society, or if a writer produces rubbish writings for money or political benefits, etc.

It seems that, in modern texts, its original meaning denoting the sad emotion associated with death or calamity has given way to its new sense to describe something which is sad, disappointing but we can do nothing about, something which should not have happened, something which will lead to very bad consequences if it continues to be ignored, especially when people are not aware of its seriousness at all. The concept of *beiai* has gone beyond its original circle and been extended to situations connected with a wider range of unfortunate events happening to people, nations, life, human beings or even the whole world. (Unfortunately, I can not find any information about this sense in the two most authoritative Chinese dictionaries.)

In its original sense, *beiai* still keeps its basic flavour of the deep sad stir, though not exclusively, due to the loss of a loved person. It is more altruistic than personal, for the focus of *beiai* is on other people, not on the experiencer. It tells us more about what the experiencer thinks about a particular sad event. It implies 'sympathy, compassion or even love, revealing a wish for bad things not to happen to the other person and a desire to do something good for the unfortunate' (Ye 2001:375). This also explains how its modern sense came into being, for its new sense is also altruistic, compassionate, sympathetic, focusing on other people or events and revealing a wish for unpleasant things not to have happened, as we discussed earlier. The following examples from the parallel corpus bear out clearly this altruistic, compassionate, more extroverted, communal and ritualized emotion concept:

(36) 在餐室里，她那么平静而又拘谨，而现在，她脸上一切伪装的悲哀都已烟消云散，双眼闪烁着生活欢乐的光辉，面部被同伴的妙语逗乐的笑纹未消
In the dining-room she had been demure and discreet. Now all pretence of grief had passed away from her. Her eyes shone with the joy of living, and her face still quivered with amusement at some remark of her companion.

(37) 许多东西会在她心里引起悲哀－那些弱者，那些凄苦无依的人，一概激起她的伤心
Sorrow in her was aroused by many a spectacle--an uncritical upwelling of grief for the weak and the helpless.

(38) '趣味要高尚一点，不要用那条纱巾来表现自己实际上从来没有过的悲哀'
And better taste than to wear that veil to advertise a grief I'm sure you never felt.

(39) 她一定要把自己渴望的勇气鼓起来，到牧师住宅去打听消息，对他的沉默表示自己的悲哀
Surely she might summon the courage of solicitude, call at the Vicarage for intelligence, and express her grief at his silence.

All pretence of in (36), *advertise* in (38), and *express* in (39) allude to the altruistic, extroverted and communal aspects of *beiai*, and *that veil* in (38), probably to ritualized aspect. In (37), *the weak and the helpless* points to its altruistic, compassionate aspects. And Example 37 seems to suggest that *beiai* could be a voluntary feeling elicited either in death-related or other situations.

3.2.3. Beishang. *Beishang* shares the common semantic core with both *sorrow* and *grief* since 27/91 occurrences of *sorrow* and 23/72 occurrences of *grief* have been translated as *beishang*. Only 101 hits of *beishang* (9.5 per million) were found in the Chinese corpus. Nothing remarkable but *chenzhong* (heavy), *fenshou* (parting), *gudu* (loneliness), *guoshi* (pass away) and *manhuai* (imbued with) appear in its collocates.

According to its concordance lines, *beishang* is a feeling frequently accompanied by loneliness, a thought stirred by some external things such as parting, an emotion not as violent as *beitong*, elicited by the death of a close relative or a friend or even a national leader. One may feel *beishang* when s/he realizes no progress has been made in his or her career after s/he struggled for ten years or when he feels inferior to others after losing the wife, family and job in his forties. Even a young sentimental boy will feel *beishang* if he has lost his favourite toy.

In a sense, *beishang* is something heavy that settles at the bottom of the heart after experiencing something unfortunate and negative. *Beishang* is a sentimental concept which highlights a sense of powerlessness due to the laws of nature and society. It is more an emotional state closely related to the attitude toward life and the world, more tragic and fatalistic, more a result of accumulation after experiencing a series of unfortunate events. It's more a long lingering haunting thought left after the sad experiences, which arises from the bottom of the heart and can be buried and hidden deep in the heart for the time being but stirred again by any possible trigger. It involves a reflection quality after the stirring.

The following examples from the corpus may shed light on the haunting and sentimental characteristics of *beishang*:

(40) 同时他也按照他混乱的和激动的思想推理，认为苔丝只是在她提到的过度悲伤下一时失去了心理平衡，才陷入这种深渊的
As well as his confused and excited ideas could reason, he supposed that in the moment of mad grief of which she spoke her mind had lost its balance, and plunged her into this abyss.

(41) 她能向瑞德说些什么才可以去缓解他的悲伤和恢复他的理智呢
What could she say to Rhett that would ease his grief and bring him back to reasoning.

(42) 苏伦和卡琳哭了一阵睡着了，她们每天至少要来这么两次，因为一想起母亲便感到悲伤，觉得自己孤苦无依，眼泪使簌簌地从深陷的两腮上往下流
Suellen and Careen had cried themselves to sleep, as they did at least twice a day when they thought of Ellen, tears of grief and weakness oozing down their sunken cheeks.

(43) 他向她走来时，思嘉发现他眼中充满了悲伤，同时也含有厌恶和轻蔑之情，这使她惊慌的心里顿时涌起满怀内疚
As he came towards her, she saw that there was grief in his eyes and also dislike and contempt that flooded her frightened heart with guilt

(44) 这里有过她的罪孽，这里有过她的悲伤，这里也还会有她的忏悔 Here had been her sin; here, her sorrow; and here was yet to be her penitence.

(45 多 少 希 望 和 惋 惜 ，多 少 悲 伤 和 痛 苦
Oh, ye legions of hope and pity – of sorrow and pain.

(46) 经理觉得这哀诉是对他个人而发，就好像他们俩单独在一起，他几乎忍不住要为他所爱的女子流泪，她是那么孤弱无助，那么悲伤凄婉，又那么妩媚动人，楚楚可怜
The manager suffered this as a personal appeal. It came to him as if they were alone, and he could hardly restrain the tears for sorrow over the hopeless, pathetic, and yet dainty and appealing woman whom he loved.

(47) 她也想到赫斯渥，但是想到他，只给她带来悲伤
Nothing but sorrow was brought her by thoughts of Hurstwood.

(48) 除了她自己而外，谁也没有看出故事中的悲伤来
None of them but herself seemed to see the sorrow of it.

(49) 一个人在悲伤停止的时候，睡眠就会乘虚而入
When sorrow ceases to be speculative sleep sees her opportunity.

Grief seems to be more closely associated with someone's death. In (42), the thought of their late mother made them feel grief, while in (47), the thought of Hurstwood would only made Sister Carrie feel sorrow. Both of them have been translated as *beishang*, but this *beishang* is not that *beishang*, which are not distinguished in the Chinese lexicon. The former is a more intense feeling, a fading version of *beitong* over time, emphasizing more on the missing element, and the latter is more lingering, haunting, sentimental and fatalistic, which explains why in (44), (45), (48), (49), *sorrow*, a more general version of *beishang* in the Chinese sense, is used instead of *grief*. The *mad grief* in (40) is inferior in intensity to the *beitong* of losing of a loved one recently. In (41) and (43), *ease his grief* and *grief in his eyes* seem to suggest that *beishang* is something haunting and introverted you need to read from the face including eyes. Rhett's explosive *beitong* towards his daughter's death has developed into longer lasting *beishang*. It takes much longer time to get over *beishang* than *beitong*. In (46), *the tears for sorrow*, which is quite different from *the tears of grief* in (42), reflects a sentimental thought typically related to powerlessness, helplessness, parting or loneliness.

4. Conclusion

In this chapter, an in-depth contrastive-semantic analysis of *sorrow* and *grief* as well as their Chinese equivalents – *beishang, beiai, beitong, shangxin* and *nanguo* (excluding *you/chou* concept) – has been made. Drawing on the statistical data and contextual information from the monolingual and parallel corpora, the discussion has focused on the distinctions between these emotions in cause, intensity, length and accompanying behaviour, etc. The study has shown that *shangxin* is a generic term for a sad feeling. *Nanguo* is less intense than *shangxin*, caused by less serious stimuli. *Beitong* is an explosive intense sadness typically associated with someone's death. *Beiai* is an altruistic, sympathetic and compassionate feeling focusing on other people or events. *Beishang* could be a less intense version than *beitong*, which will develop into *beishang* over time, or a long lingering haunting thought as a result of accumulation of unfortunate experiences, closely related to a fatalistic outlook. The lexical set of sadness shares basically the same semantic core but each focuses on different elements.

Table 2 shows that the Chinese counterparts of *sorrow* and *grief* share *beishang* and *shangxin*. It is not surprising to find *shangxin* is one of them since *shangxin* can be seen as a generic term for sadness in Chinese. To facilitate further comparison, I summarize the features of these confusing emotion terms in a table according to the previous discussion:

Table 5 Features of *sadness* terms

	Extroverted	Communal	Altruistic	Explosive	Intense
beishang					less
beiai	√	√	√		less
beitong	√			√	√
sorrow					less
grief	√	√		√	√

Obviously, the concepts of emotions are categorized differently in different languages. The Chinese language distinguishes sadness between whether it is extroverted or introverted, whether it is individual or communal, whether it is altruistic or personal, whether it is explosive or long lingering, or whether it is intense or not, while English lacks the dimension of being altruistic or personal. The feature of being altruistic is Chinese-specific in the domain of emotion. Table 2 reveals that three different Chinese *sadness* concepts (*beishang, beiai,* and *beitong*) are encoded in the same word in English – *grief*. This is because, according to the above table, *grief* overlaps much with *beitong* for their both being extroverted, personal, explosive and intense. *Beiai* was selected by the translators to express the concept of grief because both are extroverted and communal, though *beiai* is less intense and altruistic. From the above table, it follows that there is no exact Chinese equivalent to *grief*. *Beiai* is the only choice when the element of being communal is emphasized. Table 2 also shows that *beishang*, a less intense feeling than *beitong*, more introverted, more personal, more individual, longer lasting feeling than *beiai*, is shared by *sorrow* and *grief*. *Beishang* is similar to *sorrow* in terms of being more introverted, individual, voluntary, lingering, haunting and less intense. However, as we discussed in section 3, it also denotes a rather intense feeling, which is a fading version of *beitong* over time, emphasizing more on the missing element. This is why it was chosen to translate *grief*.

It appears that the problem of establishing equivalence of lexical items across languages can best be tackled by an approach based on corpus linguistics. As long as our monolingual and parallel corpora are large enough, our quantitative tools will yield sufficient data, on the basis of which the exact meanings of these emotion terms and the finer distinctions between them can be accurately captured. Corpus-based analyses can clearly reveal how they are matched with each other, how much they overlap with each other and how they should be translated into the other language.

Lexical innovations in the multimodal Corpus of Asian Magazine Advertising

Andrew Moody
University of Macau
amoody@umac.mo

Azirah Hashim
University of Malaya
azirahh@um.edu.my

1. Introduction

The growth of advertising in Asia presents several sociolinguistic avenues for the investigation of Asian cultures generally, and Asian lexicography specifically. The Corpus of Asian Magazine Advertising (CAMA) responds to the growing role of advertising in Asia and how it represents Asian cultural similarities and differences. Because advertising explicitly appeals to consumers' values, similarities or differences between cultures influence whether particular advertisements are appropriate or inappropriate within different cultures, and correspondingly different sets of values. There are obvious ethnic, religious and linguistic differences across Asia. For example, although Asia is not usually characterized in scholarly writing in the West as an Islamic region, the South East Asian (SEA) nation of Indonesia has the largest population of Muslims worldwide; more than 207 million Muslims make up 88% of the population of the world's fourth largest country (*World Factbook*). Likewise, Buddhism is widely practised throughout East and South East Asia and Christianity has an especially large number of followers in Singapore and the Philippines. In addition to the variety of religious values across Asia, ethnic and linguistic diversity also characterizes Asian societies. Ethnic diversity within the region has been complicated by a number of diasporas, most notably the diasporas of ethnic Chinese and Indians throughout the region. Because cultural and linguistic diversity are characteristic of Asia's growing consumer markets, lexical innovation is expected to be driven by and to reflect social diversity.

Although there has been little description of the values that are uniquely Asian, there are a number of values that have been called predominantly Asian values. By this we mean that they are found throughout the diverse region, although with varying degrees of commitment. For example, various scholars and observers of Asia have noted that the values of 'family', 'filial piety' and 'conformity' play important roles in most Asian cultures. The degree that these stereotypical Asian values truly are unique to Asia or not, however, is not really a question that concerns us when looking for cultural unification across Asia. Instead, the fact that many Asian cultures see these values as characteristically Asian cultural values is significant because these values may then be taken as symbols of cultural unity within the region (see Bhatia and Moody forthcoming).

While examining advertising in Asia, therefore, some observers have noted unique cultural characteristics that might identify similarities across diverse Asian cultures. Don Schultz writes:

> Asian advertising reflects the Asian cultures that make up the region. It is holistic, inventive, often reflective and sometimes even whimsical, qualities that often baffle the western observer. Asian advertising is, for the most part, holistic because that's what the cultures are, holistic from religions to everyday activities. (Aitchison 2002:xi-xii)

In addition, observers of Asian advertising sometimes note the importance of humour in Asian culture, and especially SEA advertising (Aitchison 2002). In particular, Aitchison argues that humour has become increasingly prevalent in Asian advertising and that "the humour is more piquant when it reflects some quirk of its local culture or society" (xvii). While this may not be unique to Asian advertising, it does seem to be one important way that Asian cultures – and especially Asian advertisers – see themselves, and one of the characteristics that is easily transmitted across Asian societies.

Asian lexicography, therefore, can be informed by lexical innovations that take place within the language of advertising. Because advertising language must appeal to diverse value systems across Asian societies, it is an especially suitable place to look for linguistic innovation, and especially lexical innovation. To the degree that there are cultural similarities across the Asian region, we would naturally expect to see the commonalities expressed within a shared lexicon related to culturally salient ideas and values. Similarly, cultural variations in Asia are also expressed in lexical variation across the region. Unfortunately, advertising language is typically overlooked in lexicographical studies as a source of lexical innovation, despite the fact that advertising language, like other popular culture genres, responds very quickly to changing social factors and developing economies. In this study we hope to demonstrate that the CAMA project offers a new and important tool for the study of Asian advertising and that this tool can be used to examine lexical innovation in Asian languages.

2. Common Asian experience

Although it may be difficult to define Asian values that are common across the region, it is not difficult to identify common features of the Asian experience. Many nations of the Asian region have recently (i.e. within the past 50 years) made the transition from kingdoms into states, and in many cases made that transition as colonial states. The development of post-colonial nations in particular illustrates the kinds of challenges that developing countries across the Asian region face. In many cases, post-colonial nations have formulated ambiguous responses to colonial languages in the attempt to support both local languages and national cohesion. Furthermore, in the same way that colonialism imposes somewhat arbitrary boundaries to territories, many Asian nations, especially those in South East and South Asia, face the challenge of building post-colonial states within regions whose ethnic and cultural diversity derives from colonial boundaries. Hence, multi-ethnic and multilingual populations are characteristic of the South East and South Asian experience, although somewhat less characteristic of East Asia.

Language use in multilingual countries like Malaysia, Singapore or India, for example, is particularly complex, especially in the use of vocabulary that is unique to one of the languages and is used to express items or events that are not shared across the multi-ethnic or multilingual population. In some cases there are no corresponding words in another language and lexical items are difficult, and at times impossible, to translate. Different images and texts written for different target audiences even within an individual country demonstrate that various values and beliefs often operate simultaneously within a single national experience. Different cultural metaphors, with which all or most of the individuals of a particular cultural group identify, reflect underlying differences in values between groups. Thus, language, and in particular lexicon, may be considered the best evidence of the reality of cultural difference. These types of cultural difference, however, are typical in many multilingual and multi-cultural South East and South Asian countries and they illustrate the importance of lexicon and lexical innovation in Asian languages.

The recent growth of consumer culture across Asia is also closely related to the shared experience of modernisation and economic growth throughout the region. The growth of consumer culture within Asia has probably had the greatest impact on the development of advertising strategies and advertising language within the region. Graddol (2006) has argued that much of the development of an urban, middle class population throughout the world – a phenomenon that is especially widespread throughout Asia – has made English an important symbol of their growth:

> English, however, is an increasingly urban language, associated with growing middle classes, metropolitan workplaces and city lifestyles. The middle class is not just a consequence of a growing economy, but also a contributory factor. (Graddol 2006:50)

It is, therefore, within the assumption of economic growth, prosperity and the rise of a middle class that advertising language has become an important factor and indicator of development throughout the region.

Batey (2002) demonstrates the degree to which advertising in Asian countries may potentially grow with Asian markets. According to statistics from ZenithMedia (see Figure 1 below), Asian advertising makes up only 22% of advertising spending worldwide.[1] However, this figure includes the already highly developed consumer market of Japan as a part of Asia. When the amount of advertising spending in Asia is broken down into individual national markets, as it is in Figure 2 below, it is clear that advertising spending in Japan makes up more than 60% of the ad spending in Asia and that there is much greater potential for growth in other Asian advertising markets.[2]

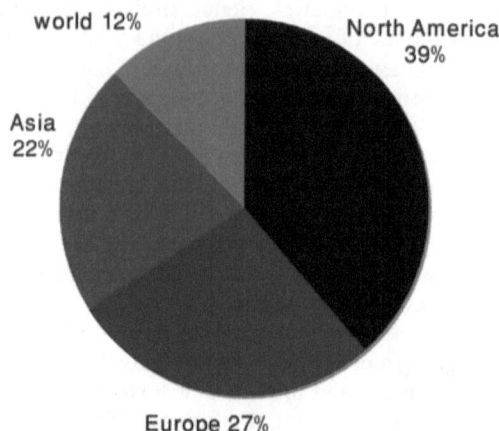

Figure 1 Global ad spending in 2000 (Batey 2002)

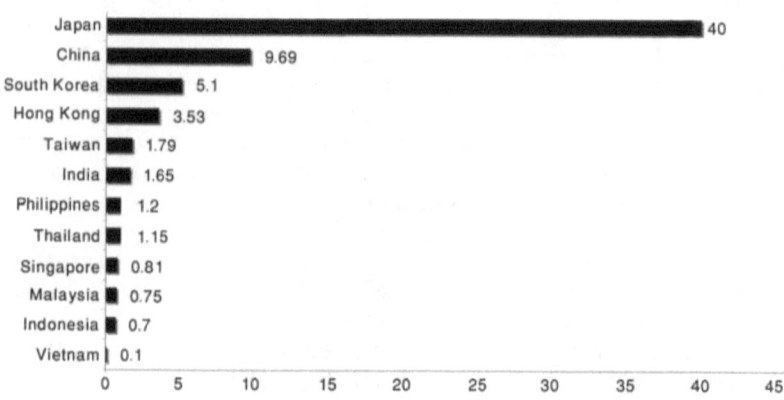

Figure 2 Asian ad spending in 2000 in US$ billions (Batey 2002)

Assuming that there will be continuing growth in the consumer markets in Asia, and especially in those of China and India, in coming decades, Batey

(2002) offers a 'bold' estimate of the increase of ad spending that is likely to take place within the developing markets of Asia. He estimates that ad spending will increase 6 fold from US$ 34 billion in 2000 to US$ 204 billion in 2020 (see Figure 3 below). The expected growth rate in Asian advertising is twice as high as the expected growth rates anywhere else, making Asia the world's most potentially dynamic advertising market.

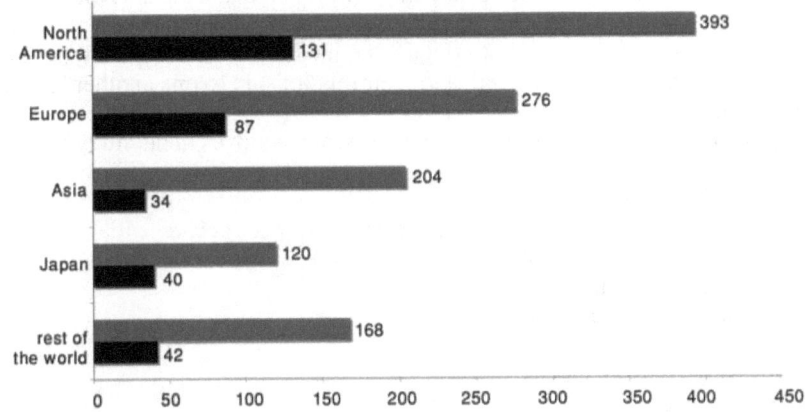

Figure 3 A bold prediction of global ad spending increases from 2000 to 2020 (Batey 2002)

3. The sociolinguistics of advertising language

Sociolinguists have long been reluctant to use data from advertising to draw conclusions about the functions, status or forms of language within a speech community, and this is largely because the data are neither spontaneous nor naturally occurring. Instead, advertising data are highly edited and not necessarily representative of the variety that is used. However, researchers have increasingly used data from advertising to understand the language functions of the speech community and innovative uses of language. Because advertising language represents a form of creative linguistic production, advertising data are especially useful for demonstrating the kinds of word formation processes that are most active within a language, or what types of lexical innovations most frequently occur. Vibrant and creative words found in advertising – as well as in other edited genres – illustrate the way that hybridized varieties derive from the multi-cultural and multilingual experience of many Asian nations. Lexical items with new meanings and rhetorical strategies such as native similes and metaphors, proverbs and idioms are often found in these emerging advertising markets. Advertisements in the market also often contain individual words that can only be understood within the cultural context of the advertising market. As consumer cultures and identities flourish throughout Asia, advertising offers a mechanism to allow linguistic expression to quickly adapt to social changes.

Although a number of studies have examined advertisements in the West, little attention has focused on advertisements in Asia. Cook (1992), for example, analyses contemporary advertisements using an approach derived from linguistics and discourse analysis. He examines advertisements as discourse, the focus of which is not only on the language, but also the context of communication: "who is communicating with whom and why; in what kind of society and situation; through what medium; how different types and acts of communication evolved, and their relationship to one another" (Cook 1992:1).

Bhatia (1993) describes the following discourse moves in his study of sales promotion letters:
1. Establishing credentials
2. Introducing the offer: offering the product or service, essential detailing of the product, indicating value of the offer
3. Offering incentive
4. Enclosing documents
5. Soliciting response
6. Using pressure tactics
7. Ending politely

The above moves are found to be used by writers of sales promotion letters to achieve their communicative purposes. However, it is not obligatory that all the moves are used in the same order and some may not appear at all (Bhatia 1993:56).

Goatly (2000) examines the obvious and less obvious ideological strategies in and behind advertisements and provides some important aspects of consumerist ideology used by copywriters. Also from the West, Bruthiaux (2000) observes the persuasion that takes place in the spatially constrained language of advertising, and the interaction between the need to persuade and the constraining contextual factors of the genre. Kress and van Leeuwen (1996) apply a theoretical framework derived from systemic functional linguistics to the analysis of images, which also focusses on Western advertisements.

In applied linguistics, advertisements have been found to be a useful resource for learning language and culture. Picken (1999) provides the main arguments for using advertisements and demonstrates some of the uses of language, visuals and culture and how they can be exploited by teachers.

In Asia, some studies on advertisements have been carried out. For example, Ramli (1993) argues that figurative language is used extensively in television advertisements in Malay and English and that strategies like metaphors and similes are most popular. Other strategies that he observed are personification, puns, parallelism and alliteration. Ariffin and Anuar (2004) focus on superiority claims in printed advertisements and argue that words like 'help', 'like' and 'special', which are found to be often used, are actually meaningless, and are followed by scientific or statistical claims that provide the evidence to support the superiority claims for the products.

Bhatia (1987) examines the role of English and the mixing of English with local languages in print advertising from six languages: Hindi, Chinese, Japanese, French, Italian and Spanish. He observes that language mixing appears to be universal and that English is often code mixed with local languages to fulfil the advertising industry's needs of having creativity and innovation in advertisements.

In addition to work on advertising language, research across languages and cultures has been carried out to prove the hypothesis that different languages have different rhetorical systems which manifest themselves in different ways in terms of organisation of ideas and linguistics features (e.g. Grabe and Kaplan 1996; Connor and Mauranen 1999; Clyne 1987; Al-Ali 2004). Findings reveal that genres are shaped and constrained by cultural variations in spite of the fact that they share the same communicative purposes.

These studies illustrate the variety of linguistic and rhetorical strategies used in advertising. Although advertising is not a genre of spontaneous speech, it can be used to examine processes such as language mixing, creative use of loan words, language choice, words used as attention-getters, choice of words for different target groups, linguistic hybridization, semantic shifts and the development of nativized varieties of English in Asia.

Given the potential importance of advertising to understanding the sociolinguistics of Asian communities, how data is gathered from these communities is also important. In studies of Asian advertising, data sets are rarely drawn from random sampling of advertising in the publishing community[3], but are instead based upon convenient samples of advertising data. Without random selection of texts it is impossible to know if the conclusions made from any data set can be generalized to the entire publishing community. In addition, previous studies have, by and large, examined the way that advertising works within individual publishing communities, not across communities.[4] Two problems derive from the lack of comparative data in Asian advertising. First, comparative studies of Asian advertising tend to compare what is done in an Asian advertising market with what appears in Western markets, thus perpetuating a Western bias into the study of the sociolinguistics of Asian societies. Second, there is no way to reasonably judge what uniquely Asian or typically Asian values are represented in advertising because comparisons rarely take place between Asian publishing communities.

4. Description of the Corpus of Asian Magazine Advertising

The Corpus of Asian Magazine Advertising (CAMA) project was initiated in 2005 as an attempt to understand the linguistic and non-linguistic structures that are part of the norm for Asian advertising. The objectives of the CAMA project are: to compile a reliably representative survey and corpus of magazine advertising in various languages and cultures across Asia; to create a database of advertisements that will allow easy access to researchers about advertising in Asia; to support comparative studies of advertising within Asian nations; to support research on Asian languages, especially English; and to create a tool for research into popular culture in Asia.

The project has been undertaken by nine teams of researchers in 10 different Asian countries. Because many of the regions are multilingual (i.e. they contain more than one publishing community), the survey has been conducted in 16 publishing communities, outlined in Table 1 below. Because previous work in advertising has demonstrated that genre is a fundamental factor in determining the type of advertisements that one is likely to find within various magazines (see relevant literature reviewed above), magazines were collected from 10 different genres, listed in Table 2 below. The corpus of advertisements was compiled within three phases. At the time of writing, two of the phases were completed within four of the publishing communities. Phase One was a survey of magazine genres across the 16 publishing communities and selection of the 10 genres listed in Table 2. During the completion of Phase One it was noted that not every genre is evenly distributed throughout the publishing communities and that, in some cases, a publishing community may not have magazines from a particular genre.

Table 1 Regions and publishing communities surveyed in the CAMA project

Region	Publishing Community
China	Chinese
Hong Kong	Chinese
Indonesia	Indonesian
Japan	Japanese
Korea	Korean
Malaysia	Malay
	Chinese
	English
The Philippines	English
	Tagalog
Singapore	Malay
	Chinese
	English
Taiwan	Chinese
Thailand	Thai

Table 2 Genres of magazines surveyed in the CAMA project

Genres
1- Women's
2- Men's
3- Home, Food, & Cooking
4- Hobbies & Special Interests
5- Travel
6- Entertainment
7- Wedding
8- News
9- Health & Fitness
10- Sports

Phase Two was the sampling of magazines from the survey conducted in Phase One. Magazines were selected as eligible for sampling according to three broadly defined criteria. First, the magazine must be published as a weekly, bi-weekly, monthly, or bimonthly publication; no daily publications were considered. Second, in order to be considered eligible for sampling a magazine must have at least 10 pages with advertising, of which at least 50% of the page is devoted to advertising. Finally, in order to ensure that publications were, in fact, being produced by publishers within the publishing community for readers within the publishing community, only magazines published within the publishing community and containing no less that 25% 'locally-oriented' advertising were considered for sampling. 'Locally-oriented' advertising is defined as goods or services that are readily available within the publishing community's region. Magazines, one from each of the 10 genres, were collected every two months, six times in a year. Every advertisement in each publication was scanned electronically and saved as a Portable Document Format (PDF) file. Each file was given a unique code that identified the sampling period and the genre sampled.

The third phase of the project — the compilation of a database of information about the ads — has not been completed at the time of writing of this chapter. The database is designed to encode three types of information about each advertisement, and all information in the database is searchable. The first type of information is about the product being advertised, and includes details such as the type of product, the advertiser, the approximate price of the product and whether it is produced locally or imported. The second type of information to be encoded within the database pertains to the non-linguistic features of each advertisement, such as the size of the ad, dominant colours and the type of text and visuals. This kind of information will allow for easy use of multi-modal analysis such as the type of analysis advocated by Kress and van Leeuwen (1996) and Picken (1999). Finally, the database will record information about language use in each advertisement. In addition to noting the matrix and, where applicable, the code-switched languages of each ad, the database will encode information about the approximate length of each ad, the language-based strategies used in the ad and the probable target audience of the ad.

Although the corpus will have broad applications across a number of different fields of linguistics (i.e. sociolinguistics, discourse analysis, language innovation, language contact, etc.) the applications within Asian lexicography are illustrated in the case study of Written Cantonese below.

5. Case study: Lexicography of written Cantonese

Despite the wide range of diversity that has developed among spoken dialects of Chinese, Cantonese is one of the few Chinese languages that has begun to develop a written form that may be used in distinction to other standardized forms of written Chinese. Chen (1999) offers a thorough description of the development of Modern Written Chinese (MWC) in the early part of the 20th century. From the end of the Tang Dynasty (9th century AD) written Chinese developed into two distinct writing styles that were used in a more or less diglossic relationship.[5] *Wenyanwen* was used within all 'high' functions of the written language (e.g. religious writings, government documents, literature, etc.) and *baihuawen* was used within 'low' functions (e.g. letter writing, diaries, folk literature, etc.). Since the 1910s, however, *baihuawen* has been selected as the standard for MWC and is used in all functions, while *wenyanwen* is no longer used as a productive standard language.

Although there is a great deal of diversity between spoken dialects of Chinese, this diversity does not usually find its way into the written language and dialect writing is usually discouraged by MWC's codification processes (Li 2000). While this may be the result of active discouragement of dialect writing because of likely unintelligibility (Scollon and Scollon 1998), it also supports what Cheung (1992) calls "the 'Great Tradition'" of a unified written language symbolizing a unified population (212). Nevertheless, there is a tradition of writing dialect literature in a number of southern Chinese dialects (e.g. Southern Min, Hakka and Cantonese) and this tradition has sometimes been used to symbolize resistance to the political forces that overtly support standardisation processes in MWC (Erbaugh 1995). Although there is a long tradition of dialect writing in Written Cantonese (WC) (see Snow 1994 and Chin 1997), recent examinations of the language claim that it is increasingly being used to symbolize an emerging Hong Kong identity that is defined in opposition to identities that use MWC exclusively (Snow 1993, Lau 1995, Li 1997).

Written Cantonese uses the same logographic writing system that is used by MWC, but with some syntactic constructions that are not usually used in MWC and, more importantly, a set of characters that uniquely represent Cantonese words and morphemes (Bauer 1995, Li 2000). Bauer (1995) offers a thorough description of WC and categorizes Cantonese words according to "orthographic conventions" that define the set of unique WC characters. Li (2000:201) groups them into the following list, based on Bauer (1995), of five conventions:

a. Chinese characters common to Cantonese and Modern Standard Chinese
b. Cantonese-specific characters inherited from classical Chinese, adapted from Modern Standard Chinese, or created to express Cantonese morpho-syllables – including borrowings from foreign languages, especially English
c. Phonetic borrowing from Modern Standard Chinese and English, used to transliterate Cantonese morpho-syllables, including those borrowed from English
d. Chinese characters borrowed from Modern Standard Chinese and Classical Chinese in the semantic capacities, but given Cantonese pronunciation
e. English letters or words used to render English elements borrowed into Cantonese

In terms of the acceptability of WC, Li (1999) notes that the WC writing style is typically used in newspapers and magazines and that its use is not associated with lower-class writing styles. However, there are certain genres (i.e. domains) of writing in which WC is more prevalent than MWC, and these genres form something of a diglossic situation in which WC is primarily used in 'low' domains and MWC in most 'high' domains.[6]

These 'high' and 'low' domains are illustrated in the various genres from which previous research on Written Cantonese has collected data. Bauer (1995) notes that Cantonese as a spoken language has become the language of "radio news programs and plays, TV news broadcasts and soap operas, live theatre, popular songs and novels, newspapers cartoons and serialized stories, and mass advertising" (246). Wu (2003) claims that WC is widely used in the "popular press" and sometimes used in the "quality press" in "less formal pages" as a way to "gain a wide readership" (59–60) and Li (2000) notes that WC is increasingly used in court proceedings involving Cantonese-speaking clients (200). Mok (1998) examines samples of WC from the popular culture genre of comic books published in Hong Kong as a typical genre that uses WC. Similarly Wong (2006) collected data from a local Hong Kong newspaper. Li (2000) also collected data from Chinese newspapers and popular magazines and notes that most of the data came from "'soft' materials – especially 'showbiz' chitchat, columns, and advertisements" (203). Li (2000) continues within his analysis to argue that WC "may be considered the unmarked writing style in those newspapers and magazines which are characterized by features of the popular press" (204). However, it should be noted that Li's methodology does not use randomized sampling; instead, he explains that "data were collected as they came to my attention"

(Li 2000:203).
The types of data that have been examined quantitatively are illustrated in the two examples below from the corpus, where some typical WC features in each sentence have been underlined:

(1) 每日　既　防哂　保護　一定　唔　可以忽視
muíhyaht <u>gei</u>　fòhngsaai　bóuwuh jātdihng　<u>mh</u>　hójíh fātsih
everyday <u>PRT</u>　sun　protection must　<u>not</u>　can　neglect
'Daily sun protection must not be neglected.' (from a cosmetic ad)

(2) 仲　愈　嚟　愈　白　添
<u>juhng</u>　jyuh　<u>làih</u>　jyuh　baahk　<u>tīm</u>
<u>still</u>　more　<u>and</u>　more　white　<u>PRT</u>

'My skin tone is brighter than before.' (from a cosmetic ad)

In (1) there are two features of Cantonese that have been rendered into the Chinese text. The first is the particle *gei*, a possessive particle that allows the adjective *mu'hyaht* 'everyday' to modify the compound noun 'sun protection'. The Cantonese negator, *mh*, also appears within this sentence in the form of a 'created' character, as are many of those listed in the Appendix below. In this form the left side of the lexical element, a 'mouth' radical, signifies that the character is meant to be read according to the pronunciation of the form on the right side of the word. This negator is a very common feature of Written Cantonese and appears in several forms in the appendix 17 times.

In (2) there are three features that may be described as Written Cantonese features that do not appear in MWC. The first is the conjunctive adverb *juhng*, which is typically used in sentences like this one that show comparison. The 'more and more' construction is similar to many comparative constructions across Chinese dialects, but the use of *làih* is unique to Cantonese. Finally, the final element of the sentence, *tīm*, is a sentence final particle that is used to show surprise.

The current case study analysis of WC in the CAMA corpus examines the advertisements collected in the final sampling period for the Hong Kong publishing community.[8] There are nine magazines, one from each of the genres listed in Table 2 above.[9] Altogether 394 advertisements were collected during this sample period. Each of the ads was examined for WC elements according to the five conventions (see above) outlined by Bauer (1995) and simplified in Li (2000). Each of the magazines had at least one ad that showed evidence of WC features, yet WC features were not prominent enough to justify the claim that Written Cantonese is the unmarked writing style of advertising. In all, only 28 ads (7.1% of all ads) were found to contain WC forms. Depending upon the genre of magazine that the ad was taken from, however, the number of ads with WC forms could be as high as 14.3% of the ads in the 'health and fitness' magazine, or as low as 2.5% of the ads in the 'wedding' magazine. There are results for individual magazines that were randomly selected to be representative of their genres and illustrate the value of the corpus to further research in this area. However, examination of ads from an entire year of sampling (i.e. six magazines in each genre) would likely yield more reliable results about the number of ads containing WC features in any particular genre.

Table 3 Written Cantonese (WC) features in Hong Kong magazine ads

Genres	Number of Ads	Ads with WC features	Number of WC features	Avg. number of WC features in an ad
(1) Women's	67	4 (6.0%)	118	29.5
(2) Men's	19	2 (5.3%)	11	5.5
(3) Home, Food & Cooking	26	2 (7.7%)	2	1
(4) Hobbies & Special Interests	30	2 (6.7%)	8	4
(5) Travel	35	1 (2.9%)	11	11
(6) Entertainment	71	7 (11.3%)	26	3.7
(7) Wedding	79	2 (2.5%)	17	8.5
(8) News	53	6 (11.3%)	33	5.5
(9) Health & Fitness	14	2 (14.3%)	4	2
TOTAL	394	28 (7.1%)	230	8.2

Although this analysis is of the writing style of advertisements, not the writing style of the magazine text, the results do suggest that the genre of magazine might affect how likely an advertiser is to use WC writing style. In the same way that Li (2000) notes that WC is more prevalent in the 'soft' sections of a Hong Kong newspaper, we would expect to find the largest number of ads with Cantonese features in some magazine genres more than others. In fact, there appear to be three distinct levels of appearance of ads with WC features. The highest levels of WC ads are found in the 'health and fitness,' 'entertainment,' and 'news' genres of magazines. While 'news' does not necessarily seem to fit Li's (2000) description of 'soft' material, the other two genres do. The lowest numbers of WC ads are found in the 'wedding' and 'travel' genres. The remaining genres all have moderate numbers of ads with WC features.

In addition, Table 3 calculates the average number of WC features that are found within the ads. This calculation measures the degree to which an ad might be affected by the norm of WC writing. Since the writing style simply means that Cantonese lexical items have been used, an ad might have only one feature to be included in this analysis, or more than 30 features, as do two cosmetics ads in the 'women's' magazine. The unusually high rate of WC features in ads in 'women's' magazines might suggest that this writing style is more acceptable to women readers, a potentially significant sociolinguistic insight.

In terms of lexicography, this analysis of Written Cantonese has yielded a list of 112 lexical items, listed below in Appendix A. Most of the lexical items are used only one time within this examination of the Hong Kong advertising data, suggesting that a more longitudinal approach to the study of WC in advertising is needed in order to understand the various ways that individual lexical items might be used. In addition, as expected when looking at a language that is based upon a spoken dialect, there is often more than one way to write the same Cantonese word. Again a study of WC over a longer period of time would likely inform about the emerging norms for the language. Finally, because there are not enough tokens for any of the lexical items, it is impossible to generalize about the stylistic characteristics of lexical items from this analysis. As noted before, however, this aspect of the study of WC would likely be informed by a broader study of the language in advertising.

6. Conclusion

While is not clear whether one can reasonably talk about such a thing as core Asian values in advertising, it is clear that there is a great deal of diversity across the whole of advertising in Asia. The Corpus of Asian Magazine Advertising (CAMA) project attempts to create a tool that will allow researchers to understand the role of advertising within a single publishing community – as illustrated in the preceding case study of Written Cantonese in Hong Kong advertising – and at the same time make comparison between publishing communities. For example, Cantonese is a language widely spoken in the Chinese diaspora across South East Asia, and it would be possible with the CAMA corpus to see if WC features have also come to influence advertising language in Taiwan, the People's Republic of China, Malaysia or Singapore. In these ways it is hoped that the corpus will prove to be a useful tool in sociolinguistic research for many years to come, especially within the study of lexicography in Asia.

Acknowledgments

Funding for the Corpus of Asian Magazine Advertising Project was supported by the University of Macau, Research Committee, Grant Number RG057/04-05s/06R38/MA/FSH. The authors would like to acknowledge the assistance of Lavania Chang Huan Hua for supplying data from an ongoing project on Written Cantonese.

Notes

1. Figures from ZenithMedia for Asia (quoted in Batey 2002) include Australia and New Zealand as part of Asia.
2. Figures for Japan and Taiwan are from ZenithMedia and Rainmaker Research respectively. Figures for other Asian countries are from AC

Nielsen. All figures are quoted in Batey (2002).
3. The term that is being coined here, 'publishing community', is meant to be parallel to the term 'speech community'. For the purposes of this study, a publishing community refers to the publications that appear within a designated territory within a particular language. This would mean, therefore, that there are at least three widely read publishing communities in Malaysia: one publishing in English, one in Malay and one in Chinese. It is noted that, while it is possible that magazines from one publishing community might be prevalent within another publishing community – e.g. Taiwan magazines in Chinese are widely available in Hong Kong – the advertising found in a magazine is primarily focused to the readers within that publishing community (which is usually a national language group).
4. Although they are not academic discussions of advertising language, exceptions include Aitchison (2002) and Batey (2002).
5. This relationship in writing is sometimes referred to as digraphia, "the use of two or more writing systems for a single language or a varieties of a language" (Cheung 1992:207–208; see also Dale 1980 and DeFrancis 1984).
6. The term digraphia has not been used here because WC does not form a clearly different writing system; instead, it is usually only the use of an additional set of characters that are not used in MWC. Cheung (1992) explains that, although the term digraphia is usually applied to writing systems that derive from different scripts, it might also be used to explain WC and MWC as writing systems in which "both forms derive from the same system but the Low form borrows foreign elements" (210). Although the borrowing of phonetic loanwords from English according to Cantonese phonology is clearly one of the features of WC, this extension of the definition of digraphia does not easily account for the other features of WC characters.
7. Cantonese words have been Romanized according to the Yale transcription method.
8. The final sampling period was chosen for this case study in the interests of brevity. This case study is related to a larger planned study of Written Cantonese in Hong Kong advertising genres (Chang and Moody in preparation).
9. The genre of 'sports' magazines is empty within the Hong Kong component of CAMA.

Appendix

Written Cantonese Element*	Yale Transcription	Number of Times Used
呀	a	3
阿	a	1
拜拜肉	bāai baai yuhk	1
爆	bāau	2
包包面	bāau bāau mihn	1
俾	béi	2
畀	béi	1
邊樣	bīn yeuhng	1
搽完	chàah yùhn	1
除咗	chèuih jó	1
黐立立	chī laahp laahp	1
瘡	chōng	1
速	chūk	2
抵	dái	1
哋	deih	7
啲	dī	5
點	dím	3
點算呀	dím syun a	1
掂	dihm	1
度尺	dohk chek	1
都	dōu	2
都係	dōu haih	1
番	fāan	1
返嚟	fāan làih	1
發燒友	faat sīu yáuh	1
㗎	ga	1
架	ga	1
加上	gâa seuhng	1
揀	gáan	4
咁	gám	4
咁多	gám dō	1
梗係	gáng haih	1
夠	gau	1
口既	ge	17
既	ge	3
幾時	géi sìh	1
勁	ging	1
嗰份	gó fahn	1
過落	gwo lohk	1
吓	há	3
慳	hāan	1
喺	háih	1
喺度	háih douh	1
係	haih	6
呵	hô	2
好	hóu	12
好多	hóu dō	2
好番	hóu fāan	1
好在	hóu joih	1
好天	hóu tîn	1
好嘢	hóu yéh	1
真係	jān hāi	1
啫	jē	1
至	ji	4
至夠	ji gau	1
即刻	jīk hāk	2
正	jing	1
蒸乾	jīng gôn	1
咗	jó	4
左	jó	1
做	jouh	1
仲	juhng	6
仲有	juhng yáuh	1
V - 住	jyuh	3
佢	kéuih	5
傾	kîng	1
狂 - V	kwòhng	1
啦	lâ	2
喇	lâ	2
嚟	làih	1
淋	làhm	1
諗著	lám jyuh	1
靚	leng	3

Lexical innovations in the multimodal CAMA

Written Cantonese Element*	Yale Transcription	Number of Times Used
料	liuh	1
籮	lòh	2
落雨	lohk jyúh	1
佬	lóu	1
唔	mh	10
唔該	mh gōi	1
唔好	mh hóu	2
唔止…仲	mh jí juhng	2
唔駛	mh sái	1
唔同	mh tùhng	1
孖住	mā jyuh	1
未	meih	1
無得	móuh dâk	1
冇你份	móuh néih fahn	1
冇哂	móuh saai	1
呢隻	nēi jek	1
啱	ngāam	3
耐	noih	1
囉	saai	3
哂	saai	3
駛乜	sái māt	1
試過	si gwo	2
睇	tái	1
添	tīm	3
條	tìuh	1
同	tùhng	5
話事	wah sih	1
喂	wai	1
搵	wán	1
屋企	wūk kéih	1
任	yahm	2
日	yaht	1
一	yât	1
一樣	yât cheung	1
一陣	yât jahn	1
又點會	yau dím wuíh	1

Written Cantonese Element*	Yale Transcription	Number of Times Used
嘢	yéh	3
依家	yî gâa	1
易	yih	1

Some Cantonese lexical items, when preceded by a 'mouth' (i.e. 口), are written as a single character with the 'mouth' radical.

EFL dictionaries on the Web: Students' appraisal and issues in the Cambridge, Longman, and Oxford dictionaries

Shigeru Yamada
Waseda University
shyamada@waseda.jp

1. Introduction

Although dictionaries still tend to be associated with printed books, it has been a while since they also became available electronically in hand-held machines and on CD-ROMs and the Internet. In fact, there are several free-of-charge EFL dictionaries on the World Wide Web (WWW). If Internet connection is not a problem, they are useful additions to learning and teaching resources. Believing in the benefits students gain from using state-of-the-art EFL dictionaries, I have been incorporating such dictionaries into my class. In 2003, I switched from using the print dictionary to web-based EFL dictionaries by Cambridge, Longman, and Oxford instead. In this chapter, I discuss the characteristics and problems of these three Web dictionaries, drawing on students' feedback and my own experience. I also offer suggestions for improving and making the most of those dictionaries. Comparisons will be made with the results obtained by Yamada (2006), who looked into the state of the same dictionaries in 2004.

2. Characteristics of the dictionaries

Despite the fact that they are all monolingual learners' dictionaries for students of English, the Web dictionaries by Cambridge, Longman, and Oxford are considerably different. I briefly describe the characteristics and the important functions of these dictionaries, mainly by taking you through the process of looking up the meaning of a word in each dictionary. Although the dictionary websites are becoming richer and more colorful, offering extra features and services[1], I limit myself to the dictionary components. General characteristics of the dictionaries are summarized in Appendix 1.

Cambridge Dictionaries Online, as its name suggests, offers six other dictionary titles[2] apart from *Cambridge Advanced Learner's Dictionary* (CALD-OL). Here I focus on this dictionary as we did in class. After you enter a word in the search box, you are usually presented with a list of

"Guidewords" and set phrases including the word (Appendix 2), from which you start your search. You select a link to click to go to the entry of a sense by way of Guidewords. If you are after a set phrase and find it in the list, just click on it. If you realize that you have clicked on a wrong link, go back to the Guideword list by the back command and start over[3]. CALD-OL maintains the policy of "one meaning, one entry"[4]. Derivatives of a word and related expressions are sometimes subsumed and presented together under a representative sense. The major challenge in consulting CALD-OL lies in the choice of an appropriate Guideword in the list which takes you to the appropriate sub-entry. Beyond this stage, all you have to do is to (determine and) interpret the relevant information.

You have the option of displaying and eliminating the pronunciation guide: you click on "Show phonetics" and "Hide phonetics"[5]. There are no usage notes or pictorial illustrations provided in the Web version.

LDOCE-OL organizes its entries by parts of speech, displaying one entry for one part of speech at a time. After a word is keyed in, a list of the parts of speech and compounds (Appendix 3) is shown if the word is used in more than one part of speech and/or makes up compounds. The knowledge of grammar – to be able to determine the part of speech of the word – is necessary to choose the relevant entry. Even if you make a wrong choice of a part of speech, you can easily make a second choice, using the list which stays on the screen of the part of speech you have just chosen.

If the word is polysemous and the entry is long, "Menu" is on. If you click on it, you are provided with the list of "Signposts" and set phrases (Appendix 4). A click on an item instantly brings the very sense or phrase onto the screen.

LDOCE-OL dramatically improved visually by adopting the interface of LDOCE4 on the CD-ROM. The Web dictionary makes available certain features from the CD-ROM version, such as Collocation Boxes and Word Focuses. Not only phonetic notations were added but the audio recordings of headwords and examples are also provided for the words beginning with "D" and "S."

In contrast to Cambridge and Longman, OALD-OL presents all senses and set phrases of all parts of speech of a headword at a time. As a result, an entry can be rather bulky. An entry is organized by parts of speech, followed by idioms; the verbal entry also by phrasal verbs. The labels of the included parts of speech are placed next to the headword, and a click on one takes you to the beginning of the part of speech entry. There is no Menu but "Short Cuts" help sub-entry search. "Select entry" lists phrasal verbs and compound expressions, including the headword with the information on their location. A click on an item takes you to the entry[6].

Notes on usage are useful; those entitled "synonyms" not only distinguish semantically between synonyms but also list grammatical and collocational patterns the synonyms can enter into. There are no pictorial illustrations.

EFL dictionaries on the Web

3. Class activities

This chapter considers the class I gave to the third and fourth year university students of Commerce in the 2007 spring semester, using the Web-based dictionaries by the three publishers. The textbook was a selection of modern British and American literature[7]. One session of the bi-weekly class dealt with pronunciation in the language laboratory and the other with the text using the Web dictionaries in the computer room. The latter consisted of a number of activities and exercises in an attempt to familiarize students with the dictionaries. Each week I prepared a handout (two-four A4 pages), containing the entries from the three Web dictionaries for important and useful words and phrases appearing in the textbook. By means of the handout, I showed the students my example of effective dictionary use: which lexical items to look up in which dictionary. And I helped them straight to the riches such dictionaries offer and the joy of using them by shouldering the burden of (sub-entry) search in the English-English dictionaries. Special exercises were devised, which required students to interpret and translate several dictionary examples into Japanese by applying the information extracted from the definitions. Towards the end I challenged the students with the comparative use of the three Web dictionaries by having them make a handout (four A4 pages or fewer, see Appendix 6 for my example) on the selected part of *Disgrace* by Coetzee (Appendix 5), putting together the best entries from those dictionaries. The students were also required to submit a report on the assignment.

4. Students' preferences of the dictionaries

Towards the end of the course I gave the students (29 present) a questionnaire which asked them to rank the three Web dictionaries in order of preference, to give the merits and limitations of each and to make other comments. The rankings are as shown in Table 1, which reveals that LDOCE-OL is by far the most popular, followed by Cambridge and Oxford.

Table 1 Students' preferences of the dictionaries

	1st	2nd	3rd
Cambridge	8	9	12
Longman	18	9	2
Oxford	3	11	15

4.1. Students' feedback on the merits and limitations of the dictionaries

Which features and functions of a Web dictionary appealed to the students? It will be helpful to have a close look at the comments the students made in response to the merits and limitations of the dictionaries. Table 2 summarizes the student feedback. The rest of the section examines their opinions in the three areas they placed special emphasis: legibility, quick retrievability of relevant information, and examples.

Table 2 Students' feedback on merits and limitations of the dictionaries

	Cambridge	Longman	Oxford
Merits	Definition (12) Guideword list (11) Easy to look at (7) One meaning, one entry (7) Examples (4) Double click to see the word's definition (2) Quick reference when meaning known (2) Useful just to check meaning (2)	Easy to look at (25) Abundant examples (9) Pictures (6) Easy to consult (5) Arrangement by parts of speech (5) Definitions easy to understand (5) Double click to see the definition (5) Useful when meaning not known (3) Examples easy to understand (3) Pronunciation can be heard (3) Easy to use without difficult words (2) Detailed definitions (2)	Definitions (9) Abundant examples (8) All shown at a time (3) More senses (3) More headwords (2) Lean (2) Definitions easy to understand (2)
Limitations	Guideword list (6) Fewer examples (6) Not easy to look at (3) Too simple definitions (3) Difficult to consult (2) No spin-offs (2) Second look-up troublesome (2) Too small characters (2) Pronunciation not shown in default setting (2) Some items lack explanation (2)	Examples (5) Time-consuming to consult (5) Too simple definitions (4) Some difficult definitions (3) Inadequate content (2) Sub-entry search difficult (2) Some lengthy definitions (2)	Not easy to look at (23) All shown at a time (4) Many difficult words involved (3) Difficult definitions (3) Fewer examples (3) Difficult to understand (2) Time-consuming to find wanted senses or examples (2) Inability to double click to see the word's definition (2)

Note: The number of students who made a particular comment is presented in the parenthesis. Opinions expressed by more than one person are included in this table.

A general survey confirms the findings made by Yamada (2006: 317): ease of reference, especially legibility, is a paramount qualification expected of a good Web dictionary. It is no exaggeration to say that the vote on legibility had a direct bearing on the preferences of dictionaries by the students. Seven students mentioned CALD-OL is easy to look at[8], while three thought otherwise. A total of 25 students (86.2%) made favourable comments on the legibility of LDOCE-OL[9] and no criticism was made in this respect. While only two students spoke well of the aesthetic aspects of OALD-OL[10], as many as 23 (79.3%) did not like the appearance of the dictionary[11,12].

Analysis of the questionnaire and the students' comments and reports has shown one basic orientation: they want to go to the (sub-)entry quickly and only want to read the information relevant for their purposes. This tendency toward time-and-energy-efficiency of retrieving relevant information seems to be stronger than in my previous study. The dictionaries with the features and functions helpful in these areas seem to enjoy more student support.

CALD-OL is structured to provide quick access to the exact entry and does not give too many definitions and examples. The Guideword list and the policy of one meaning, one entry were commended by 11 and 7 students[13] respectively, but are double-edged swords. "Guide Words do not show parts of speech explicitly ..., users are required to closely examine each Guideword when they cannot depend on the meaning" (ibid.: 315). While three students say that quick reference is possible with CALD-OL if meaning can be guessed, four of the five students who are against the Guideword list found it only detrimental to consultation without having the meaning as a clue[14]. It is true that a dictionary is a tool for quick reference but it is not all when it comes to learners' dictionaries. Two insightful students criticized the one-meaning-one-entry organization for denying users chances to get spin-off information[15]. Out of the 12 students who highly rated the definition, seven attributed the beauty to its conciseness; one referred to the just-right length of definition[16]. On the other hand, three found the definition too simple. Two concluded that CALD-OL was ideal for just checking meaning; another made an interesting comment: the dictionary was most helpful when you only needed to come up with equivalents in Japanese while reading[17]. CALD-OL's simplicity and directness also have plusses and minuses.

It appears that moderation in the access structure and information dosage put Longman at an advantage. Many students found the dictionary's part-of-speech principle and the amount and depth of information to be just right. Five students found the dictionary easy to consult, and the part-of-speech arrangement was supported by another five. A comment "useful when meaning not known" by three students may have been made with CALD-OL in mind. On the other hand, five students considered LDOCE-OL time-consuming to consult: two referred to skimming through entries, another two to searching for relevant information in entries with many definitions and examples, and one to consulting polysemous entries. A separate two complained of the difficulty in sub-entry search[18]. The dictionary is praised for ease of use: five mentioned easy-to-understand definitions, and two the absence of difficult words. However, several of the students were divided over the amount and depth of information: two praised the detailed definitions; four found them too simple, and two too lengthy. Reconciling these matters with ease of reference and understanding remains a problem.

OALD-OL's policy of presenting all related information under a headword did not meet with much support from the students, though the definition did fairly well. Only three students favoured the organizing principle and four otherwise[19]. The principle has both advantages and disadvantages: users are not confronted with the choice of parts of speech and senses at the outset and they feel assured that the answer is somewhere in the dictionary text as long as an entry word was keyed in correctly, but they are required to wade through the not necessarily easy-to-look-at dictionary text (ibid.: 316). Two of the critics found that the organization led to troublesome look-ups; another pointed to time-consuming ones. In addition, two said "time-consuming to find wanted senses or examples" and one complained of the difficulty of sub-entry search. Many students found OALD-OL's organization awkward to handle and not conducive to quick reference. Overall, the definition was fairly well-received. Out of the nine students who brought this up as a plus, seven suggested detailedness. Two thought that OALD-OL included more senses. Whereas a total of eight students mentioned difficulty as a down side, one welcomed the use of "high-level words." The following adjectives which occurred in the questionnaire may partly represent how students see the dictionary: "formal" (made by one student), "lean" (2), "solid" (1, mentioned as to definition).

It has been shown that students attach more importance to examples than in my previous study. More opinions were expressed though there was a discrepancy. Four students applauded CALD-OL for their examples[20] and six denounced the dictionary for giving few examples[21]. Nine and three students praised LDOCE-OL for its abundant and easy examples, respectively, but five made criticisms related to examples. Two students mentioned the scarcity of examples, one excessive ease, and another both[22]. OALD-OL was praised by eight students for its abundant examples[23] but was criticized by three for offering few examples. The importance and usefulness of examples in dictionary consultation have been suggested. A few students revealed in the questionnaire and in the reports attached to the handout-making assignment that they relied on examples in an effort to figure out meaning (when they did not understand the definition or found it unhelpful).

5. Longman's boosted popularity

In the present study, LDOCE-OL was the sole leader in the students' popularity vote, while the dictionary almost shared the lead with CALD-OL in my previous study (see Appendix 7). The Longman Web dictionary underwent several changes in the space of two and a half years. A look into these changes will give clues as to what can be thought to have boosted the dictionary's popularity among the students. As was touched upon in the second section, the online version has become generous, offering non-paying users some of the privileges of the purchasers of LDOCE4 in book and CD-ROM forms: phonetic notations, collocation boxes, and Word Focuses, and the audio recordings of some of the headwords and examples. The Web dictionary has

EFL dictionaries on the Web   93

improved in the reaction to misspelled entry words since it used to just show "No results!" The dictionary lacked flexibility by showing search results only in a pop-up window but this has been changed. In the questionnaire of my previous study, 12 (42.3%) and 7 (25%) of the 28 students found inconvenient the fixed window size and the lack of pronunciation notations, respectively (Yamada 2006: 314, see Appendix 8). The improvement in these areas, as well as added features, can be assumed to have worked positively and increased the dictionary's popularity.

6. Problems with the dictionaries

Ways of access to an entry differ between the print dictionary and the electronic dictionary. You flip through pages of the former, while you type a word on the keyboard with the latter. This allows the users of Web dictionaries quicker reference but can cause problems because of search programming and the degree of its sophistication. There are problems, specific to individual dictionaries, found especially in Cambridge's and Longman's. This section looks at such problems, based on my experience.

LDOCE-OL lacks flexibility and shows only main headwords in response to the search word keyed in. For example, if you type in *tang.* the dictionary coolly says "No result!" even though the adjective is run on under the entry for *tang*. CALD-OL and OALD-OL are kind enough to show the entry for *tang* which subsumes the adjective. Unlike these dictionaries, LDOCE-OL fails to serve the user who enters *latticework*, the alternative spelling of *lattice*[24,25].

There is room for improvement in the access to multi-word items in Web dictionaries. LDOCE-OL seems to be the weakest in that it only exhibits those items that are entered as a main headword (e.g. *point of view*). The dictionary only responds with "No result!" when it is fed "as it were," for example, while CALD-OL shows a long list including the item and OALD-OL the entry for the first word *as*.

CALD-OL's characteristic Guideword list can be problematic. If you enter two or more words into the search box you can end up at a loss with too long a list. If you enter all the three words in search of "of all people," for instance, you are given a dauntingly long list to go through. You can tackle a lengthy list with the use of the "Find" command on the Edit menu of MS Word (Yamada 2006: 319, Note 8). But you should first try cutting the search words down to one ("people" in this case) to get a manageable list. A second problem is that you can not apply a grammar-oriented search method because Guidewords consist basically of synonyms (see the second section)[26]. Identifying the appropriate Guideword for "get" as in "get to thinking"[27] in the list entails great pains. A third problem is to do with sense discrimination[28] and "Guidewording" itself. Choose the appropriate Guideword for "relieve" below in the list at Appendix 2:

And, always as one writes, there is the temptation to hurry the book to its end to <u>relieve</u> the suspense about one's ability to finish it. (*Write On* [1986] by David Lodge, as included in Saito and Kamioka [2004: 127]; emphasis added)

How many can click on "relief (HAPPINESS)" for the appropriate sense of the word at the first attempt (Yamada 2007)?

The combination of Cambridge's one-meaning-one-entry policy, displaying of one entry at a time, and difficulty of moving from one entry to another backfires when comparison of entries is necessary. Users are put off when they need a close, comparative look at entries for referencing and learning purposes, as in the case of consulting *relieve* above when the list of Guidewords does not turn out to be helpful.

LDOCE-OL shares the interface with its CD-ROM version as mentioned in the second section. The Web (and CD-ROM) dictionary needs fine-tuning because it does not allow users to view pages in the way the print version does. The dictionary amalgamates the adverbial and prepositional uses of a word (e.g. *above*) in an entry but the list users are shown right after entering a search word indicates only the adverb (see Appendix 3). Menus fail to display the alternative spelling: for example, "by way of" is in but "in the way of" is not (see Sense 25 in Appendix 4). Where there is more than one entry for a word, only the first comes with pronunciation. Since the dictionary shows entries by parts of speech, pronunciation should be provided for each entry. When you are at the second nominal entry for *reverse*, for instance, it is troublesome to have to refer to the first verbal entry just to check the pronunciation. It may be a good idea to provide pronunciation on to the list, especially in the cases of homographs with different pronunciations, such as *row* ('line') and *row* ('quarrel'). This can make for quick reference, saving one unnecessary look-up. The second verbal entry for *void* defines the word by means of the adjective sense of the word, which is treated in the first entry. In these areas, adopting the part-of-speech principle, LDOCE-OL lacks consideration and service for online users.

The function of double clicking to find the word's definition was appreciated by students. It is unfortunate that the function is operable only on one-word items with both Cambridge and Longman. It is hoped that the function is so improved as to take care of hyphenated and multi-word lexical items.

7. Suggestions for teaching dictionary use

I have been firmly convinced the assignment of dictionary handout making is effective in many ways – which forced students to consult the three Web dictionaries on each look-up to prepare a handout including the best entries for words and phrases appearing in the textbook. The assignment taught the students important lessons to become well-informed dictionary users in a short time. Many students found the assignment "time-" and "energy-consuming" but "beneficial." Many encouraging and reassuring comments were expressed in the accompanying reports[29]:

(1) The assignment gave me some/better idea of the characteristics of the dictionaries.

The comparative use of the dictionaries provided a fresh idea for the students, who usually do not practice it:

(2) I was surprised to find that there are differences in description and approach between dictionaries.
(3) Each dictionary has both plusses and minuses.
(4) The "best" dictionary varies with entries.

Practice makes perfect – the assignment offered a useful intensive training in the use of English-English dictionaries:

(5) Thanks to the assignment, it became fairly comfortable to deal with the Web dictionaries.
(6) The assignment helped me to develop a feel for the Web dictionaries.
(7) This assignment helped me to get rid of the allergy to Web dictionaries.

Dealing with multiple EFL dictionaries enhanced vocabulary learning:

(8) Exposed to three definitions, I was able to form well-rounded images of word meanings.
(9) I was able to get to the heart of English words by using those dictionaries.

The assignment gave the students knowledge which enabled them to make judgments about the dictionaries and helped to devise strategies for their own effective usage[30]:

(10) I thought Longman was for elementary students, Cambridge for those intermediate, and Oxford for those advanced.
(11) I found Cambridge useful for looking up single-word items and Longman for multi-word ones.
(12) The assignment helped me find out about the characteristics – advantages and disadvantages – of the Web dictionaries and which dictionary is the easiest for me to use. As far as I am concerned, it is best to use Longman and Oxford, depending on what to look up.
(13) I developed a dictionary-using strategy suited to me: use Longman for full understanding of the meaning and usage of words, Cambridge to think of Japanese translations of especially nouns, and Oxford supplementarily.
(14) There are differences between Web dictionaries. If you use the dictionaries, bearing the differences in mind, you will be able to make the most of them.
(15) You make full use of the Web dictionaries by using them in combination, making up for the minuses of a dictionary with the others. For example, use the comprehensive Oxford when you can not consult Cambridge on the basis of parts of speech. Follow up quick reference with Longman with Oxford for grasping nuances.

The assignment made the students face the dictionaries squarely and helped to get rid of prejudice, leading to second thoughts, especially about OALD-OL:
(16) I found Oxford the worst visually. However, the more I used the dictionary, the less of an obstacle consultation became.
(17) This assignment has made me realize that Oxford is my favourite[31].

I gave the assignment of handout-making toward the end of the class as the final homework because of its difficulty, and so as to estimate what progress they had made as a dictionary user and on what level they stood. Considering the effect the assignment had on the students and the implications for their future dictionary use, I think that assignments of this kind which involve (voluntary) multiple-dictionary use could be introduced at an earlier stage, for better effect, before they form and consolidate their judgments of dictionaries[32].

Reading the students' feedback has left me skeptical about how much they are aware of and are actually able to use the look-up supporting devices. I am under the impression that a fairly large number of students are familiar with the function of clicking on a word to find its definition because there are seven praises and two criticisms concerning the function in the questionnaire. What about Signposts, Menus, Short Cuts, and the Select entry? Also, what about the function of clicking on a part-of-speech label to go to the relevant part in the entry of OALD-OL[33]? From the fact that these functions were not mentioned in the students' feedback as frequently as they should, I suspect that they are considerably underused or largely ignored. I suggested the importance of intensive practical session at the introductory stage which ideally make everyone try out every function and feature at least once (Yamada 2006: 317) but the number must be increased to several times until they master the use.

8. Conclusion

Following my previous study of the 2004 situation, this chapter investigates the status quo of Cambridge's, Longman's, and Oxford's Web dictionaries. The study confirmed and discovered the value the students attached to legibility, quick retrievability of relevant information, and examples. LDOCE-OL commanded the most student support – approachable and well-balanced with its easy-to-look-at layout and manageability of access structure and information presentation. As pointed out, however, each dictionary has both strengths and problems. The problems are general, dictionary-specific, and unique to the electronic medium, the last requiring due technical attention from designers. More meticulous study that will yield results is necessary, informing dictionary makers of specific ways to improve their products: for example, which entry of a dictionary is preferred over the others in what look-up situations, because of what factors? There could be follow-up interviews over areas where the students' reactions were mixed.

Whatever the reason behind it, it is a blessing that students have free access to the sophisticated EFL dictionaries by the three leading publishers. Before this, how many, other than professionals, afforded this luxury? Teaching effective dictionary usage can allow the students to enjoy the luxury of multiple-dictionary use, as well as teach them to make informed choices of these dictionaries based on the situation and need. Of the benevolent publishers, would it be too much to ask to make more functions available on the Web from the CD-ROM versions? And the dictionaries for production, though in less demand they may contribute less to the purposes of promotion and marketing?

Although this chapter has focused on Web dictionaries, the reality of dictionary use should be considered in a much wider context. In Japan, there are several free Web bilingual dictionaries with English. Nevertheless, almost all university students own a hand-held electronic dictionary, carrying a number of titles, one EFL dictionary included. Murata, Osaki, and Kokawa (2007: 86-87) report that four of the five electronic dictionaries for advanced students of English include OALD6. Critical of the fact, they point out that it severely restricts choice for purchasers and recommend inclusion of more than one title from one genre. The free Web EFL dictionaries can help rectify this unsatisfactory situation. To better serve this purpose, it is to be hoped that EFL dictionaries, as a whole, regain variety that they lost in the mid 1990s when they blatantly started copying each other's successful features at the expense of individuality.

Notes

1. Included are teachers' resources, educational materials, information on the dictionary and other materials, and so on.
2. They are those for learners, American English, idioms, phrasal verbs, French/English, Spanish/English. You can designate the dictionary to use through the "Select another dictionary" pull-down.
3. Two students commented that this was troublesome in my questionnaire.
4. There are some headwords that present multiple senses with sense numbers (e.g. *relieve* under "relief (HELP)").
5. The pronunciation is not displayed in the default setting. Two students stated in the questionnaire that they preferred pronunciation to be on the default screen.
6. But not to the exact sense or place within the entry, unlike LDOCE-OL.
7. *Eigo Tatsujin Dokuhon* (*English Master's Reader*) by Saito, Yoshifumi and Nobuo Kamioka, 2004, Tokyo: Chuo Koron Shinsha. The class dealt with a couple of pages from the works below as included in the textbook, at the pace of one work per week:
Daisetz T. Suzuki, *Zen and Japanese Culture* (1959)
John Fowles, *The French Lieutenant's Woman* (1969)
Agatha Christie, *An Autobiography* (1977)
Raymond Carver, "A Small, Good Thing" (1983)

Paul Auster, *City of Glass* (1985)
David Lodge, 'Why Do I Write?' from *Write On* (1986)
Kazuo Ishiguro, *The Remains of the Day* (1989)
Tim O'Brien, *The Things They Carried* (1990)
J. M. Coetzee, *Disgrace* (1999).

8. Five of them gave specific reasons: fonts (2), colors (2), character size (2), new lines for each definition and example (1), headwords standing out (1), and optional pronunciation indication (1).
9. Twenty of them made specific references: layout (8), large and colorful characters (5), use of colors (3), large characters (3), and fonts (1).
10. One mentioned the page design and the other the layout.
11. Twenty students stated specific reasons: small characters (7), fonts (5), use of colors (4), crowded (4), characters (3), layout (2), and no new lines for each definition and example (2).
12. One remarked that he could not bring himself to use OALD-OL because of the illegibility caused by too small characters.
13. Two spoke of ease of locating a sense, and another two of trouble being saved.
14. Another brought up the difficulty of tracking down a sense in CALD-OL. He mentioned that sense discrimination is not fine enough (cf. Note 28).
15. In this regard, one student spoke highly of OALD-OL's all-inclusive organizing principle.
16. He expressed the same opinion about examples.
17. Another found the dictionary fell short of his expectations in consulting basic words and those with multiple senses.
18. There was only one student who mentioned Signposts as an advantage.
19. In my previous study, the opinion was almost evenly split with 11 ayes and 10 nays (Yamada 2006: 314, see Appendix 8).
20. One felt that the dictionary went out of the way to provide examples for words and senses where the other dictionaries do not.
21. Two students made this comment in comparison with Longman, and one with both Longman and Oxford. Another observed that lack of examples got in the way of understanding of the meaning of a new word, consulting CALD-OL.
22. One student thought that the dictionary offered less content and the other the least content of the three dictionaries.
23. In this connection, one said the examples were helpful in understanding fine usage differences. Another found Longman even better, offering more examples. There was one who found the Oxford examples easy to understand.
24. LDOCE4 on the CD-ROM does the job when both "tangy" and "latticework" are typed in. So do the CALD and OALD7 counterparts.
25. If you enter "a" into LDOCE-OL you are warned "Your search must contain more than 1 character and less than 10 words." It is strange that if

you type in "minute" OALD-OL turns up *minute*² first.
26. An exception can be found in the list for *squeeze*, which includes grammatical collocations of the verb.
27. "And you get to thinking about a different life, a *better* life you might have had." In *The Remains of the Day* by Kazuo Ishiguro (1989) as included in Saito and Kamioka (2004: 133).
28. CALD-OL tends to discriminate senses coarsely rather than finely. This allows relatively high information content per entry, which can give the dictionary an educational edge. Because of this, there were occasions where I chose the entry from the dictionary over the others for inclusion in my handout (for example, that for Sense 1 of *transpose*).
29. Several students thankfully acknowledged my effort for handout making after they experienced it for themselves.
30. Views on dictionaries and dictionary consultation are highly personal matters. I do not necessarily agree with each of the students' opinions.
31. This view was shared by two students. The assignment converted them to OALD-OL and they rated the dictionary as the best in the questionnaire.
32. I suspect that they do so rather too quickly (Yamada 2006: 317).
33. One student mentioned this in his report accompanying the dictionary handout assignment.

Appendices
1. Three Web-based EFL dictionaries

	Cambridge	Longman	Oxford
Source dictionaries	[CALD (2003), etc. =>] CALD (2005), etc	LDOCE4 (2003), LAAD (2000)	[OALD6 (2000)=>] OALD7 (2005)
Number of entries	[170,000 words, phrases and examples]	[106,000 words and phrases (incl. 7,000 encyclopedic items)]	[80,000 references]
Defining vocabulary	[2,000 words (?)]	2,000 words	3,000 words
Search method (after entering entry word)	- Choose from list of Guidewords and set phrases - More than one part of speech and derivatives are included under one Guideword - Set phrases can be typed into search box	- List of parts of speech and compounds appears if applicable - Consult polysemous entry by Signposts. Menu (when it is on) shows Signposts and set phrases; click one to go to appropriate sub-entry [- Click left- and right-pointing arrow to go to previous and next entry] - [Set phrases cannot be typed into search box=>] Multi-word headwords are indicated	- All parts of speech and derivatives are shown under one headword - Consult polysemous entry by Short Cuts - Select entry shows compounds and set phrases - [Set phrases cannot be typed into search box=>] Multi-word headwords are indicated; otherwise, entry for first words are shown

	Cambridge	Longman	Oxford
For misspelled entry words	Candidates shown	[No candidates shown=>] Candidates shown	Candidates shown if approximate enough
Legibility	Very good: effective use of fonts and colors, new lines for each definition and example	Very good: effective use of colors and typefaces, new lines for each definition and example	OK: definitions and examples run on
Pronunciation	Optionally indicated	[N.A.=>] Available; recordings of headwords and examples of D-and S-words are provided	Available
Frequency information	N.A.	Three levels for the 3,000 most common spoken and written words each	N.A.
Usage notes	N.A.	[N.A. in Web version =>] Available	Available
Double click to see the word's definition	Available	Available	N.A.
Other features	- Other dictionaries included [- With cursor automatically moved into search box, next search easy]	- Color illustrations	

Based on Yamada (2006: 322); what were applicable to the 2004 versions appear in square brackets.

2. CALD-OL's list of guidewords and phrases for "relieve"

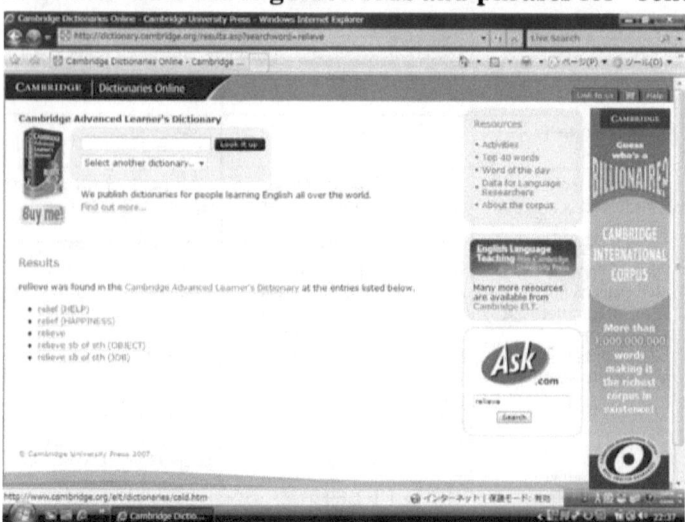

EFL dictionaries on the Web

3. LDOCE-OL's list of parts of speech and compounds for "above"

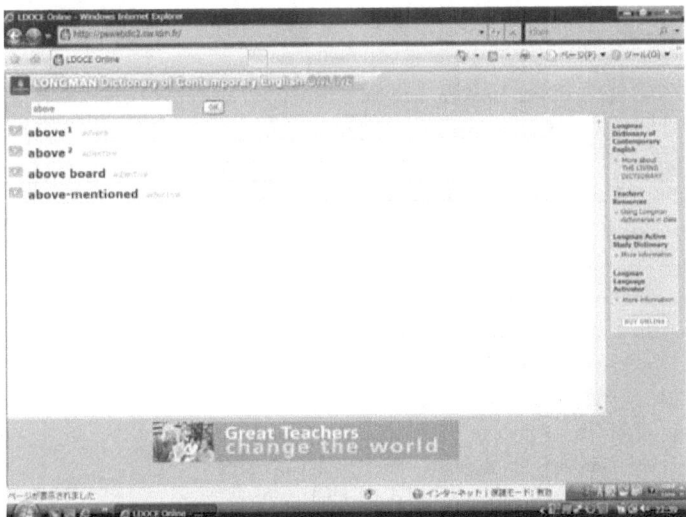

4. LDOCE-OL's menu for "way"

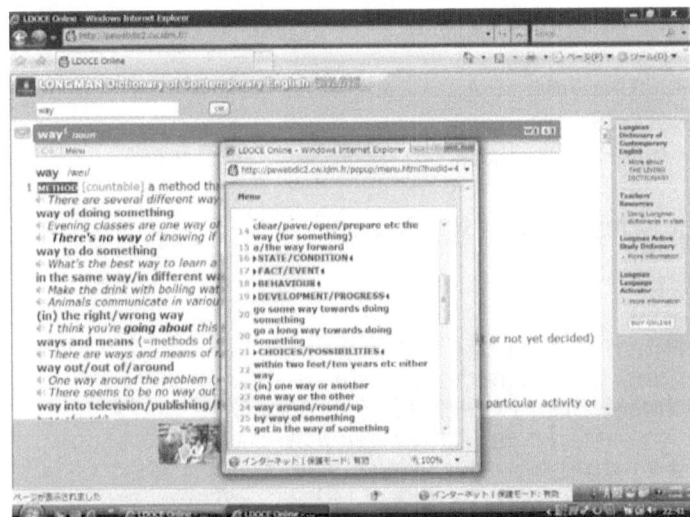

5. *Disgrace* (1999) by J. M. Coetzee, as included in Saito and Kamioka (2004: 144)

In the old days one could have had it out with Petrus. In the old days one could have had it out to the extent of losing one's temper and sending him packing and hiring someone in his place. But though Petrus is paid a wage, Petrus is no longer, strictly speaking, hired help. It is hard to say what Petrus is, strictly speaking. The word that seems to serve best, however, is *neighbour*. Petrus is a neighbour who at present happens to sell his labour, because that is what suits him. He sells his labour under contract, unwritten contract, and that contract makes no provision for dismissal on grounds of suspicion. It is a new world they live in, he and Lucy and Petrus. Petrus knows it, and he knows it, and Petrus knows that he knows it.

In spite of which he feels at home with Petrus, is even prepared, however guardedly, to like him. Petrus is a man of his generation. Doubtless Petrus has been through a lot, doubtless he has a story to tell. He would not mind hearing Petrus's story one day. But preferably not reduced to English. More and more he is convinced that English is an unfit medium for the truth of South Africa. Stretches of English code whole sentences long have thickened, lost their articulations, their articulateness, their articulatedness. Like a dinosaur expiring and settling in the mud, the language has stiffened. Pressed into the mould of English, Petrus's story would come out arthritic, bygone.

6. First page of my handout for *Disgrace*

27 J. M. Coetzee, *Disgrace* **(1999)**

have it out with *sb*
to talk to someone about something they have done which makes you angry, in order to try to solve the problem:
She'd been late for work every morning that week and I thought I'd better have it out with her. [CALD-OL]
IDM **to ... extent** used to show how far sth is true or how great an effect it has: *To a **certain extent**, we are all responsible for this tragic situation.* ◊*He had changed **to such an extent** (= so much) that I no longer recognized him.* ◊***To some extent*** *what she argues is true.* ◊*The pollution of the forest has seriously*

affected plant life and, **to a lesser extent**, *wildlife*. ○**To what extent** *is this true of all schools?* ○*The book discusses* **the extent to which** *(= how much) family life has changed over the past 50 years*. [OALD-OL]
11 send somebody packing *informal* to tell someone who is not wanted that they must leave at once:
◀ *After his four years as governor, the voters sent him packing.* [LDOCE-OL]
pack (PUT INTO) kp/ Hide phonetics
verb
1 [I or T] to put something into a bag, box, etc:
We're leaving early tomorrow morning, so you'd better pack (= put clothes and other possessions into a bag or bags) tonight.
*She packed a small **suitcase** for the weekend.*
*He just packed his **bags** and walked out on his wife and children.*
I haven't packed my clothes (= put them into a bag etc.) yet.
*[+ two objects] Could you pack me a spare pair of shoes, please/pack a spare pair of shoes **for** me, please?*
*These books need to be packed **in/into** a box.* [CALD-OL]
IDM **in place of sb/sth** |
IDM **in sb's / sth's place** instead of sb/sth: *You can use milk in place of cream in this recipe.* ○*He was unable to come to the ceremony, but he sent his son to accept the award in his place.* [OALD-OL]

7. 2004 Students' preferences of the dictionaries after 1.5 months and toward the end of semester (Yamada 2006: 313)

	After 1.5 months			End of semester		
	1st	2nd	3rd	1st	2nd	3rd
Cambridge	13	10	5	12	11	5
Longman	14	10	4	13	11	4
Oxford	3	6	19	5	6	17

Five of the 28 students designated two dictionaries as equal in rank.

8. 2004 Students' feedback on merits and limitations of the dictionaries (Yamada 2006: 314)
Merits

Cambridge	Longman	Oxford
"Guide Word" list (20) Easy to look at (17) Pronunciation (8) Double click to see the word's definition (5) Candidates shown when entry words misspelled (5) Examples (5) Easy to consult (4)	Easy to look at (23) Indication of list (13) Definition (8) Arrangement by parts of speech (7) Color illustrations (6) "Menu" (6) Examples (5) "Signposts" (4) Easy to understand (3) Collocation (3)	All shown at a time (11) Idioms (7) Use of color/bold (4) "Select entry" (3) Definition (3) Examples (3)

Limitations

Cambridge	Longman	Oxford
"Guide Word" list (20)	Window not to be enlarged (12) Difficult to consult (8) No pronunciation (7)	Not easy to look at (22) All shown at a time (10) No double-click-to-see-the-word's-definition function (5) Advertisement nuisance (4) No candidates shown when entry words misspelled (3) Examples (3)

Note: The numbers of students who mentioned it are presented in the brackets. Opinions expressed by more than two are included in the table.

The potential of learner corpora for pedagogical lexicography

Yukio Tono
Tokyo University of Foreign Studies
y.tono@tufs.ac.jp

1. Research paradigm shift in pedagogical lexicography

Lexicography covers a broad range of interdisciplinary areas in linguistics, reference sciences, language teaching and learning, and more recently natural language processing. A common approach in lexicography is to try to apply knowledge and facts found in these disparate areas to the production of dictionaries. These facts are mainly concerned with linguistic observations or theoretical analyses of the system of a language as well as its use. Linguists study languages and inform lexicographers on better or more innovative ways of describing a word, providing usage information, giving illustrative examples and so on.

In the last two decades, however, this traditional approach to dictionary-making has been taken over by a more data-oriented approach to lexicography, which is based upon empirical research on language corpora, dictionary users and language learners. This is particularly true in the field of pedagogical lexicography. In this chapter, I will summarise recent developments in pedagogical lexicography with special reference to the three areas mentioned above (language corpora, dictionary users and language learners) and argue that significant improvements in user-friendliness could be achieved by using second language (L2 henceforth) learner corpora to inform the making of learners' dictionaries.

2. A data-oriented approach to pedagogical lexicography

In a sense, lexicography has always been 'data oriented'. Lexicographers investigate the use of words and phrases by what lexicographers at Merriam-Webster's call 'reading and marking'. The way lexicographers access language use data, however, has dramatically changed since computerised corpora became available in the early 1960s. The first fully corpus-based monolingual dictionary was the *COBUILD English Dictionary* (1987), which was radically different from existing monolingual learners' dictionaries and enthusiastically welcomed among linguists and language educators in Japan as well as in the rest of the world. All the other major monolingual learners' dictionaries have more or less followed this trend and lexicographers have been using KWIC (keyword in context) concordances as their primary tool for finding out how a word behaves ever since. After Church and Hanks (1989) introduced the notion of Mutual Information (a measure of the salience of the association between any two words), lexicographers became more interested in identifying statistically salient collocates. Every publisher started to compile its own corpus (e.g. the Cambridge International Corpus, the Longman Corpus Network, among others) and even its own corpus query system (a set of tools to help lexicographers use corpus data effectively). By 1995, the revised Big 4 (COBUILD, OALD, LDOCE, and CIDE) claimed that they were all so-called 'corpus-based'. Since then, using corpora for dictionary-making has become standard practice, at least for the major dictionary publishers in the UK.

Recently, a more sophisticated approach to using corpora has been proposed, mainly to deal with larger sets of data or more detailed grammatical relations in the text (e.g. the Sketch Engine (Kilgarriff, et al. 2004) and the Shogakukan Language Toolbox (Nakamura and Tono 2003) among others). Papers presented at Euralex 2004 or 2006 showed that dictionary publishers are shifting their attention from using general mega-corpora to more specialised corpora and from the ordinary use of corpora to more purpose-specific uses.

Another important area which underwent a marked shift in the past two decades is research into dictionary use. Up until the 1980s, very little attention was paid to the needs and skills of dictionary users. Reinhart Hartmann was one of the first to enlighten us on the importance of research into dictionary use (Hartmann 1979, 1983). I myself was one of the few researchers who started to conduct experimental studies on dictionary reference skills in the 1980s (Tono 1984, 1986, 1988). There is now a growing body of literature in this field and major works are reviewed in my book in Lexicographica series (Tono 2001).

Whilst lexicographers are aware of the importance of user studies, it takes time to apply research findings to the actual production of dictionaries. Some notable successful applications of research findings to dictionary-making include the provision of a 'menu' at the beginning of dictionary entries. With the menu, users can first browse through the various meanings of any given word, which is a feature widely introduced after a study confirmed the fact that the users only look at the beginning of dictionary entries (Tono 1984). Dictionary makers are also taking note of research in dictionary use where the effectiveness of newly introduced organizational devices are put to the test. For example, I conducted an experiment to investigate the effects of 'Signposts' in LDOCE and 'Guidewords' in CIDE and found that the terms used for signposts in LDOCE were more effective in directing users to the right meanings while the terms used for Guidewords were often too abstract to 'signpost' meanings in the dictionary (Tono 1992).

More recently, there has been a renewed interest in the role of dictionaries in language learning since electronic dictionaries began growing in popularity in Japan several years ago. The market is constantly increasing in size, and major manufacturers such as Casio, Seiko, Sharp, and Canon are competing on the development of new types of hand-held e-dictionaries. As the number of university and high school students who own pocket e-dictionaries grows rapidly, more research has been conducted on the effects of using pocket e-dictionaries in reading and writing. The dictionary workshop organised by the JACET Lexicography SIG has been very well attended, where around 50-60 paper presentations are given, in which the use of pocket e-dictionaries has become a favourite theme. The time is ripe for further research on the effects of using pocket e-dictionaries in terms of the medium or interface (paper vs. electronic), L2 vocabulary learning, and dictionary skills training.

The above two factors, the advent of language corpora and research into dictionary use, have contributed greatly to the improvement of learners' dictionaries. The third area which I will now focus on is the study of language learners themselves. Dictionaries serve many different purposes. Pedagogical lexicography is mainly concerned with dictionaries designed to help foreign learners of the language. Language learners as dictionary users need to be investigated more seriously. Pedagogical lexicography should take into account L2 learners' learning habits, learning styles, learning strategies and learning processes. There is a large body of research in the field of foreign language learning and second language acquisition (SLA henceforth), but unfortunately very little effort has been made to apply SLA research findings to the study of dictionary-making and on how language learners actually use dictionaries.

For the past 20 years, I have been conducting research in all the above three areas. At the beginning of my research career in the 1980s, my primary interest was in the role of dictionary use in language learning. When COBUILD was published in 1987, I realised the potential of corpus-based approach in language studies and this led me to pursue my doctoral research at Lancaster in the 1990s. There I learned about the various branches of corpus-based research and saw examples of corpus applications in different fields. I became convinced that the use of corpora would make a major difference in the field of English language teaching in Japan. At that time, I had an opportunity to collect English essays written by Japanese learners of English as part of a large-scale research project on the effects of teacher feedback in L2 writing. I started turning this valuable data into a corpus so that I could more systematically investigate the characteristic features of the writing of Japanese learners of English. This corpus, the Japanese EFL Learner (JEFLL hereafter) Corpus, has been one of the primary sources of learner corpus research in Japan at present.

3. Learner corpora and L2 lexicography

A learner corpus is a collection of speech or writing by foreign language learners. By looking at the learner performance data, we can find many interesting patterns of use which are quite different from those of native speakers. In many cases, these differences are due to the fact that learners are still in the process of acquiring a language, and they naturally make errors or mistakes. In other cases, learners will underuse or overuse particular linguistic items or constructions, which is again the sign of on-going process of learning the target language.

Studying learner errors is not new. The research area called 'Error Analysis' has been around for more than 30 years. What is new is that we can now investigate learner language by employing techniques of large-scale textual analysis by computer. What sort of information can we extract from learner corpora? How can we apply such findings to pedagogical dictionary-making? Let me describe some of these areas in detail.

3.1. Source of vocabulary selection for L2 learners

One way of analysing learner corpora is to analyse the vocabulary used in the learner production data and compare it with the vocabulary used by native speakers. I worked for NHK (Nihon Hoso Kyokai, Japan Broadcasting Centre) in developing a television English conversation programme (titled *Hyakugo de sutato eikaiwa* which means 'Let's start with 100 basic words in English'). This programme was unique in the sense that it was the first 'corpus-based' English conversation programme on television. It consists of a 100 lessons based on the 100 key vocabulary items which were chosen based on corpus analysis. It is a well-known fact that the high-frequency lexical items in English (or any language) will cover a very high proportion of the words in any text; the most frequent 100 words (lemmas) in English, for example, will cover approximately 70% of words in a spoken corpus[1]. Many of these are core lexical items (verbs, prepositions, personal and *wh*-pronouns, determiners, adverbs and conjunctions) that play a crucial role in constructing basic English structures (See Lee 2001 for more discussion on core vocabulary). There are relatively few nouns (only six!) and adjectives in the top 100 words. In this television programme, I focused on the most frequent 100 keywords and designed the programme in a lexical syllabus. As I worked on this programme, I became convinced that beginning-level students should study a set of basic core vocabulary again and again in a series of different language tasks. These core vocabulary items are at the heart of English grammar and are rich in meanings and functions, and it takes time to acquire a satisfactory productive and receptive grasp of them.

One hundred words might seem too few in number and some people claim that to be functional in English one should know at least the top 2000 words, which would typically cover about 90% of the words in a spoken corpus. Leftover words (i.e. those below the 2000 word level) are said to be mostly those which are affected by particular topics or situations and which can therefore be learned independently from the first 2000 basic items. However, how exactly can we determine the next set of words to learn (after the first

The potential of learner corpora for pedagogical lexicography 109

2000)? In an EFL environment like Japan, most L2 input will come from the classroom especially for beginning-level learners. The language spoken and written in the classroom is different from that of everyday conversations encountered by native speakers. It is natural, therefore, that the vocabulary covered in classroom settings will be different from those used in everyday life in Britain, and EFL learners' dictionaries should meet the specific communicative needs of L2 learners in terms of vocabulary selection. For such purposes, learner corpora collected from particular L2 learner groups would be most useful. By comparing well-balanced learner corpora with native-speaker corpora, both in spoken and written modes, we can possibly identify a list of words which are significantly more frequently used by L2 learners. These are the candidate words that learners want to express in English. In this way, we could exploit learner corpora to improve the selection of vocabulary for more user-friendly teaching materials, including textbooks, grammar books and dictionaries.

3.2. Identifying L2 learners' common errors

Recently, monolingual dictionaries such as LDOCE, CALD, and *Longman Essential Activator* all feature common learner errors as part of the usage information. The primary aim of this information is to give learners information on correct usage based on common errors as shown in the learner corpus data collected by the dictionary publishers. The types of errors highlighted in learners' dictionaries may be classified as follows:

(i) *Lexical choice*
e.g. Do not say '**injure** someone's health'. Say '**damage** someone's health'.
(*LDOCE*)
e.g. The words '*not ... either*' are used to add another piece of negative information.
    Helen didn't enjoy it either.
    ~~Helen didn't enjoy it too~~.
(*CALD*)

(ii) *Verb forms*
e.g. You can '**have** problems doing something'. Do not use 'to do'.
(*LDOCE*)

(iii) *Verb patterns*
e.g. You **propose** something to someone: *He proposed a possible solution to me*.
    (NOT *He proposed me a possible solution.*)
(*LDOCE*)

(iv) *Word position*
e.g. **Especially** never comes at the start of a sentence: *He loves fruit. He especially likes kiwis.* (NOT *Especially he likes ...*)
(*LDOCE*)

(v) *Grammatical/lexical collocation*
e.g. Be careful to use the correct verb.
  I have to make a speech.
  ~~I have to do a speech.~~
(*CALD*)

Whilst such error information is valuable in itself, the way the information is provided in pedagogical dictionaries still needs to be refined. Firstly, the selection of errors is not always appropriate. Some information is too basic for those who would use monolingual dictionaries. There is a trend to provide simple error information in beginners' monolingual dictionaries such as the *Longman Active Study Dictionary (LASD)* and the *Cambridge Learner's Dictionary (CLD)*, but most of those who would dare to use a monolingual dictionary are likely to be already familiar with such usage. The error information should be tuned to the level of learners who would venture to use monolingual dictionaries. The analysis of the JEFLL Corpus shows that there are significant relationships between particular error patterns and stages of acquisition. For example, verb morphology errors are relatively more common for beginning- to intermediate-stage learners than for more advanced learners, while lexical-choice errors are observed more commonly in advanced learners. This is due to the fact that beginning-level learners had difficulties in constructing a longer sentence that contains complex noun phrases, thus there are a smaller number of errors in nouns in comparison to verb errors. For advanced learners, on the other hand, they produce more complex sentences, containing more noun phrases in verb object or prepositional object positions, which produce more noun-related lexical errors, rather than verb errors. In contrast to these, the article (*the, a, an*) errors are persistent throughout the acquisition levels, which shows that there are some errors that are very difficult to overcome for Japanese learners of English.

Secondly, it is difficult to deal with L1-related errors in general-purpose monolingual dictionaries which are not aimed at particular L1-speaking learners. For example, Japanese-speaking learners of English often made the following ungrammatical sentences (examples are taken from JEFLL):
(1) My house is Shinjuku.
(2) We are very hard life everyday.
(3) Keitai is kakaru a lot of money. ('keitai' = 'mobile phone'; 'kakaru' = 'cost')
All these sentences have the 'subject + *be* + predicate' pattern, whose

corrected versions are listed as follows:
(4) I live in Shinjuku.
(5) We have a very hard life every day.
(6) Mobile phones cost a lot of money.

It is interesting that each pattern involves slightly different patterns of errors. The sentence (1) needs a human subject as in 'I live in ...', whereas the original sentence starts with 'my house'. This is very common in Japanese, for in Japanese sentences do not always require a subject. The sentence in (7), for example, means 'I live in Shinjuku':

(7) Watashi-no ie-wa Shinjuku-desu.
    I-GEN house-TOP Shinjuku-DECL

In (7), 'Watashi-no ie-ha' works as topicalisation, not the subject of the sentence. Many students get confused about the role of a copula *be* in this kind of construction. The problem is that a direct translation sometimes works, as in (8), but sometimes not, as in (9):

(8) Watashi-wa kanemochi-desu. (= I am rich.)
    I- SUB rich-DECL
(9) Watashi-wa kohi. (=*I am coffee.)
    I-TOP coffee (DECL-omitted)

Japanese learners of English often confuse subject-predicate constructions with topic-comment constructions, which is one of the very common error patterns in learner writings.

The second error above in (2) shows a slightly different pattern. In this case, the Japanese equivalent is also a topic-comment structure as in (10):

(10) Mainichi   taihen kibishii seikatu desu.
    everyday   very   hard   life   DECL

The sentence (10) could be translated using a pronoun *it*, as in (11), or a personal pronoun *we*, as in (12):
(11) It is a very hard life.
(12) We have a very hard life.

In the sentence (2), the student successfully chose the personal pronoun we, but could not select a right verb to express the message (12). Here there is a strong tendency that Japanese learners of English stick to the 'subject + be + predicate' construction whenever they can express the message by the topic-comment construction in L1.

The sentence (3) also shows the evidence that Japanese learners of English heavily depend on the topic-comment structure whenever they cannot find right words. Here, the student could not come up with words like 'mobile phone' or 'cost', so she or he used the Japanese equivalents in a sentence. To realise the proposition into English, he deliberately used a copula *be* because again the Japanese translation for the sentence (3) could be expressed using topical particle '*wa*':

(13) Keitai-wa   okane ga   kakaru.
    mobile phone-TOP   money-SUB   cost

Here it is a little tricky, since, in Japanese, the noun *okane* (i.e. *money*) can become a subject for the verb *kakaru* (i.e. *cost*) whereas in English it should be placed in the object position. Thus, this student gets confused and simply connect 'mobile phone' and 'cost' with a copula ***be***.

This type of error cannot be adequately described in monolingual dictionaries because it is often caused by learners' L1 knowledge and error patterns are different from L1 to L1. Thus, these kinds of L1-related errors should be treated more extensively in bilingual learners' dictionaries. Without a careful examination of learner production data, it would not be possible to incorporate such information in learners' dictionaries. Learner corpora should play an important role here as well.

3.3. Identifying the weak areas of learners: underuse of collocations

It is not sufficient to use learner corpora to provide error information only. Another significant application of corpus-based techniques would be to show L2 learners the gap in performance between native speakers and learners and thus encourage them to perform in a more target-like manner. One typical example would be the pattern of use in grammatical and lexical collocations. Table 1 shows the comparison in object-noun collocates of the verb ***make*** between the British National Corpus and the JEFLL Corpus.

Table 1 Object-noun collocates of the verb make in BNC and JEFLL

Rank by Freq.	BNC	JEFLL
1	sense	money
2	way	food
3	use	breakfast
4	decision	friends
5	mistake	story

Japanese EFL learners tend to use, as collocates of *make*, relatively concrete objects such as ***money***, ***food***, and ***friends***, among others. These collocates are considered to be free combinations with the verb *make* in the sense of 'to produce'. On the other hand, native speakers use the verb *make* with more abstract nouns such as ***sense***, ***way***, *use, decision* and the like. Since phrases such as *make sense, make a decision*, etc. are all highly frequent collocations used by native speakers of English, but constantly underused by Japanese EFL learners, it would be desirable to highlight these differences in dictionaries and to advise learners to use the keyword in a more target-like manner. One way to do this is to allocate more space to the item which needs more attention. In this particular case, one could describe the basic use of the verb ***make*** (i.e. the core meaning of 'produce') more extensively in a beginner's dictionary and give more space and treatment to the extended and often metaphorical meanings in advanced learners' dictionaries. In this way, we can take into account the gap between native speakers and L2 learners (Tono 2001:203ff).

4. Profiling learner language for pedagogical lexicography

So far I have discussed the potential of learner corpus research for pedagogical lexicography in three major areas. The contribution of learner corpora sorely depends on the quality of the data. I have recently completed the projects of compiling two different corpora of Japanese EFL learners. One is called the NICT JLE Corpus (Izumi et al. 2004)[2], the world's largest spoken learner corpus to date. The total size is approximately 2 million words. It comprises 1,281 subjects' transcripts of 15-minute oral proficiency interviews taken as part of the Standard Speaking Test, the localised version of the ACTFL Oral Proficiency Interview, developed by ALC Press. Each subject's transcript is tagged for nine spoken English proficiency levels, which makes it possible to investigate characteristics of learner language based on proficiency. The second corpus is called the JEFLL Corpus (c. 700,000 words; see Tono 2007 for more details), which is a corpus of free compositions (in-class, timed essays written without recourse to dictionaries) by approximately 10,000 students.

By comparing spoken and written productions by Japanese-speaking learners of English in terms of overuse, underuse, and misuse in lexis and structures, we could provide systematic usage notes in learners' dictionaries. They are not just common errors, but errors characterising particular proficiency groups of learners in spoken and written modes, which would be very different from the common learner error notes provided in LDOCE, CALD and so forth.

Another breakthrough has come when lexical profiling tools such as the Sketch Engine (See Figure 1) and the Shogakukan Corpus Network (See Figure 2) became available these past several years. Both interfaces can deal with not only learner corpora[3] but also native-speaker corpora such as BNC, making it possible to compare native vs. non-native performance in various linguistic features. The Sketch Engine is especially useful to analyse the grammatical relations of the target word, such as verb and prepositional complements, adjectival and adverbial modifiers, etc. It is now possible to gain an overall picture of learners' use of core and specialised vocabularies at various proficiency levels. This will provide very useful input for vocabulary learning theories and for syllabus design.

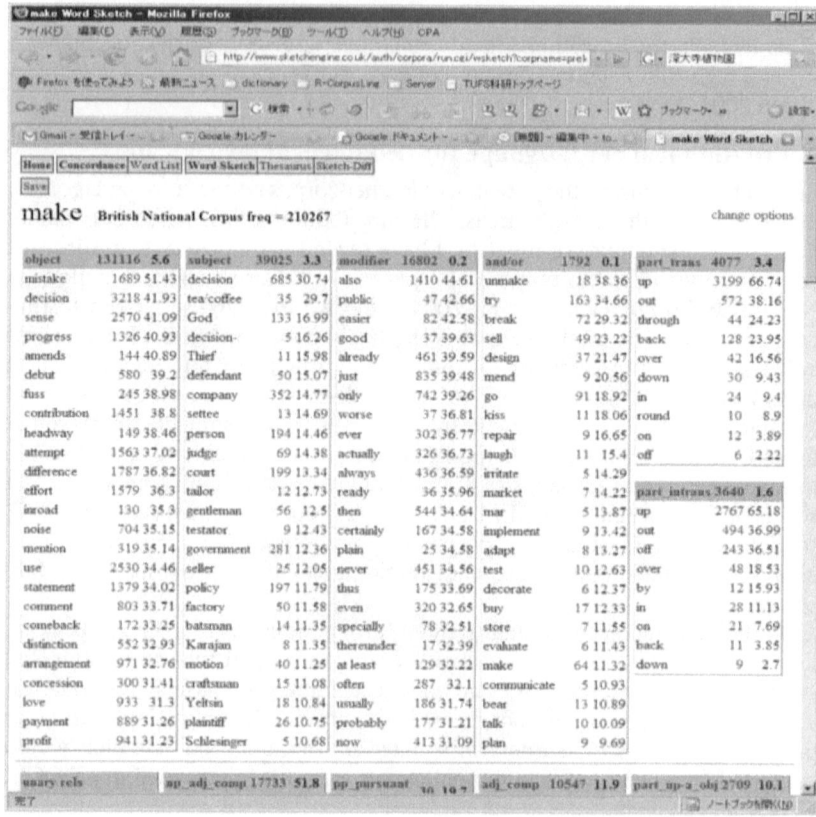

Figure 1 The Sketch Engine (word sketch on BNC)

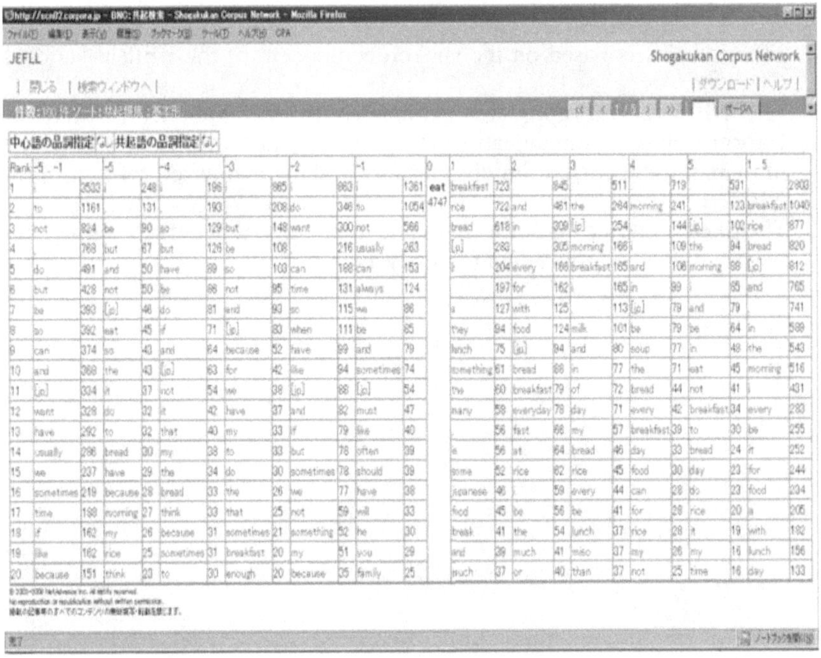

The potential of learner corpora for pedagogical lexicography   115

Figure 2 The Shogakukan Corpus Network (JEFLL Corpus on the Web)

5. Conclusion

In this chapter, I have argued that a computational analysis of a large amount of L2 learner language will shed light on better understanding of language learning processes and incorporation of such information into pedagogical lexicography will improve learners' dictionaries tremendously.

If developmental errors are identified for each proficiency level, dictionaries can then be customised to specifically address the relevant weak points for different levels of users. Electronic dictionaries, in particular, could change their interfaces and even their content according to individual user settings. It would be ideal to have multiple-levels of information in a dictionary, leaving it to end-users to choose the level, amount and type of content they see according to their needs. At the moment, we have very little of this sort of proficiency level-based information, but as relevant corpora grow in size and coverage, the type of customisable dictionary described above should become a reality in the foreseeable future. Pedagogical dictionaries should deal with all the issues I have discussed in this chapter and provide necessary support. One last point to be made, however, is that proper dictionary training also needs to be given so that learners can learn to access and exploit such information for their own ends and thus become more successful language users.

Notes

1. The statistics is based on the spoken component of the British National Corpus.
2. The NICT JLE Corpus was completed by the National Institute of Information & Communications Technology, but I was heavily involved in planning the corpus building project initially and asked for help from NICT.
3. The Sketch Engine does not contain learner corpora at default setting, but we can upload our own data for analysis.

A trilingual dictionary for learners of Cantonese, English and Putonghua

Jacqueline Kam-mei Lam
jacqui.lam.mcarthur@gmail.com

Lan Li
Hong Kong Polytechnic University
eglilan@polyu.edu.hk

Tom McArthur
scotsway@aol.com

1. Introduction: Sociolinguistic development in Hong Kong

Hong Kong has long been described as an 'international city', 'Asian's world city', a 'cosmopolitan city', a 'cosmopolitan trading hub' and 'an international cultural metropolis' (Lau 1995, Tung 2003 & 2005, SCOLAR, 2005). From a demographic point of view, although the population is mostly Chinese (some 95% of its 6.8 million people: 2004 Population Census), Hong Kong has always been more than simply a Chinese city, because its residents include individuals of British, North American, mainland European, and various Asian backgrounds. From a majority perspective, however, Hong Kong is a Chinese city, in which Cantonese is the mother tongue of the majority and a lingua franca for Chinese people of all backgrounds. After the 1997 hand-over from the UK to China, more and more business transactions and other kinds of co-operation with the mainland have triggered a surge in using Putonghua, especially after the implementation in 2003 of the Closer Economic Partnership Arrangement (CEPA) between the mainland and Hong Kong.

As a British colony and afterwards, Hong Kong has undergone various language policies. Although 95% of the population speak Cantonese, English was, for many years, the only language used by the civil service and in law, business, and education (cf. Lethbridge 1976). Although the social gulf between the Cantonese and British communities began to narrow in the inter-war years, it was not until well after World War II that members of the Chinese community began to attain positions of power and prestige in the colonial establishment (Tsang 1995). The past three decades have however witnessed a steady re-alignment of the roles of English and Chinese. In 1974, the colonial government enacted the Official Languages Ordinance, which declared that English and Chinese (in effect Cantonese) were the official languages of Hong Kong for the purposes of communication between the government or any public officer and members of the public (So 1996, Poon 2004).

In 1995, the Government began to develop an explicitly biliterate and trilingual civil service, and Lau (1995) states, 'In essence, the *Report of the Working Group on the Use of Chinese in the Civil Service* foreshadows a fundamental change in the language orientation of the Government'. A biliterate and trilingual educational policy was first proposed in the *Education Commission Report* (1996), without however providing any description of a framework or plan for implementation.

Since the 1997 return of sovereignty to China, this policy has been further clarified and strengthened. In the last ten years, the annual policy address by the Chief Executive has repeatedly re-stated that 'Hong Kong's development is geared towards the provision of quality services to the Mainland and the rest of the world' and noted that '[t]o achieve this, we must upgrade our biliterate and trilingual proficiency' (Tseng 2005:25).

Since 2002, the determination of the government to implement a biliterate and trilingual (BL/TL) policy has intensified, and by and large the community, where and whenever it thinks about such things, has appeared to share the sentiment. Such an interest is for example explicitly and constantly demonstrated by calls for bi-tri skills in job advertisements in the *South China Morning Post*.

In June 2003, the Standing Committee on Language Education and Research (SCOLAR[1]) released its *Action Plan to Raise Language Standards in Hong Kong*: in effect a plan for implementing a BL/TL policy. Unlike former language policies, most of which focused only on English, the *Action Plan* pays heed to Chinese, notably emphasizing the use of simplified Chinese characters in writing and of both Putonghua and Cantonese in speech. In addition, departing from previous language policy, the plan adopted the perspective of employers and sought to motivate the business world to join hands with the government to reform the education system[2] (SCOLAR, 2003 pp. 45-6, Poon, 2004).

In December 2004, the Education and Manpower Bureau (EMB) issued its third progress report on education reform, again making it clear, in Section 2: Language Education that 'the language policy of the Government is to enable students and the working population to be biliterate (in written Chinese and English) and trilingual (in Cantonese, Putonghua and English)'.

In February 2005, Chris Wardlaw, Deputy Secretary for Education and Manpower, stated that there are rising expectations regarding language skills in Hong Kong. In his paper *Supporting language learning in Hong Kong: Are we doing enough?*, he notes that 'whatever past language standards have been, current community needs and expectations place a premium on higher levels of trilingualism (Cantonese, Putonghua and English) and biliteracy (Chinese and English) to support the rapid restructuring of Hong Kong, its rich culture, and global inter-connectedness. Together, the government, education and business sectors and the wider community are investing heavily in the aspirational goal of a trilingual and biliterate Hong Kong.'

In March 2005, SCOLAR issued a final report regarding its Second Action Plan to Raise Language Standards in Hong Kong, calling for a two-month period of public consultation in January. The report once more reminded Hong Kongers that being biliterate and trilingual is to our competitive advantage, because such language ability helps bridge the gap between an English-speaking global business community and Chinese-speaking merchants and traders in both Hong Kong and on the mainland of China, a factor strongly contributing to Hong Kong's success as an international city. The report further emphasizes that proficiency in Cantonese, English and Putonghua is 'essential for life-long learning and the communication of knowledge, ideas, values, attitudes and experience' (p.7).

At the same time, although English continues to be widely used in such public domains as government, law, and education, it often interfaces with Chinese through code-switching and code-mixing, both at the spoken and the written level. If Hong Kong is to live up to its wish to be 'international', 'cosmopolitan' and 'Asia's world city', its people will by and large need to become proficient biliterates and trilinguals, and it is with this necessity in mind that our idea of a set of BiTri dictionaries has been evolving.

In creating such products, the language base has necessarily been English, because more work has been done on the teaching, learning, and lexicography of English as a second or foreign language (ESL, EFL) than on any other language. As a result, English has a stronger tradition of learners' dictionaries than any other language. In addition, since Putonghua and its romanization (Hanyu Pinyin) have in recent years received considerable linguistic and lexicographical attention in Hong Kong, we do not anticipate any problems in compiling the component that focuses on mainland China. The most innovative and demanding element, however, has been the foregrounding and in effect the 'upward equalization' of Cantonese, on the basis that it is the key linguistic medium of Hong Kong, Macau, Shenzhen and Guangdong province. As the mother tongue of the vast majority of Hong Kong people, it is spoken by over seven million people and should therefore serve as the lexicographical anchor point for the majority of users.

However, the sad fact is that, although Cantonese is hardly likely to die out, and although the two SCOLAR *Action Plan*s recommend that 'teachers should master and teach students standard Cantonese pronunciation' (2003), a majority of Chinese (including the Cantonese community at large and Cantonese scholars in particular) thinks that Cantonese is no more than a dialect and that its distinctive written form is of doubtful status (Harrison et al., 1996). As a result, Cantonese gets little objective attention in its own community. In Europe, however, one time-honoured way of turning a 'dialect' into a 'language' has been to give it a dictionary, and Cantonese certainly has dictionaries. The first was published in 1877 by Ernest John Eitel, a German missionary, with distinct characters, such as 喥*dou*⁶, 嘢*ya*⁵, 嘛*ma*³ *and* 佢*keoi*⁵, that are not part of the traditional set of characters. In this graphic sense, Cantonese is certainly a language in its own right, with more than twenty often very different systems of romanization. In addition, the widely varied and non-standardized systems for reflecting its pronunciation in writing have unfortunately made the language difficult to learn. The *BiTri Basic* aims to address this issue, among others.

First, we have adopted a mildly modified form of the Jyutping system of romanization that has been developed and promoted in recent years by the Linguistic Society of Hong Kong.

The Society's *Jyutping Pronunciation Guide* 粵 語 拼 音 字 表 (jyut⁶jyu⁵ ping³yam¹ zi⁶biu²) has been developed by a group of academics working over the past ten years in five universities in Hong Kong, and recently the Hong Kong Government adopted it as the default Cantonese romanization system for its civil service.

This is the system we use in the *BiTri Basic*. Moreover, our research to date shows that such a modified Jyutping system brings its learners closer to the native Cantonese pronunciation than any other romanization systems currently available.

Second, if Hong Kong wishes to live up to its claim of being 'Asia's world city', its citizens will need to be able to communicate with both non-Cantonese users of English worldwide and in Putonghua with mainlanders who do not know Cantonese (that is, the vast majority). Any system of language education with such a goal in mind should start early, and because of this the target users of the *BiTri Basic* are lower-secondary students (Secondary 1 to 3, aged 13 to 16), almost all of whom are mother-tongue speakers of Cantonese who need to build up a sound basic vocabulary in English and in Putonghua. To fulfil the city's claim that Hong Kong is an 'international cultural metropolis', they also need recognition and reading skills in the roman alphabet for English, in Hanyu Pinyin for Putonghua, and, importantly, we would argue, in a Jyutping-based romanization for Cantonese so that they will be able to help non-Cantonese with Hong Kong's key language.

Third, it is time to unify the romanization of Cantonese, an aim that can be achieved by supplementing the *BiTri Basic* with sets of practice materials that turn it into a workbook for teaching children one system of Cantonese romanization after they have learned to read and write in the traditional way. This is in effect an attempt to match the basic language-teaching approach in the mainland, where Hanyu Pinyin for Putonghua is taught to students as early as their kindergarten years and serves as a base for learning to read and write characters.

2. Aligning the languages

Such very different languages as English, Cantonese, and Putonghua/Mandarin are by no means easy to align, but in our view such alignment is a most interesting and useful lexicographical exercise at the beginning of the twenty-first century. During the twentieth century, a great deal of lexicographical attention was lavished on English, in the United Kingdom (UK), the United States (US) and indeed worldwide, and in both the native area of dictionary-making and the booming field of ELT lexicography. This last was not only a commercially attractive undertaking but also an area of considerable innovation, particularly with regard to handling the divide between UK and US usage (in terms particularly of differences in pronunciation, spelling and the use of particular words).

As a result, in creating the base list of English words for the *BiTri* project, we first needed to establish what, for our purposes, the key words of English might be – both internationally and in terms of an English/Chinese interface.

One advantage in this regard is that Tom McArthur has long been interested in the nature and history of English word lists as developed: (1) for graded readers serving both native-speaking children and foreign learners of various ages, and (2) as a defining vocabulary for dictionaries of English as a second or foreign language. Even if such word lists have never actually represented the minimum essential words for children growing up in the world's native English-speaking milieux, there is a century-old tradition of making, using, and researching lists of this kind for educational purposes. As a result, an integrated list of this kind would appear to be the firmest available base for the purpose that interests us here.

3. Selecting the words

Our starting point was therefore a synthesis of the lexis in five well-grounded dictionary-linked word lists: the first two, Ogden's Basic English and Michael West's General Service List, are the outcome of work begun in the first half of the twentieth century (and are classics of their kind); the remaining three, the defining vocabularies of the key Longman, Macmillan, and Cambridge ELT dictionaries, were published late in the second half of the century. The outcome is a list of some 3,500 words widely used in basic ELT courses and publications. In this regard, the *Bi-Tri Basic* draws upon a successful and long-established ELT tradition.

In continuing and extending this tradition, the *Basic* list responds to both the perceived needs and expectations of Hong Kong users and word lists that have emerged for the two Chinese languages. While based on, but not restricted to, *The Oxford 3000* word list (OALD, 7th Edition, 2005), the words in the *BiTri Basic* English list are manifestly common and used in a wide range of contexts and texts, including words that do not necessarily have a high frequency but are important and familiar to users of English worldwide. Such words cover everyday themes like parts of the body and household contents and appliances. At the moment, although the overall list is most easily conceived in terms of English, we now have three parallel mutually-re-enforcing learners' lists, the words in each serving to 'define' the words in the others. This is, as far as we know, a unique development.

A second (minor but significant) source of English material is specific to Hong Kong and its people, and includes such manifestly English items as *bird's nest* and *Canto-pop* as well as such borrowings from Chinese as 大排檔 *daai6paai4dong³* and 利是 *lai⁶si⁶*. Local material of this kind is being culled from the *South China Morning Post*, the major English newspaper in Hong Kong, and other reliable and typical local sources, and will tie in with a concise set of appended themes that includes aspects of local geography, travel, transport, food, restaurants, and education.

In addition, however, there are some aspects of language that we want to emphasize, so as to provide the most practical service possible. For example, we want to ensure that learners become acquainted early on with key English phrasal verbs and some of their commoner idioms. As a result, we have incorporated them under key headwords, as follows:

- BE *be in, be out, be up, be down, be off*
- CALL *call in, call out, call up, call down, call off*
- GET *get in, get out, get up, get down, get on, get off*

And so on through *lay* and *lie* to *see, set,* and *take*.

4. Adjustments

In the course of compilation, adjustments need to be made, in order to refine our approach, especially as a consequence of the interaction of material in and across English, Cantonese, and Putonghua/Mandarin, especially so as to adapt any inadequate preconceptions that we started with, as regard the basic vocabulary of each language and adjusting it to the realities of putting everything together in two 'delivery systems': one, with printed English as the entry point, the other with character-based Chinese as the entry point. In addition to this dual system there are likely to be some supplementary lists (at the back of the book) to help users get as quickly and painlessly as possible from what they know to what they want to know. In effect, the entire procedure (as in any work of reference) systematizes three fundamentals: easy access, adequate presentation, and (all going well) acquisition and assimilation.

Such a plan requires cross-checks and adjustments among the representatives of the two writing systems and three spoken languages that we cover. In addition, we will need procedures for adding further words that seem for good reasons to be essential at the level we are aiming at: the basic operating vocabularies of the three languages. Inevitably, further words will present themselves, but we consider that a point will arrive where the circle of interacting basic vocabulary is as complete as we need it to be for such a beginners' book.

5. A triangular balance of entries

The principle we have kept in mind is that the three languages are equal in microstructural terms. Each entry is therefore organized according to the following scheme:

Table 1 The micro-structure of an entry

• Headword • Parts of speech • British and American variants (if any)	English
• Equivalent in traditional Chinese characters (in mainland terms: complex Chinese) • Equivalent in simplified Chinese characters • Hanyu Pinyin • Colloquial Putonghua characters and Hanyu Pinyin (if any: shaded) • Cantonese romanization (a variant of the Jyutping system) • Colloquial Cantonese characters and its romanization (if any: shaded)	Chinese Putonghua Cantonese
• Examples	
• Derivatives	

Many of the basic words of English are well known for their multiple meanings. Thus, in the *Collins English Dictionary* (CED, Millennium Edition), the noun 'case' has eighteen senses relating to 'instance' and ten to 'container'. The *Macmillan English Dictionary for Advanced Learners* (MED) does not separate 'case' in this way, but provides seven senses that include phrases relating to 'case'. In its turn, the *Oxford Advanced Learner's English Chinese Dictionary* (OALECD, 2004 edition) has ten senses of 'case', from 'situations' in sense 1 to 'container' in sense 8. This indicates that, even with a carefully selected wordlist, decision-making regarding the number of senses for any entry is a serious challenge. The *BiTri Basic*, however, with secondary students as its key end users, draws on a long-established tradition of covering only the commoner senses and uses of words, and moves from the generic and concrete to the specialized and abstract. As an example, the current entry for the word 'case' is shown below:

case *n*

1 箱[子] **P.** xiāng[zi] **C.** soeng^1[zi^2]

pencil case 筆(笔)盒 **P.** bǐhé **C.** bat^{1}hap^2

suitcase 旅行箱 **P.** lǚxíngxiāng **C.** leoi^{5}haang^{4}soeng^1; 旅行 • leoi^{5}haang^{4}gip^1

2 情況, 事件 **P.** qíngkuàng, shìjiàn **C.** cin^{4}fong^3, si^{6}gin^2

in any case 無論(无论)如何 **P.** wúlùn rúhé **C.** mou^{4}leon^6 yu^{4}ho^4

in that case 既然那樣(样) **P.** jìrán nàyang **C.** gei^{3}yin^4 naa^{5}yoeng^6

Figure 1 A sample entry: the word *case*

In dictionary compilation, frequency and usage are always the first selection criteria. However, the frequency information (of a word in a corpus) is not difficult to obtain in this hi-tech era by means of natural-language processing software. Leading dictionaries nowadays, in both the UK and the US, emphasize that their content is buttressed by corpora of contemporary English, and some (including *Collins and Macmillan*) have used symbols (such as one or more asterisks) to indicate the frequency levels of headwords.

Although one kind of information, word frequency, has been available to lexicographers for some time, sense frequency (which is just as useful) has not been well-documented. Considerable effort has however been expended by computational linguists on both semantic annotation and the classification of word senses through computational algorithms, so as to disambiguate words by means of glosses, as for example with the word *justice*:

```
Sense 1
justice, justness
     => righteousness
        => morality
           => quality
              => attribute
                 => abstraction
Sense 2
virtue
  => natural virtue
     => cardinal virtue
        => virtue
           => good, goodness
              => morality
                 => quality
                    => attribute
                       => abstraction
```
(from WordNet 2005)

Figure 2 A sample algorithm of the word *justice* (from WordNet 2005)

Sense frequencies can be obtained automatically by computing algorithms of this kind, even though tagging a corpus is by no means an easy task. However, more extensive experiments are under way, including for example part-of-speech (POS) tagging glosses of all *WordNet* nouns (Rosso 2003). The literature to date has not however provided a satisfactory picture of sense discrimination and frequency. Such activity in dictionary compilation is largely still based on looking at concordances of a word, using personal experience and intuition to make a decision regarding meaning, and ordering a word's different senses. We have checked with frequency-based lists from different resources and compared them in order to select the most frequently used sense(s), as with the word *degree* (included in the *BiTri*), as illustrated in Figure 3:

A trilingual dictionary for learners of Cantonese, English and Putonghua

degree *n*
    1 程度 **P.** chéngdù **C.** cing⁴dou⁶
    degree of accuracy 準確(准确)程度 **P.** zhǔnquè chéngdù **C.** zeon²kok³ cing⁴dou⁶
    2 溫(温)度 **P.** wēndù **C.** wan¹dou⁶
    five degrees Celsius 攝氏五度 **P.** shèshì wǔdù **C.** sip³si⁶ ng⁵dou⁶
    3 角度 **P.** jiǎodù **C.** gok³dou⁶
    an angle of 40 degrees四十度角 **P.** sìshídù jiǎo **C.** sei³sap⁶dou⁶ gok³

Figure 3 The word *degree*

Bearing in mind that the *Bi-Tri Basic* is a localized dictionary, we have added elements of special interest to Hong Kong people, as in the entry *dollar*, in Figure 4:

dollar *n* 元/圓(圆) **P.** yuán **C.** yun⁴
    American /US dollar 美元, 美金 **P.** měiyuán, měijīn **C.** mei⁵yun⁴, mei⁵gam¹
    Hong Kong dollar 港幣(币) **P.** gǎngbì **C.** gong²bai⁶, 港元 gong²yun⁴; 港紙 gong²zi²

Figure 4 The word *dollar*

Written characters are generally the same throughout China, but, whereas mainland Chinese generally read them in terms of Putonghua, the vast majority of Hong Kong people read them in terms of Cantonese, and may not know how to read them in Putonghua. In addition, some Putonghua expressions are not shared with Cantonese, and some expressions used in Cantonese do not occur in Putonghua. On occasion, Cantonese and Putonghua speakers use different sets of vocabulary items (written and/or spoken) to represent the same things or concepts. In these cases, we will try to include the most frequently used variants for each language, as in the words *paint* and *plastic*:

paint *n* 顏(颜)料 **P.** yánliào, 油漆 yóuqī **C.** ngaan⁴liu², 漆油 cat¹yau²
plastic *n* 塑膠 **P.** suòjiāo **C.** sou/<u>sok</u>³gaau¹
    plastic bag **P.** 塑料袋 suòliàodà **C.** 膠袋 gaau¹doi²

Figure 5 Translation difference between Cantonese and Putonghua

The Chinese equivalent for paint 顏(颜)料 is shared by both Putonghua yánliào, and Cantonese ngaan⁴liu², but paint can also be rendered differently in these two languages: 油漆 yóuqī in Putonghua, and 漆油 cat¹yau² in Cantonese. Similarly, plastic bag is 塑料袋 suòliàodà in Putonghua, but 膠袋 gaau¹doi² in Cantonese.

So as to avoid using more symbols and contrasts than users can comfortably handle, the *BiTri Basic* does not include English phonetic pronunciations. Hanyu Pinyin is used for Putonghua and a modified form of Jyutping for Cantonese. Hanyu Pinyin has been standardized by the mainland government for nearly fifty years with the result that phoneticizing characters is straightforward. With regard to Cantonese, however, there are over thirty notations for marking its sound system. Jyutping is a system that has been developed and promoted by a group of Hong Kong academics over the past ten years.

Hanyu Pinyin came into use in 1958 under the guidance of an institution of central government but even so, confusions, especially in segmentation, still exist when it is used in texts. Words with one or two characters are not difficult to handle, but when a word has more than three syllables, or when a Chinese idiom is brought into a text, the compiler must follow certain rules to stay consistent. Consider, for example,

careless *adj* 不小心的, 粗心大意的 **P.** bùxǎoxīn de, cūxīndàyì de **C.** bat[1]siu[2]sam[1] dik[1], cou[1]sam[1]daai[6]yi[3] dik[3]; 唔小心嘅 ng[4]siu[2]sam[1]ge[3]

partly *adv* 部份地, 在一定程度上 **P.** bùfèn de, zài yīdìng chéngdù shàng **C.** bou[6]fan[6] dei[6], zoi[6] yat[1]ding[6] cing[4]dou[6] soeng[6]

Figure 6 Segmentation of Hanyu Pinyin and Jyutping

When Pinyin is added after the character group 不小心的, we have to decide whether it is in the form *bùxǎo xīnde*, or *bùxǎoxīn de*, or *bù xǎoxīn de*; for 粗心大意的 *cūxīn dàyì de*, or *cūxīndàyì de*, or *cūxīndàyìde*. The standard we have adopted is the Chinese Pinyin Glossary published by the Committee for Language Reform of China (CLRC) in 1965, which includes 59,100 words with 2,100 single syllabic words, 35,000 double syllabic words, 15,000 triple syllabic, and 6,000 phrases and idioms with four or more syllables. We have also followed the *Basic Rules for Hanyu Pinyin Orthography* provided by the CLRC in 1996, which advocates such an arrangement as 分詞連寫, *fēncí liánxiě,* which puts multi-syllabic words together and separates parts of speech. For example, the word *broad* in English is one word, but its equivalent in Putonghua/Mandarin is 廣闊的 *guǎngkùo de* (N + particle), which separates off the particle *de*.

It has been noticed that various Cantonese romanization systems, mainly appearing in glossaries, do not have segmentations when they phoneticize sentences. Such a long string of letters without separation must however be hard work for learners. We have therefore adapted Pinyin rules to fit Jyutping, so that the segmentation alignment of Putonghua and Cantonese are identical.

Pinyin not only serves as a pronunciation guide but also promulgates the romanization of Chinese. As such, it has been used alongside Chinese characters at sentence level, with capitalisation and punctuation, in children's reading. When we began compiling the *BiTri Basic,* we used Pinyin and Jyutping only at the word level, to indicate the sound of a word. When more content and examples were added, however, we integrated the rules of the Pinyin and English writing systems at the sentence level, which means that we capitalize the first letter (of the romanization) of a sentence, and add punctuations to the sentence whenever is appropriate.

In all probability the neatest ultimate solution to the problem of representing the pronunciation of all three languages would be to have both the print and spoken versions available in electronic form, a level of sophistication we may not reach for some time.

6. Conclusion

Bringing Cantonese, English and Putonghua together in the way we envisage is hardly simple, but we believe that it *can* be done, and that it responds to the Hong Kong government's policy regarding language and education. At the very least, it sets the three systems side by side, and allows comparisons to be made and parallel learning to take place. At its best, if the idea catches on, it could serve to promote a new way of learning the three languages *together* that Hong Kong citizens have to use *together*.

Notes

1. SCOLAR was set up in early 2001 by the Hong Kong Government to review language education in both schools and the wider community. Its aim is to develop a set of recommendations on ways of raising language standards in Hong Kong.
2. A coalition on Education in the Business Sector was formed by the Federation of Hong Kong Industry and 10 Chambers of Commerce to examine Hong Kong education system and propose ways to improve it from the perspective of the business sector (*Ming Pao Daily*, 3 September 1999).

Electronic dictionaries in the classroom

Shinya Ozawa
Hiroshima Shudo University
ozawa@shudo-u.ac.jp

James Ronald
Hiroshima Shudo University
ronald@shudo-u.ac.jp

1. Introduction

In recent years, especially in a number of Asian countries, we have witnessed unprecedented student ownership of, and widespread reliance on, handheld electronic dictionaries in the foreign language classroom. In many Japanese universities, for example, ownership was already in the range of 75% a few years ago (Kobayashi 2004). Within that overall figure, there will be variation according to the students' academic disciplines, as well as ability and interest in foreign language learning. A small investigation of 150 freshman students at the authors' university in 2004 revealed that almost 90% of English major students possessed an electronic dictionary (henceforth ED), as compared with 50% of Commercial Science majors.

The quiet classroom revolution wrought by the ED has been largely student-led, with the language teacher often left as a bemused bystander: witnessing these changes, and the challenges they bring in their wake, but unsure about how to respond. A number of studies have investigated the ED use of foreign language learners: comparing learners' use of EDs and paper dictionaries (Osaki et al. 2003), or considering their use by different learners (Kobayashi 2004). Self-evidently, the ED is a tool that is in the hands of individual learners, and it is clear that ED use may affect individual language learning in various ways. On a wider scale, the widespread presence of EDs in the foreign language classroom continues to have a fundamental impact on whole classrooms: affecting student classroom behaviour and learning styles, affecting student-student and student-teacher interaction, and affecting the role and status of the teacher in the language classroom. Despite their importance, these classroom-related issues have received relatively little attention from researchers.

Language teachers do devote much thought to the growing presence of the ED in their classrooms, together with the gradual disappearance of paper dictionaries. They are concerned about the effect of these dictionaries on various aspects of language teaching and learning, and reflect on these issues both alone and in staffroom conversations with other teachers. The aim of the research described in this study has been to gather these private beliefs and opinions, analyse them, and consider their implications for language teaching. There are two main reasons for pursuing this goal. First, teachers vary widely in their attitudes and behaviour towards ED use in the classroom, and these differences may depend in part on factors such as the teacher's age, native tongue, or teaching environment. As teachers, we have a lot to learn from each other, not least the understanding and appreciation of each other's differing perspectives.

Second, while some teachers may feel that to interfere with students' ED use in the classroom is to impede learner independence, as language teaching professionals we do need to be able to offer informed guidance to students who very often may not know how best to learn a foreign language. To be able to do this, we need to know about the different issues raised by the presence and use of EDs in the language classroom.

This chapter begins by reporting a survey of the attitudes and practices of university-level language teachers in regard to handheld EDs. We will describe how the survey was conducted and present an analysis of the results. This will be followed by a discussion of the findings of the survey in which we will consider the consequences of the various issues raised by these as they affect language learning, classroom roles and dynamics, and teacher development.

2. The survey

As Hatherall (1984), Lew (2002) and others have noted, questionnaire-based research into dictionary use is not always the best means of investigating dictionary use. Dictionary users cannot, for example, be expected to recall with accuracy how often they use dictionaries, to estimate how successful their dictionary use has been, or to be able to deal with the technical vocabulary or concepts that may be used in surveys. These include *headword, register, defining style, example sentence,* and *collocation*. At the same time, questionnaires do provide an important means of gathering information, especially attitudes, from large numbers of people. This is especially valid for language teachers, rather than students, in that they are themselves language professionals and are familiar with many of the language-related vocabulary and issues addressed in surveys relating to dictionary use.

With reference to Dörnyei's (2003) general guidelines for questionnaire design, and Lew's (2002) specific recommendations in the context of dictionary use, a questionnaire for English teachers was prepared in both Japanese and English. It was composed of three sections: questions which would provide a profile of the respondent, including their ownership and use of EDs; questions about the respondent's attitudes towards EDs in the classroom; and questions about the respondent's behaviour with regard to student ED use in the classroom. Both Japanese and English versions of the questionnaire were piloted then revised with the help of university-level English teachers not involved in the survey itself.

The survey was conducted with all the English teachers, both full-time and part-time, at a middle-ranking Japanese university, Hiroshima Shudo University. Questionnaires were distributed to each of the fifty-six Japanese teachers of English and twenty-three non-Japanese teachers of English, with all but one of the latter being native speakers of English. Response rates were 50% for Japanese teachers and 61% for non-Japanese teachers. While these response rates were disappointingly low, there is still much that we can learn from this survey.

We will begin by briefly summarizing the profiles of teachers who responded before going on to focus on the behaviour and attitudes of the teachers towards student ED use. After this, we will investigate what relationships there may be between individual teacher profiles and behaviour or attitudes regarding EDs in the classroom. Finally, we will look at Japanese and non-Japanese perceptions of the merits and demerits of EDs in the classroom.

Respondent profiles are summarized in Table 1, with figures for Japanese (J) and non-Japanese (N-J) respondents presented separately. At once we can see that there are major differences between Japanese and non-Japanese teachers in terms of their typical ages, sex, subjects taught, and dictionary ownership. Most notably, over half the Japanese teachers possess and use an ED, usually of a model similar to that used by their students, while few of the non-Japanese teachers have access to such dictionaries.

Table 1 Profiles of teachers in ED survey

	J	N-J		J	N-J		J	N-J		J	N-J
Age			Sex			Subject			Own ED		
20~	1	0	*M*	15	13	Language	13	13	*Yes*	15	4
30~	6	6	*F*	13	2	Literature	8	1	*No*	13	11
40~	5	5				Culture	0	1			
50~	8	3				Linguistics	3	0			
60~	8	1				Other	4	0			
Totals	28	15		28	15		28	15		28	15

The next issue is that of teacher behaviour regarding ED use in the classroom. Here we will seek to identify correlations between behaviour and other factors, focusing mainly on the responses of Japanese teachers. Teacher ED ownership and use in class is an important factor, with fifteen of the twenty-eight teachers owning an ED and six of these using the ED in class. As we can see from Table 2, there is a clear relationship between whether teachers use their ED in class and what they use their ED for. ED-owning teachers who don't bring their ED to class typically only use it for simple or basic uses such as checking meanings or spellings while those who bring their ED to class all use the dictionary for more elaborate or sophisticated purposes.

Table 2 Japanese teachers' ED use

	Teachers' ED use purposes			
	Elaborate	Simple	N/A	Totals
ED use in class				
Yes	6	0	0	6
No	3	7	2	12
N/A			10	10
Totals	9	7	12	28

There is a similar relationship between teacher use of EDs in class and teachers' regulation of student ED in class. As we can see from Table 3, teachers who use the EDs in class allow their students to do so as well, while those who do not are much more likely to restrict or forbid student ED use.

Table 3 Japanese teachers' regulation of student classroom ED use

	Teacher regulation of student classroom ED use				
	Allow	It depends	Forbid	N/A	Totals
ED use in class					
Yes	5	0	0	1	6
No	3	5	4	0	12
N/A	2	2	5	1	10
Totals	10	7	9	2	28

We might expect that teachers who use and allow the use of EDs in class would also be likely to provide ED use guidance or training for students. This is true in some cases but as Table 4 shows, as many do this as do not. Interestingly, a more significant correlation is between teacher age and dictionary training, with five of the nine Japanese teachers who provide some kind of training being in their sixties. This tendency is also found in older non-Japanese teachers, with the only two who do provide training being in their fifties or sixties.

Five out of the twenty-eight Japanese teachers of English reported that they provide dictionary use guidance in the classroom, with most of these focusing on paper dictionaries and telling students how to use different dictionaries for different purposes. Only one of the teachers suggested that teachers need to provide dictionary use guidance because most students do not know how to use their ED. Most of the teachers who have not provided guidance regarding dictionary use believe that it is part of the learner's own development to learn how to use their dictionary. Some teachers even admitted that they didn't have sufficient knowledge of EDs to provide guidance. Generally speaking, most of the teachers have a negative attitude towards students' possession of ED and do not want to encourage their use by guidance in the classroom. As for more focused dictionary training, nine of the twenty-eight Japanese teachers answered that they do provide it in the classroom, with the aims of showing students how to use their dictionaries appropriately or find meanings in the dictionary that match those words encountered in their contexts. None of the teachers reported focusing on, or providing training, for the specific characteristics of handheld EDs.

Table 4 Japanese teachers' provision of dictionary use guidance

	Dictionary use guidance		
	Yes	*No*	Totals
ED use in class			
Yes	3	3	6
No	1	11	12
N/A	1	9	10
Totals	5	23	28

We will now go on to look at teachers' attitudes towards EDs in the classroom. Specifically, we will focus on the perceived merits and demerits of student ED use. Answers from Japanese teachers were given in Japanese and summaries are presented here in English. The most often cited merits of EDs for both Japanese and non-Japanese teachers are listed in Table 5. The numbers in brackets indicate the number of respondents giving a particular answer. Here, the answers given by Japanese and non-Japanese teachers are largely similar, with both most commonly citing convenience to carry and speed of access. One difference between the two groups of teachers, expressed in relation to ease of use and ED contents, is the Japanese teachers' familiarity with the EDs the students use. The opposite is evident for many non-Japanese teachers from their use of hedges, not included in these summaries, such as 'I guess', 'appear to be' or 'from what I've seen'. A further difference, although only cited by two non-Japanese teachers, is the issue of learner autonomy.

Table 5 Perceived merits of EDs in the classroom

Japanese teachers	Non-Japanese teachers
Easy to carry (10) (they bring it to class) **Quick for looking up (9)** (saves time, students can look up a lot) **Easy to use (5), like a mobile phone (4)** (use more often, like a game, satisfying) **Contact with various dictionaries (6)** (easy to consult various dictionaries, good for preparation)	**Quick for looking up (9)** (easier than paper, more words in less time) **Easy to carry (5)** (most students won't bring heavy paper dictionaries) **Learner autonomy (2)** (students have control over a very useful tool)

As we go on to consider the perceived demerits of EDs in the classroom, we can see, in Table 6, that the perspectives of the two groups of teachers on the demerits of classroom ED use are very different. The two main concerns of the Japanese teachers relate to the experience of getting lexical information from the ED and to the effect of ED use on vocabulary acquisition. Again, we can see that these are the views of teachers many of whom are themselves ED users. The widespread consideration given by Japanese teachers to vocabulary acquisition-related issues is also related to these teachers' own experience as both teachers and learners of the foreign language. This will be considered in more detail below.

For the non-Japanese teachers, the majority of answers regarding demerits are concerned with the practice of communicating in English: the interruption of classroom conversation by ED use, or the inability to use or develop other communication strategies when students resort to ED use without reflection. A further issue includes implicit recognition, and criticism, of the fact that most ED use in Japan means bilingual dictionary use. The criticisms, then, are both towards the unwelcome intrusion of ED use into classroom communication and towards the deleterious effects of the repeated intrusion of Japanese into English learning environments. It is interesting to note that, in contrast with the Japanese teachers, there is little direct reference by the non-Japanese teachers to the effect of ED use on L2 vocabulary acquisition, although the objection to Japanese in the classroom is, in part at least, due to the perception of the L1 as an obstacle to acquisition of the target language.

Table 6 Perceived demerits of EDs in the classroom

Japanese teachers	Non-Japanese teachers
Difficult to get the full picture on the small screen (8) (only see top of entry, not example sentences, grammar, words either side) **Easy but no retention (6)** (no vocabulary growth, no effort to memorize) **Use without thinking (4)** (paper dictionary use time is important: learning depends on time and effort) **Too convenient (4)** (fuzzy spelling inhibits learning, not quick for example sentences, idioms)	**Disrupts flow of class/conversation (4)** (breaks flow of conversations, focus on English) **Hinders students' creativity, natural self-expression (4)** (don't try to use vocabulary they know, EDs discourage students from finding a natural way to negotiate generation of ideas) **Danger of overuse, dependency, too much Japanese (4)** (easy to use so danger of automatic/ reflexive use, don't guess meanings from context)

3. Discussion

We will now go on to consider the changes in learning environment brought about by the presence of students' EDs in the language classroom, as reflected in the data reported above. We will suggest ways in which teachers may respond to the various challenges brought to the classroom by the ED.

As Kent (2001) observes, the presence of the dictionary in the language classroom represents a challenge to the authority and language expertise of the teacher. This arguably applies with even greater force to the ED, with its increased presence and more frequent use in the classroom. The issues of challenged authority and questioned expertise affect both Japanese and non-Japanese teachers, but the issues affect them differently. Their responses both to these challenges, and to the challenges and opportunities presented by EDs in the classroom, will undoubtedly also be different. We will consider each of these in turn.

Japanese teachers' relatively widespread ownership and use of EDs gives them a greater understanding both of the ED and of their students' ED use than is generally true for teachers who do not share the students' mother tongue or their adoption of this technology. One way by which these teachers may regain the status of classroom expert is by being an ED specialist: more familiar with the technology in the students' hands than the students are, and more knowledgeable about how to best use the ED as a tool for learning the foreign language. In this way, although the teacher may lose the role of all-knowing linguistic authority, this is exchanged for that of guide or *sempai* for the students to follow. Another way that Japanese teachers may retain authority is by maintaining control of ED use in the classroom, coupled with expertise regarding language learning. They may advise their students about how, when and where to gain the greatest benefit from their ED use. A third way is to ban the use of EDs for a particular class or course, and to insist on the use of paper dictionaries. While to some this may seem a retrogressive, if not actually Luddite, response, it may in fact represent recognition by teachers of the need to focus on information finding skills that are being lost in this age of electronic information media. Students nowadays are increasingly skilled at finding information quickly, although uncritically, through their ED, through Google, or in Wikipedia. At the same time they are increasingly unable to find and assess information in journals or academic books, in encyclopaedias or in paper dictionaries. One class in which the teacher insists on paper dictionaries will not affect students' freedom in other classes to use their EDs, but it will give them the opportunity to learn, or relearn, the essential academic skill of seeking out and evaluating information from non-electronic sources.

For the teacher who is not a native speaker of the students' language, solutions are not so easy to find. Twice alienated by the ED – 'It's the technology of the students' generation and it's in their language' – responses have been various and many teachers are still not sure about how to respond to these aliens/alienators in the classroom. One worthwhile response to this situation may be to set students language tasks that both encourage reflective ED use by the language learners and inform the teacher about the ED as part of their students' world. In a writing class, they could be asked to describe the contents and functions of their ED. Alternatively, they could keep a record of their use of their ED over a whole day and then make a report of this: how often, for what purpose and which words, with which particular dictionary, and with what degree of success. In a speaking class, 'Electronic vs. paper dictionaries' could be a topic for presentations or discussions, together with class surveys. Or students could brainstorm, discuss, and compile a reasoned set of guidelines for their own ED use: etiquette for when to use or not to use their ED in and out of class. In a way similar to that proposed for Japanese teachers, non-Japanese teachers could insist on a particular dictionary type in the classroom. In this case, teachers could insist on monolingual dictionaries in their class, whether electronic or paper. This would introduce many learners to a resource that is new to them and which contains much information that they would find both accessible and useful. The increased effort and time required for this information source may also help learners break the damaging ED-reflex habit of looking up every unfamiliar word they encounter, while the reasoned investment of this time and effort for the words they choose to look up may lead to greater retention of the looked-up lexical information.

Finally, ED training is worth considering for both Japanese and non-Japanese teachers, especially in environments where ED ownership is approaching 100%. These could be in the form of word information tasks that students are set, and for which they need to exploit the various resources available to them within their ED. Increased learner autonomy is an important goal, and one directly related to ED use, but it only becomes more than a fashionable catchphrase when students are enabled to make best use of the resources available to them. As teachers themselves learn more about the benefits and weaknesses of classroom ED use, they will be better able to instruct their students in using their EDs wisely.

4. Conclusion

The survey of English teachers' attitudes and experiences reported in this chapter confirms the belief that widespread use of electronic dictionaries by language learners has wrought profound changes to the language learning environment. These changes and their consequences have remained largely unexamined, despite the relevance that they have for many aspects of language learning and impinging directly on the practice of language learning and teaching. This chapter has also included practical suggestions by which language teachers may facilitate language learners' wise use of the electronic dictionary so that it may fulfil its potential as a powerful language learning tool.

The benefits of CD-ROM dictionaries in teaching

Monika Szirmai
Hiroshima International University
monika@hw.hirokoku-u.ac.jp

1. Introduction

Dictionaries have always been considered as essential tools for helping communication in a foreign language. In spite of their widely acknowledged importance, according to student questionnaires at the Japanese university I work at, only a negligible few of the students have ever actually been taught how to use a dictionary, which most often meant using the hard copy of bilingual dictionaries. This leaves them ill-equipped to cope with their current learning situation and unprepared for future use of English in academic and specialist work situations. As schools should provide students with skills that they can use in the future, it is essential not only to teach and practise dictionary skills but also to do this using the format that students will most likely need and benefit the most from. Considering that modern companies are highly computerized, and most of their everyday communication is done through electronic messages, CD-ROM dictionaries seem to fulfil both expectations. After a brief overview of the teaching situation and of the different types of dictionaries, this chapter will discuss the main benefits of using CD-ROM dictionaries in regular language classes, such as integration of skills, visual aids, cross-referencing, ease and speed of searching, integration into learning activities, portability, and extra exercises.

2. Teaching English at college level in Japan

At university level in Japan, English is usually taught skills-based, with little or no coordination between the different courses: reading, writing, and oral communication. The latter may also be divided into listening and speaking. Sometimes reading and writing classes are run in a teacher-centred way because these classes often accommodate more than fifty students. If students work individually, they have to rely on their dictionaries and work silently until they finish the task and check it. As Japanese universities are highly computerized, reading and especially writing classes often take place in computer labs. In fact, this chapter is also based on information gathered in a reading class for first year non-English major students. For three years, there were more than sixty students in the class, for one year only forty, and the CLD-SBV (*Cambridge Learner's Dictionary: Semi-Bilingual Version* with

CD-ROM) was used as a course textbook. From April 2005, there have been forty students in the reading class, and a new course textbook was required, making the dictionary only a recommended textbook. Thus classroom activities have been based on the electronic version of the dictionary from this April.

Dictionaries are generally considered reference books that should be consulted occasionally rather than books that should be used for everyday studies. Nowadays, students do not even have to look up words in dictionaries as most textbooks have a word list either right at the end of each unit or at the back of the textbook. However, being a non-native speaker of English, my personal experience as a language learner using the OALD (*Oxford Advanced Learner's Dictionary of Current English*), popularly called 'The Hornby' at the time, encouraged me to set a dictionary as a course textbook for several years. Although the dictionary became a recommended, optional textbook in 2005, it has not altered the content of the course compared to previous years.

As mentioned above, very few students have ever been taught how to use the dictionary, in spite of the fact that language learners usually heavily rely on it. This, together with the knowledge that university courses are their last chance to learn dictionary skills that would be useful even after finishing their formal studies, urged me to make teaching dictionary skills a priority in my reading class, even if it meant neglecting reading skills in the first semester. Although all the students have dictionaries at home that they occasionally use, they are almost exclusively bilingual ones. The mere idea of using an 'English only' textbook often scares students, and dictionaries all the more so as they are supposed to explain words that they do not understand in the foreign language. Even students whose English is relatively good lack the confidence to start using monolingual dictionaries on their own. They believe that it would be too difficult for them. So, first, the emotional and psychological barriers created by this preconception must be overcome in order to create a positive learning atmosphere. It is well-known that people who are ill but firmly believe in their recovery can recover even if they do not take medicine. It is the same with learning. Students who believe in themselves are more successful learners. Therefore, as there are many different monolingual dictionaries, it is essential that teachers should choose carefully according to the level of their students. In order to help overcome students' fears, I deliberately chose the CLD-SBV (*Cambridge Learner's Dictionary*, with CD-ROM) because it is a semi-bilingual dictionary, which means that at each entry, students can find a translation equivalent in the hard copy of the dictionary but not in the CD-ROM version. Before we go on, it must be clarified that as our main concern is the use of monolingual learner dictionaries, this is what is meant by the term 'dictionary' in most cases. If not, it will be specified.

Another reason why dictionary skills and learning vocabulary using traditional word lists are important in Japan is the fact that students are exposed to English almost exclusively at school or in a non-natural situation specifically created for learning. British Hills in Fukushima Prefecture is a perfect example of such an effort. As its name suggests, it aims to make you believe that you have arrived in Britain without even leaving Japan. However, in everyday life, Japanese students cannot just 'pick up' vocabulary by seeing or hearing English in natural conversations around them. In Europe, people travel more extensively in wide multi-lingual areas, making it possible to interact in a more natural way in a foreign language, although not necessarily with native speakers.

As I have been teaching this reading class for five years, every year I tried to improve class management, grading, feedback and also the content of the course. In the first four years, during the first semester, students learnt what information was available in the dictionary and how they could find it. As at this stage, students were usually not so familiar with computers, I believed that using the paper dictionary would take some unnecessary burden off the students. However, even then the worksheets were in an electronic form, so they had to type their answers, which helped with learning spelling. Once the students were familiar with the hard copy, it took only one or two classes in the second semester to change to using the CD-ROM version of the same dictionary. In the second semester, texts were chosen both for intensive and extensive reading, so that the students could learn different ways of reading and of using the dictionary.

The most important changes during the five years of the reading course seem to be related to the growing use of computers and electronic information, leading to the complete change from the paper version of the dictionary to the CD-ROM right from the beginning of the course, rather than introducing it only in the second semester as in the previous years. Originally, the course was not set up with the intention of answering a particular research question, so I did not start to collect data from the very beginning or in a very rigorous manner.

3. Differences between types of dictionaries

Basically, dictionaries today are available in four media: 1. as a traditional paper dictionary; 2. as a handheld electronic dictionary; 3. as a CD-ROM dictionary; and 4. as a Web-based dictionary. The information contained in each type does not vary so much, as the information is usually just transferred from one platform to another. Printed versions of dictionaries are just as well based on corpus research; the results are organized on the computer, and the actual hard copy is created using computers before it is printed. However, some changes in the content are necessary for each type of publication. Just to give an example, handheld dictionaries may not have any illustrations or just very few, whereas both hard copies and CD-ROMs do. Dictionaries may have more black and white pictures but CD-ROMs are usually very colourful.

All dictionaries contain or come with some kind of user's guide that explains how information is displayed and encoded in the given dictionary. Entries provide information about pronunciation, meaning, grammar, collocations, etc., some even about frequency (e.g. COBUILD, *Longman Dictionary of Contemporary English* (LDOCE)). Most publishers use a defining vocabulary of two or three thousand words for the explanations in the dictionary. Probably it is not necessary to go through the whole list to prove that it is not so much what is different but how the content is organized and how the information is presented and can be accessed. It must be mentioned though that right now CD-ROMs can and do hold much more information than printed books, and also include sounds, pictures and moving pictures. In this respect, the CD-ROM offers much more to the user because it contains additional learning material in addition to the dictionary itself.

4. Benefits of CD-ROM dictionaries in teaching

The strengths of using CD-ROM dictionaries come from the nature of the medium itself. As mentioned above, CD-ROMs can hold text, pictures, moving pictures, and sound, all of which can be displayed and used simultaneously. Very often control over functions is given to the user. For example in the case of pictures, the user can decide whether to see labels or use a quasi test mode where pictures must be matched to the labels by the user. With paper dictionaries, there is no option for how much information is shown at once because the printed form has a fixed amount of information presented on each page regardless of individual users' preferences. There also seems to be a tendency to combine dictionaries in the CD-ROM versions. For example, the *Longman Dictionary of Contemporary English* and the *Longman Language Activator* are two different publications in their paper version but the CD-ROM of the LDOCE4 contains both of them. Let us look at different aspects of how CD-ROMs enhance teaching.

4.1. Integration of skills

As CD-ROMs combine text with sound, oral skills can be integrated to some extent to the silent reading and writing classes. Students can listen to and practice the pronunciation of words or phrases they have just encountered for the first time. This is very important because many Japanese students have problems with matching spelling and sound. It is common knowledge that the Japanese language does not make a distinction between the sounds '*r*' and '*l*'. As a result, if a Japanese speaker uses '*r*'-like sounds, the word '*lamb*' will sound like '*ram*'. On the other hand, if a speaker uses '*l*'-like sounds, we might hear a confusing sentence like: '*I eat lice every day.*' This problem is aggravated by the frequent use of English words in everyday Japanese.

English words are written down using the Japanese katakana syllabary and pronounced accordingly. That is why this kind of pronunciation is called 'katakana pronunciation'. Another obstacle for Japanese students in acquiring the right pronunciation without an aural model is that phonetic transcriptions, such as IPA, are not taught at school. So consulting a paper dictionary may not result in being able to say or understand a word they have looked up if it is only seen but not heard. CD-ROM dictionaries contain sound files as models, usually spoken by both an American and a British native speaker.

These dictionaries often have a recording function as well where students can listen to the model and record their own speech for comparison.

4.2. Visual aids

Visual aids fall into two categories: one helps navigation and cross-referencing in the dictionary, the other explains the meaning of words by showing the objects, animals, actions, etc. A clear layout can also increase the speed with which one can find the right information. Figure 1 shows the same entry in the paper version (left) and the CD-ROM version of CLD. The paper version uses light blue for the headword and no other colours, while the CD-ROM version uses dark blue for the headword and red for the guidewords. Even a quick glance at the two versions can convince us that the one on the top looks crammed and information can be found much easier in the one on the bottom.

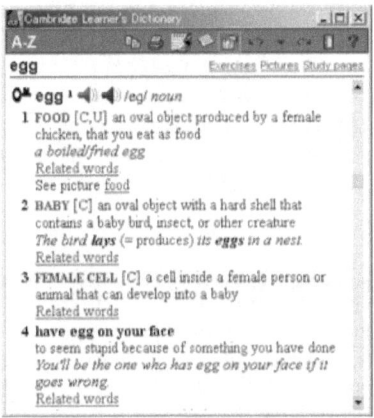

Figure 1 A comparison of visual clarity in a hard copy (above) and a CD-ROM (below)

One might think that these seemingly slight differences do not make any difference, but in fact they do, especially for students who are usually slower at finding information in an English text. In the paper version, the symbol informs the user that related information is available at a different place. In the CD-ROM, according to the conventions of links, blue underlined words serve the same purpose. In this case, at the end of the first sense of *egg*, there are two such links: one for 'Related words' and one for the illustration of 'food'.

4.3. Cross-referencing

If we take another look at Figure 1, it becomes clear that in total there are only two signals for cross referencing in the paper version but there are five in the CD-ROM, which means that each sense has at least one link to other related words. As a matter of fact, everything is related to something, even the letters of the alphabet. This is another strength of the CD-ROM version. If students have to find the related information by turning the pages, that may take quite some time. So students tend to look up pictures but they rarely look up other entries. With the CD-ROM, because this can be done simply by clicking on the link, students are curious enough to carry out such an effortless action. Even if they do not read or understand the whole list of words that comes up, they might either just skim through it or choose one or two that they look up. Most students like this kind of browsing in the dictionary, which means that studying English can become more enjoyable, and may improve the students' motivation or at least increase their level of tolerance with English-only texts.

Other colour-coded links available are: Word Building, Collocation, Learner Error, and Verb Ending. If students regularly look up, for example, Word Building, it will be easier for them to discover known elements in unfamiliar words as well, and by doing that, guessing from context becomes easier. For the word *work*, the following list came up: *Nouns: work, workaholic, worker, workings; Adjectives: workable, unworkable, overwork, working; Verbs: work* and *rework*. The Learner Error section pointed out the difference between *job* and *work*, which are often used incorrectly by students. In addition to that, *career, profession* and *occupation* were also mentioned.

4.4. Searching for words

Using a paper dictionary can help users memorize the alphabet, so students who are used to using the dictionary can find information relatively fast. However, students who would need the help of the dictionary the most often get lost in the dictionary and give up their word hunt. With the CD-ROM, these students can search for words just as fast as the other students. By saving time on using the dictionary, students can accomplish more work in one class.

In order to illustrate the speed of searching, Table 1 shows the time needed

The benefits of CD-ROM dictionaries in teaching 145

for the completion of worksheets last year and this year in the reading class. Time was recorded automatically by the Internet hosting service offered by the company FSCreations[1] for the software called ExamView (1999-2006). The same software was used for creating the worksheets and also for class management. Last year (2006), all the students had to use the paper version of the dictionary. This year (2007), with very few exceptions, all the students used the electronic version of the dictionary. Worksheets were identical in most cases. In all cases, students using the CD-ROM version finished their task faster; on average they needed seven minutes and thirty-five seconds less than students using the paper version.

Table 1 Time needed to complete worksheets

Worksheet	1	2	3	4	5	6
2006 (mm:ss)	26:38	36:16	19:45	29:29	50:36	29:41
2007 (mm:ss)	20:44	24:45	15:13	24:25	40:30	21:14
Difference (mm:ss)	5:54	11:29	4:32	5:04	10:06	8:27

Students are also encouraged to create word lists for themselves. By copying words in their notebook by hand in the traditional way, they may, of course, memorize some of them during this process. However, in most cases, students tend to write down the minimum information they need and very often not very neatly, without any example sentences. The CD-ROM version makes it possible to copy either the whole entry or part of it by the click of a button. This way, although they may not memorize anything immediately, students can create a more complete list of words, expressions or collocations, with more example sentences for studying. As many students in Japan spend several hours on commuting every day, studying vocabulary seems to be a good way of utilizing this time.

When students try to produce a text in a foreign language, they usually use only a bilingual dictionary to look up the word in the mother tongue and find the translation equivalents in the target language. After that, very few would go as far as checking the equivalents they have found in a monolingual dictionary, mostly because of the time and effort involved. However, students tend to use the thematic picture pages because they can quickly identify what they are looking for. With the help of the CD-ROM dictionary, students can also find synonyms for words, related word forms, and many example sentences to help production. Although I had taught writing classes in the past, CD-ROM dictionaries were not available at that time. This April, I started teaching writing again, and I have been experimenting with ways of integrating the CD-ROM dictionary into the writing process.

Japanese students have difficulties in spelling words they have only heard but not seen. Some CD-ROM dictionaries, for example the LDOCE4, make it possible to search for words based on their pronunciation. Of course, this can only be done if students are familiar with the phonetic symbols.

4.5. Integrating the dictionary into the reading activity

When reading text on the computer screen, it is even easier to integrate CD-ROM dictionaries into the task, as some have a function which makes it possible to look up words by moving the pointer over the word (Figure 2). This is extremely useful because students can look up all the words they want to without spending a lot of time typing the words into the dictionary program. Students tend to look up more words than they would without this function. I firmly believe that this doubles or even triples students' exposure to the defining style of the dictionary, which helps linguistic skills in a holistic way. As students very often look up familiar words that they cannot fully remember, they get to understand monolingual definitions better, which in turn encourages them to use the dictionary more often. The small quick look up window can be moved anywhere in the screen. Here, as well, students have instant access to the sound files by clicking on the speaker marks, one of which is for the British pronunciation and the other for the American one.

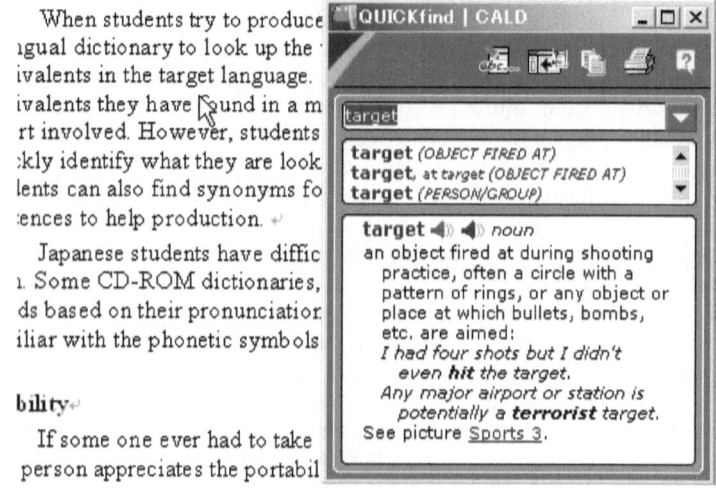

When students try to produce [text in a monoli]ngual dictionary to look up the [equ]ivalents in the target language. [The equ]ivalents they have found in a m[ono]rt involved. However, students [can qui]ckly identify what they are look[ing for. Stud]ents can also find synonyms fo[r senten]ences to help production.

Japanese students have diffic[ulty with this]. Some CD-ROM dictionaries, [have wor]ds based on their pronunciation[, for students not fam]iliar with the phonetic symbols.

bility

If some one ever had to take [two or more big dictionaries to school from home, that] person appreciates the portabil[ity...]

Figure 2 Quick look up window in CALD

4.6. Portability

If someone ever had to take two or more big dictionaries to school from home, that person will appreciate the portability of CD-ROM dictionaries. Even if students are required to bring their own dictionaries to classes, very often they turn up without them. A CD-ROM hardly weighs anything and takes up very little space. Many schools have dictionaries already installed in their computer labs, which also solves the problem of students' possible forgetfulness.

4.7. Extra activities

CD-ROM dictionaries contain exercises related to different areas. Some are designed to help learning grammar, others for vocabulary. Some also contain corpus examples and corpus related activities. These activities can be done individually as the student can also see the right answers after finishing the task.

5. Conclusion

Based on my experience as a teacher and a language learner, it does not seem to be an exaggeration to say that a good dictionary and dictionary skills are the pillars of language learning. Although dictionaries are available in many different formats, CD-ROM dictionaries are superior to other formats because of the nature of the medium. Their relational database structure, which allows words to be linked in many different ways, the ease and speed with which information can be accessed, and the capability of integrating sound cannot be matched by any other media. In addition, if they are used in regular language classes, they can be smoothly integrated into learning activities regardless of whether students are decoding the foreign language or encoding into it. Preparing students for autonomous learning in the future is one of the key tasks of schools. In language learning, that means helping students acquire good dictionary skills by using CD-ROM dictionaries.

Notes

1. FSCreations. Inc. 1999-2006. ExamView. (software) ver.5.0.0.

Dictionary use strategies by EFL learners in Taiwan

Da-Fu Huang
Southern Taiwan University
dfjhuang@mail.stut.edu.tw

1. Introduction

Research on dictionaries is incomplete without research on dictionaries from the user perspective. Despite the increasing studies on dictionary use and some evidence of positive association between dictionary use and language learning or teaching (Tono 1989, McCreary and Dolezal 1999, Knight 1994, Summers 1988, Hustijin et al. 1996, Laufer and Hill 2000, Notohara 1987, Kipfer 1987, Huang 2003, Lai 2006, etc.), our understanding of dictionary use by EFL learners and the contexts of dictionary use in an EFL setting is fairly limited.

Unlike ESL learners, EFL learners learn the target language in a linguistic environment where English is not used for communicative needs in the daily social, economic, or political lives. Typically situated in what Kouraogo (1993) dubbed an 'input-poor' English learning environment and exposed to meagre target language input, EFL learners consequently have fewer opportunities to use and communicate in the target language, which in turn leads to less availability of authentic language input or exposure to authentic language materials. For EFL learners, as a result, reading and print exposure tend to be the major source of input of English and the dominant mode of language comprehension and learning. In an EFL learning or teaching context where learners lack the opportunities to use English in the authentic situations and negotiate meanings or resolve their learning difficulties by or in the direct use of the target language, it should come as no surprise that such learners use their native language to assist in learning English and turn to other self-directed options such as dictionaries or translation machines to gain more access to the language input and solicit more aid in various English learning tasks. Accordingly, EFL learners such as those in Taiwan are reasonably expected to experience more dictionary use than, and have different dictionary beliefs and dictionary strategy use from, ESL learners.

Prior studies (Béjoint 1981, Tono 1988, Atkins and Varantola 1998a, etc.) were also unsatisfactory in that they focused only on dictionary skills while neglecting dictionary strategies and the distinction between the two. Skills are cognitive routines or capacities that have been honed or developed through practice and can be expressed in behaviour at any time whereas strategies involve conscious decisions to select, combine, or redesign those routines or implement those skills (Schmeck 1988, Kirby 1988). In the same vein, dictionary skills involve understanding dictionary conventions or routines, using dictionaries the way the dictionary editors expected them to be used in order to efficiently arrive at the target linguistic units. Dictionary strategies, in contrast, may involve choice or decision making as to dictionary use which may necessitate implementation of dictionary skills, and tend to be task-driven or tied to specific learning contexts. Since language learners use dictionaries in language learning contexts or for the purposes of performing specific language tasks, it is important to understand not only how learners use dictionary skills to target and retrieve linguistic information in dictionaries, but also how they process, interpret, analyze, or transform the sought information to facilitate language learning or tackle contextually-based learning tasks. When reading or writing English, learners are likely to use lookup methods such as cognitive, note-taking, cross-referencing, memory, or social strategies to help complete a learning task. Unexplored in prior studies, this wide spectrum of dictionary strategy use can be fitted well into, and should be examined within, an overarching and more comprehensive learning strategy classification scheme such as the strategy systems in Oxford (1990), O'Malley et al. (1985a) and O'Malley & Chamot (1990). The purpose of this chapter is therefore to understand Taiwanese EFL learners' lookup strategies and how they can be incorporated into the existing foreign language learning strategy system.

2. Methodology

This study employed quantitative and qualitative approaches to understand Taiwanese university English majors' dictionary strategies. The major research method used in the study involved the administration of the English Dictionary Strategy Questionnaire (EDSQ; v. Appendix 1) to assess students' English dictionary strategy use. Around 400 English majors of Southern Taiwan University were requested to respond to the items on dictionary strategy use on a Likert scale from (1) Always to (5) Never, thus demonstrating how frequently they used the strategy. The mean score reflected how frequently students report using dictionary strategies in English learning.

In addition, qualitative interviews of some participants and the participants' responses to the open-ended questions included in the strategy questionnaire further delineated the context of the participants' dictionary and hence crosschecked the quantitative data. Semi-structured interviews of twelve of the participants were conducted to understand their dictionary use while reading and writing English.

3. Descriptive statistics of the EDSQ

The students were requested to respond to a strategy question item on a Likert scale from (1) Always to (5) Never, thus demonstrating how frequently they used the strategy. Students' total scores of the EDSQ were derived by adding up the sub-scores of each question item of the questionnaire. The mean score of the EDSQ for a respondent was available by dividing the total score by the number of the question items (i.e. 29). The mean score reflected how frequently students report using dictionary strategies in English learning. In agreement with how Oxford (1990) conceptualized the continuum of strategy use, a mean between 2.6 and 3.5 should be considered as medium level of strategy use, a mean between 1.0 and 2.5 as high level of strategy use, while a mean between 3.6 and 5.0 as low level of strategy use. As shown in Table 1, the participants of this study therefore demonstrated a medium level of dictionary strategy use with an overall mean of 2.73, close to 2.5, the threshold into the high level of strategy use.

Table 1 Means and standard deviations for the overall dictionary strategy use

	N	Minimum	Maximum	Mean	Std. Deviation
Dictionary Strategy Use	414	1.21	3.72	2.73	.40

In addition, among the twenty-nine question items on the strategy questionnaire, twenty-two items had a mean lower than 3.0, and among these twenty-two items, ten items (items 10, 11, 12, 17, 19, 21, 22, 24, 25, 26) had a mean lower than 2.5. These ten items represented the ten most frequently used dictionary strategies, which could be further categorized into two groups: (1) general cognitive strategies, and (2) task-bound cognitive strategies.

In terms of general cognitive dictionary strategies, about 63% of the participants would always or often try to read each sense of an English word (item 11), and 55% of the students would read all the example sentences of an English word (item 12) when looking up the word in a dictionary. Moreover, the overwhelming majority of the participants (approximately 95%) tried to select one most suitable sense, rather than pick one randomly without differentiation, to understand the text they were reading if an English dictionary gave several senses for an English word they were looking up (item 17). Responses to item 10 also indicated that around half of the participants always or often tried to learn an English word by heart at the same time that they looked up the word in a dictionary.

As for task-bound cognitive dictionary strategies, most participants (79%) would look up an English word to retrieve more senses of usage although a word was familiar or known to them when reading an English text (item 25). When it comes to consulting dictionaries upon encountering unknown words in reading or when not knowing how to write something in English, about half of the participants expressed a tendency to check out an unknown word's meanings instantaneously in a dictionary whenever they came across the word in reading (item 24), while a great majority of the participants (ca. 82%) would use Chinese-English dictionaries to find out the English form for a Chinese expression they did not know how to express in English (item 26).

However, when reading an English passage, about 57% of the participants tended to underline unknown words and look them up in a dictionary only after they had read one or several paragraphs (item 22). When it comes to looking up an English word and reading the dictionary content, a great majority of the participants (86%) always or often tried to check out meanings of an English word from a dictionary and then copied the Chinese glosses of the word into the margins of the English passage they were reading (item 19). About half of the participants also reported looking up an unknown word and writing all or a part (e.g. stress mark) of its phonetic symbols in the margins of an English passage they were reading to learn how to pronounce the word.

Table 2 The ten most frequently used dictionary strategies reported by the participants

Rank	Item Description	Mean
1	17. If a paper or electronic English-Chinese dictionary gives several senses for an English word I am looking up, I try to select one most suitable sense to understand the text I am reading.	1.46
2	19. When reading an English passage, I check out meanings of an English word from a dictionary and copy the Chinese glosses of the word in the margins of the passage.	1.60
3	25. When reading English, although an English word is familiar to me, I look it up in a dictionary to retrieve more senses or usage of the word.	1.93
4	26. When writing English, I use a paper or electronic Chinese-English dictionary to find out the English for a Chinese expression every time I don't know how to express it in English.	1.94
5	11. When looking up an English word in a dictionary, I try to read each sense of the word.	2.24
6	22. When reading an English passage, I underline unknown words, and look them up in a dictionary only after I have read one or several paragraphs.	2.34
7	12. When looking up an English word in a dictionary, I try to read all the example sentences of the word.	2.40
8	24. Whenever I come across an unknown English word in reading, I check out its meanings right away in a dictionary.	2.46
9	10. When I look up an English word in a dictionary, I try to learn the word by heart at the same time.	2.49
10	21. When reading an English passage, I look up an unknown word and write in the margins of the passage all or a part of its phonetic symbols to help pronounce the word.	2.50

Table 2 presents the ten most frequently used dictionary strategies reported in the present study (M < 2.50). The results of the descriptive analysis of the EDSQ shed light on the overall dictionary strategy use by Taiwanese university English majors.

4. Discussion

The ten most often used dictionary strategies pertained exclusively to general cognitive (items 10, 11, 12) and task-bound cognitive strategies (items 17, 19, 21, 22, 24, 25, 26). The use of general cognitive strategies reflected students' prevalent lookup behaviours of reading as many example sentences (item 12) and word senses (item 11) as possible as well as memorizing the word at the same time when looking it up in a dictionary (item 10). When engaging in English reading and writing tasks, these lookup behaviours typically would go hand in hand with the follow-up task-bound strategies, such as selecting one most suitable sense to understand the context of a passage being read (item 17), copying and writing the checked out Chinese glosses (item 19) or phonetic information (item 21) in the margins of the text. Besides, while reading or writing, students tended to check out its meanings immediately upon encountering an unknown word (item 24) or when not knowing how to express in English a Chinese thought (item 26).

From a functional perspective, there appears to be two underlying motivations for students' common use of the aforementioned dictionary strategies. The first motivation essentially involves translation as a reading or writing aid. Specifically, students checked out word meanings of an unknown word immediately and wrote the Chinese glosses into the margins of a text, or consulted a Chinese-English dictionary to check out English equivalents for a Chinese concept, to facilitate their translation between English and Chinese in order to better comprehend or produce English.

The motivation for dictionary use in aiding translation in reading or writing should come as no surprise considering that English is a foreign language for Taiwanese students and that they were previously found to use English dictionaries as one of the most commonly used translation strategies (Liao 2002). As also shown in their responses to the BAEDQ, the majority of the students believed that it was important to use dictionaries to help them translate while reading and writing English. It is reasonable to say that such a firm belief is likely to lead them to use dictionaries to translate between English and Chinese to facilitate English writing or reading tasks. This propensity is particularly evident in English writing tasks. While working on an English writing assignment, students would typically first think in Chinese and draft an outline in mind or in paper, and then contrive various ways to translate Chinese thoughts into English with the aid of the dictionary that could involve using different types of English dictionaries in the entire translation and word searching process. This common practice of using dictionaries for translation in English writing was indicated directly or indirectly by almost every one of the twelve interviewees.

In addition to referring to more types of dictionaries, high proficiency respondents also reported trying to search for more clues to help produce English, such as deriving associations or inspiration from example sentences in order to help them put the Chinese thoughts in their minds into smooth English expressions. In contrast, in similar writing situations, respondents with lower proficiency tended to rely more on electronic dictionaries for fast access to English translations and make less reference to other types of dictionaries, and also reflected less on the appropriateness of the supplied translations. More importantly, less proficient respondents tended to copy separate translations they found and entire or chunks of example sentences and insert them directly into their writing without processing such raw materials into more natural English.

The preceding as well as similar responses made by proficient and less proficient learners portrayed not only how they perceived the relative strengths of different types of English dictionaries (i.e. Chinese-English, English-English, and English-Chinese dictionaries), but also how they used dictionaries as a form of translation tool to guide them in locating the raw or ready-made materials contained in the dictionaries for their writing assignment.

Apparently, for EFL learners in Taiwan, back translation plays a vital role in English writing, and Chinese-English dictionaries coupled with other types of dictionaries become an indispensable translation aid to facilitate English production. Dictionary strategies employed to facilitate back translation and other comprehension processes therefore constitute an essential part of the writing strategy system for many students.

The second and probably more important motivation underlying these most frequently used dictionary strategies by Taiwanese University English majors is associated with conscious learning of English vocabulary. In other words, students used different dictionary strategies with the objective of aiding them in learning English vocabulary better by building up more word knowledge, or learning English words by rote. More precisely, there are two salient and distinct facets to learning English words as far as these Taiwanese English learners are concerned. The first aspect involves learning exactly how an English word is spelled as well as what it means. It is therefore important for Taiwanese students to learn by rote the spelling of a word along with its meanings because the vocabulary test is a fairly common test type in many English tests. In most of the written exams or tests of English, in particular, misspelling, among other errors including mistakes in word meanings, could cost them all or some points of a vocabulary test item. Therefore, when it comes to learning English vocabulary, memorizing word spellings and meanings plays a vital role in Taiwanese EFL students' English learning process, and they may use a wide variety of learning strategies to help memorize the spelling and meaning of English vocabulary. One such strategy that is widely accepted and used is tied to dictionary use. As evidenced in this study, the majority of the respondents reported that they attempt to learn a word by heart at the same time they look it up in an English dictionary.

Moreover, while reading an English text, students tended to write in the margins of the text a part or all of the located phonetic information including phonetic transcriptions and stress mark of an English word, since a common belief amongst Taiwanese EFL learners was that the better one knows how to pronounce a word, the more easily he/she would be able to memorize it. As a proficient learner remarked in the interview, 'you don't have to memorize each English word, but you have to learn how to say or pronounce it. In saying or pronouncing a word, you are strengthening your memory of this word, thus making it easier to learn the word by heart.'

The other salient element to conscious learning of vocabulary for EFL students involves memorizing the usage and grammatical aspects of a word. Accordingly, students attempted to read as many example sentences and word senses as possible while consulting a dictionary, which they believe enables them to understand more senses and usage of a word and better appreciate the subtle differences of similar words, thus helping them not only to comprehend better but to write better as well.

Aside from the motivations underlying the frequently used dictionary strategies, there seems to be reasonable associations between these dictionary strategies and the English proficiency of the participants. English proficiency was found to have negative correlations with most of the ten most frequently used strategies except items 19, 21, 24, and 26 (see Appendix 2 for more details about the correlations among English proficiency and items on the EDSQ). More importantly, among these six negative correlations, five correlations were statistically significant, namely, correlations between English proficiency and items 10 (learn a word by rote simultaneously when looking it up; $r = -0.23$, $p < 0.01$), 11 (read each sense of a word when looking it up; $r = -0.24$, $p < 0.01$), 12 (read all example sentences of a word when looking it up; $r = -0.25$, $p < 0.01$), 17 (select a most suitable sense to understand a text; $r = -0.18$, $p < 0.01$), and 22 (underline an unknown word and look it up after reading several paragraphs; $r = -0.19$, $p < 0.01$). These relationships suggested that the more English proficient a student is, the more likely he/she would try to memorize a word simultaneously when consulting it in a dictionary (item 10), read each sense of a word in a dictionary (item 11), read all the example sentences in the dictionary (item 12), try to select one best suitable sense to fit the reading context (item 17), and underline unknown words and look them up only after reading one or several paragraphs (item 22).

More significantly, the general or task-bound cognitive strategies such as strategies 10, 11, 12, 17, and 22 also turned out to be what Taiwanese English teachers believe are effective and thoughtful strategies. In other words, proficient students tended to use supposedly more effective and sensible strategies than less proficient students. Proficient students, for example, tended not to look up an unknown word immediately, but check the word in a dictionary only after reading several paragraphs or the entire text, or use contextual guessing to get at the word meaning. A number of highly proficient interviewees recounted their progression to maturity in terms of dictionary use when encountering unknown words, reporting their shift from impulsive, ill-advised dictionary use to more sensible, effective dictionary strategy use as their English proficiency advanced to a higher level.

Moreover, while learning or, more realistically, memorizing English vocabulary, highly proficient learners tended not to be content with merely learning word meanings and spellings by heart to facilitate reading comprehension. Rather, they tended to invest appreciable effort in checking out additional senses and example sentences of a word to gain deeper understanding of word usage and make more subtle word distinctions with the goal of enhancing their English writing ability as well. This propensity of higher proficiency students to focus more on word usage and distinction than on word spelling and meaning, or more on writing than on reading comprehension, seems to support the results of the positive significant correlation ($r = 0.14$, $p < 0.01$) between English proficiency and tendency to check out and take notes of phonetic transcriptions (item 21 of the EDSQ), and negative significant correlation ($r = -0.23$, $p < 0.01$) between English proficiency and the tendency to learn a word by rote while looking it up in a dictionary (item 10 of the EDSQ). That is, high proficiency students are more likely to learn a word by rote when looking it up in a dictionary than low proficiency students, but less likely to check out and take notes of phonetic transcriptions in the margins of a text. It follows that when looking up a word and attempting to memorize the word simultaneously, proficient students tended to focus more on example sentences and grammatical aspects of words, or sentence-level information, while low proficiency students tended to care more about word pronunciation, spelling and meaning, or word-level information. It should be noted, however, that although significant correlations exist between English proficiency and the above strategies, these correlations are low and thus the preceding inferences concerning the relationship between English proficiency and dictionary strategies should be taken cautiously.

In contrast with the negative significant correlations between English proficiency and strategy items 10, 11, 12, 17, and 22, English proficiency was found to have positive significant correlations with strategy items 24 ($r = 0.21$, $p < 0.01$) and 26 ($r = 0.17$, $p < 0.01$), suggesting that the more proficient the students are, the less readily they are to resort to dictionaries whenever encountering unknown words while reading (item 24) or uncertainty about how to back translate Chinese into English while writing (item 26). These two strategies happen to be the strategies considered ill-advised and ineffective by EFL teachers in Taiwan.

To sum up, the dictionary strategies frequently used by students seem to facilitate their use of translation in reading and writing English as well as to foster their conscious learning of English vocabulary. Some of these strategies are thought of as effective, while others are considered less effective and discouraged by Taiwanese EFL teachers. More importantly, it was found that as students' English proficiency increased, they were more likely to use what

EFL teachers generally thought of as effective and thoughtful strategies, and less likely to use the supposedly ineffective strategies.

5. Results of the interview data

The qualitative data also showed that interviewees took notes in the margins of a reading text or kept additional notebooks or index cards to collect word information, marking in a dictionary, reading and analyzing different word senses and determining a best sense that fits in the reading context, referring to more than one dictionary to resolve reading difficulties, checking out phonetic transcriptions or example sentences to help learning words by rote, and so on. Besides, both proficient and less proficient students would typically use Chinese to a differing extent to help them write English by using Chinese-English dictionaries for the English translation of a Chinese thought which they had no idea how to express in English. However, proficient learners were more inclined to proceed to English-Chinese or English-English dictionaries to clarify and distinguish the meanings of the English translations, which were usually unclear for most students. Following Oxford's (1990) strategy system, proficient interviewees tended to use metacognitive strategies (e.g. cross-reference), general cognitive strategies (e.g. checking out example sentences or phonetic transcriptions for word memorization), and memory strategies (e.g. keeping additional notes to refresh word memories) more than less proficient ones.

6. Conclusion

The results of the study suggested that the students used a wide variety of lookup strategies during English reading and writing, and that the higher the students' English proficiency was, the more thoughtful and reflective they tended to be in using dictionaries.

Since learners were found in this study to use a series of cognitive strategies, including note-taking, which remained unexplored in previous dictionary use studies, any previous understanding of dictionary use as only a cognitive, referencing strategy (e.g. Scholfield 1997) needs to be modified to include memory strategies, social strategies, and metacognitive strategies as evidenced in cross-referencing, self-evaluating and monitoring learning progress. These findings of learners' dictionary strategy use add a new dimension to our understanding of the second/foreign language learning strategies, since previous strategy research did not take learners' dictionary use into consideration.

The findings of this study also suggested that the effective learning strategies typically used by the more proficient language learners reported in prior strategy research on good language learners (e.g. Rubin 1975, Stern 1975, Naiman et al. 1978) appear to parallel the case of effective dictionary strategies, thus implying that good language learners are also good dictionary users, and vice versa.

An important pedagogical implication derived from the above finding is the emerging need of the dictionary education in the spirit of Huang (2007), which champions the incorporation of dictionary strategy and skill instruction into the English curriculum to foster effecitve dictionary use and learner autonomy and facilitate foreign language learning.

Appendix 1

English Dictionary Strategy Questionnaire (EDSQ)

A. General Strategies

1. When looking up meanings of an English word in a dictionary, I also check out derivatives of the word.
2. I browse a dictionary randomly to learn English vocabulary.
3. When I look up an English word, I make a mark beside the headword in a dictionary, so that if I look up the word again, I know I have looked it up before.
4. I notice if Chinese translations strike me as awkward or inappropriate when using an English-Chinese dictionary.
5. When encountering unknown English words in the dictionary, I keep looking up those words in the same dictionary or in other dictionaries.
6. When consulting an English-English dictionary, I underline, circle, or highlight words or segments of an English definition that I think are worth learning.
7. When consulting a dictionary, I underline, circle, or highlight those English example sentences that I think are worth learning.
8. I consider or notice strengths and limitations of different dictionaries.
9. I use different dictionaries on different occasions or during different learning tasks.
10. When I look up an English word in a dictionary, I try to learn the word by heart at the same time.
11. When looking up an English word in a dictionary, I try to read each sense of the word.
12. When looking up an English word in a dictionary, I try to read all the example sentences of the word.
13. If I can't retrieve the needed information in a dictionary, I ask for help from my English teacher or from classmates.
14. I keep an additional notebook to collect English words or phrases checked out from dictionaries and worth learning to me.
15. I write on index cards the English words or phrases checked out from dictionaries and worth learning to me.
16. Do you use or know about other general dictionary strategies that are not included in the preceding statements? Please describe them in the following space.

B. Strategies Used in Reading and Writing

17. If a paper or electronic English-Chinese dictionary gives several senses for an English word I am looking up, I try to select one most suitable sense to understand the text I am reading.
18. If I can't find the suitable meaning of a word in one dictionary to fit into a reading context, I keep searching in another or other dictionaries.
19. When reading an English passage, I check out meanings of an English word from a dictionary and copy the Chinese glosses of the word in the margins of the passage.
20. When reading an English passage, I check out meanings of an English word from a dictionary and copy the English glosses in the margins of the passage.
21. When reading an English passage, I look up an unknown word and write in the margins of the passage all or a part of its phonetic symbols to help pronounce the word.
22. When reading an English passage, I underline unknown words, and look them up in a dictionary only after I have read one or several paragraphs.
23. If I am not sure which of the senses of the word I am looking up fits in the reading context, I pick one of the senses randomly to understand the reading.
24. Whenever I come across an unknown English word in reading, I check out its meanings right away in a dictionary.
25. When reading English, although an English word is familiar to me, I look it up in a dictionary to retrieve more senses or usage of the word.
26. When writing English, I use a paper or electronic Chinese-English dictionary to find out the English for a Chinese expression every time I don't know how to express it in English.
27. When writing English, after checking out the English words for Chinese from a paper or electronic Chinese-English dictionary, I keep checking the usage or meanings of the English words in an English-English or English-Chinese dictionary.
28. I use a portion of the word definitions or example sentences checked out from a dictionary in the sentences I am writing.
29. When trying to avoid repeating an English word in my writing, I search for synonyms of the word in a dictionary.
30. When writing English, although I am ready to use an English word that is familiar to me, I still look it up in dictionaries to make sure of its usage.
31. Pretend that you are at home and reading an English textbook's chapter on American culture for tomorrow's English class. What would you do when you encounter unknown words? Please describe all the things you would do in this situation.
32. Pretend that you are at home and working on an assignment that asks you to write in English your English learning experience. What would you

do when you don't know how to express some ideas in English? Please describe all the things you would do in this situation.

33. Pretend that you are in an English conversation class, and waiting for your turn to talk in English about your hobbies. What would you do when you don't know how to say some of your hobbies in English? Please describe all the things you would do in this situation.

Appendix 2

Pearson Correlations between English Proficiency and the Items on the EDSQ

Pearson correlations among English proficiency and the items of the EDSQ subsumed under each of the four composite strategy variables (S1, S2, S3, and S4)

S1	English Proficiency	S2	English Proficiency	S3	English Proficiency	S4	English Proficiency
S2	-.24**	S1	-.19**	S10	-.23**	S19	.07
S3	-.14**	S5	-.21**	S11	-.24**	S21	.14**
S6	-.22**	S8	-.28**	S12	-.25**	S24	.21**
S7	-.15**	S9	-.24**	S13	-.18**	S25	-.10
S14	-.23**	S18	-.21**	S17	-.18**	S26	.17**
S15	-.09	S27	-.22**				
		S28	-.23**				
		S29	-.24**				
		S30	.01				

* Correlation is significant at the 0.05 level (2-tailed)
** Correlation is significant at the 0.01 level (2-tailed)

English learners' dictionaries: An undervalued resource

Julia Miller
Adelaide University
julia.miller@adelaide.edu.au

1. Introduction

Most ESL students will assert that the prerequisites for tertiary study in Australia are an IELTS certificate, a theoretical knowledge of the English language and a bilingual electronic dictionary. In practice, however, the IELTS test is not always an accurate indicator of academic success (Feast 2002), English knowledge is usually incomplete, and recourse to a grammar book or dictionary is frequently necessary. Most students therefore rely on their bilingual dictionaries, which provide a quick and easy translation, often suitable for what Béjoint terms 'decoding' (translating into L1), but inadequate for the intricacies of 'encoding' (writing in L2) (Béjoint 1981: 210). However, monolingual English learners' dictionaries (henceforth referred to simply as learners' dictionaries) present a resource which gives information on grammar, pronunciation and register, as well as meaning. If students were aware of the range of information provided by such dictionaries, they might be able to use a learners' dictionary to improve their vocabulary, grammar and contextual knowledge, and thereby enhance their academic writing skills. While studies on learners' use of dictionaries have been conducted in Europe and Israel, little research has yet been done in other countries (Chi 2003). This pilot study was undertaken in order to determine if students in an Australian university setting were aware of the contents of learners' dictionaries and to examine their evaluation of this resource.

2. Literature review

Previous studies suggest that learners do not fully understand the range of resources offered by their dictionaries. Lemmens (1996) indicates that of the 112 translation studies students in his study, 46.5% did not know what grammatical information could be found in the bilingual dictionaries which they used regularly. Indeed, many students assume that they already know how to use dictionaries and do not take the trouble to investigate further (Bensoussan et al. 1984).

There is also a general reluctance among students to use learners' dictionaries rather than bilingual dictionaries. Atkins and Varantola (1998b) and Bensoussan et al. (1984) found that, even when shown the advantages of using a learners' dictionary, the majority of students still preferred to use their bilingual dictionaries. In some cases this was for pragmatic reasons, the student's bilingual electronic dictionary proving easier to transport than a more cumbersome hard copy. Even training in dictionary use, however, did not increase students' desire to use a learners' dictionary (Atkins & Varantola 1998b). Bogaards (1995, as cited in Hulstijn & Atkins 1998) suggests that this reluctance on the part of the students may be due to ignorance of correct and effective dictionary skills.

One problem outlined by Cowie (1980, as cited in Béjoint 1981) is that learners' dictionaries demand reference skills beyond the capabilities of many of their users. The coding systems used by dictionaries vary in complexity and depth, making it difficult for students to use them effectively and to switch easily between dictionaries. A study by Béjoint revealed that 89% of those surveyed had not studied their dictionary's introductory matter, and 55% did not use the coded information on word usage (Béjoint 1981). Béjoint's conclusion, like that of Atkins and Varantola (1998b), was that students should be guided in their use of learners' dictionaries.

The type of learners' dictionary used (for example Collins COBUILD, Longman or Oxford) seems to have little effect on users' accuracy, according to Nesi (1998). Students are more often hindered due to their own poor knowledge of grammar. In Nesi and Haill's study (2002: 282), students often failed to 'identify the word class of the look-up word', confusing nouns, verbs and adjectives. Bensoussan et al. (1984: 269) found that most students ignored the part of speech of a given word and felt that they 'merely [needed] to look up words in order to understand the text', leading the researchers to the conclusion that teachers need to make students more grammatically aware when using dictionaries.

The above studies were conducted in European and Israeli universities, with predominantly European or Israeli students. In Australia, the majority of international university students come from Asian countries. The study which follows aimed to discover whether these students knew what was in a learners' dictionary, and to ascertain whether, once exposed to this resource, they thought it would be helpful for encoding tasks.

3. Participants

Forty-two students participated in the study. They were all studying an ESL topic at an Australian university and were in their first or second year of tertiary study in Australia. The ESL topic was a credit-bearing course which students studied concurrently with other topics. Forty of the students were undergraduates; the remaining two were postgraduates. All had a minimum global IELTS score of 6 and had been in the ESL class for three months, receiving instruction in academic writing skills, vocabulary and grammar. There was an almost equal number of male (23) and female (19) students, most of them aged in their early twenties. Thirty-one of the participants spoke Chinese as a first language. The other participants were L1 speakers of Amharic (1), Arabic (2), Japanese (3), Khmer (1), Portuguese (2), Swedish (1) and Tagalog (1).

4. Method

The ESL students were taught in three separate classes, each student having enrolled in the class which best suited his or her own timetable. The same material was taught in each class, at the same level of difficulty. This study was conducted with each class individually.

At the first stage, after a brief discussion of the different kinds of dictionaries available (bilingual, electronic, monolingual and learners'), the students were introduced to a selection of learners' dictionaries. These were limited to the hard copies available in the Student Learning Centre and comprised: *Collins COBUILD* (1987, 1995 and 1996 editions); CALD (*Cambridge Advanced Learner's Dictionary*, 2003), CLD (*Cambridge Learner's Dictionary*, 2004) and LDOCE (*Longman Dictionary of Contemporary English*, 2003). The coding information was briefly explained.

In Stage Two, the students were asked to use either a learners' dictionary or a bilingual dictionary (their own or that of a classmate) and complete a gapfill exercise, using ten words to complete ten sentences (see Appendix 1). Students were reminded to fit the words into the sentences grammatically. Each word was to be used only once. The words used were *accentuate, discrepancy, elaborate, elucidate, epitome, euphemistically, idiosyncratically, myriad, panacea* and *paucity*. These words were chosen from a list devised by Nesi and Haill (2002) of vocabulary looked up by students and felt to be commonly used by English-speaking lecturers, and were deemed to be those that students might not know but which would be useful to them in their studies.

For Stage Three of the study, as they completed the gapfill exercise, students were also required to fill in a chart (see Appendix 2) which listed the ten words and asked for details of word class (adjective/adverb/noun/verb), context (formal/informal/scientific), collocation (such as prepositions) and pronunciation.

In Stage Four, after finishing the exercise, the participants were invited to complete a questionnaire on dictionary usage (based on Nesi and Haill 2002) designed to investigate the students' prior knowledge of dictionaries, the ease with which they had completed the exercise and the attitude which they now had to learners' dictionaries (see Appendix 3). The questionnaire enabled the students to articulate their attitudes to bilingual dictionaries or learners' dictionaries, allowing the researcher to compare rates of satisfaction with the two types of dictionaries.

5. Findings

The questionnaire revealed that each student owned on average two dictionaries. It is not clear, however, whether the students interpreted 'own' as 'possess' or 'have on the desk before me now', since several who claimed to 'own' a learners' dictionary said they had never used one before the exercise. (This may perhaps reflect the fact that they had a dictionary but did not use it.) Nineteen students (45% of the sample) specified that they had at least one electronic dictionary (usually Chinese/English, but three of these incorporated a learners' dictionary). Twenty-two students (52% of the sample) said they had used learners' dictionaries before. Of those used, eleven were Oxford learners' dictionaries, two were Collins COBUILD, two were published by Longman and four were published by Cambridge University Press (the exact names and editions were usually not specified). A short discussion, however, revealed that although these students claimed prior use of learners' dictionaries, they were not familiar with the full range of their dictionaries' contents. Nineteen students (45%) used a bilingual dictionary to do the exercise (seventeen of these dictionaries were electronic and two were paper dictionaries), while twenty (48%) used learners' dictionaries (one of which was part of an electronic bilingual dictionary). Three students (7%) did not use a dictionary.

Students were asked whether the dictionary they had used in the exercise explained all the words correctly and, if not, which words were not explained and what was not clear in the explanation. Since students had been given a chart to fill in, described in Stage Three of the Method section above, it is likely that most students used the chart's criteria to determine whether the information they had gained was sufficiently comprehensive. The students were required to fill in one column of the chart only, answering questions on either bilingual or learners' dictionaries. However, sixteen students filled in both columns, and their results are not included in Tables 1 and 2, which summarize students' comments on information provided in the two kinds of dictionaries.

Table 1 Students' opinions about bilingual (BLD) and learners' (LD) dictionaries used in a class vocabulary exercise (0=no comment made)

	BLD (n=10)	LD (n=12)
Words correctly explained	8	11
Words not explained correctly	2	1
Words which caused problems	Idiosyncratically (2) Euphemistically (1) Elucidate (1)	Paucity (2) Elaborate (1) Euphemistically (1)
Formal/informal not indicated	0	4
Usage or context not indicated	0	0
Countability status of nouns not given	1	0
Pronunciation system too complicated	0	1

While none of the users of bilingual dictionaries commented on register, four users of learners' dictionaries complained that the formal or informal status of a word was not given. Answers to this question may have been influenced by the chart the students filled in during the exercise, and by the fact that distinctions in formal/informal usage were pointed out to the students as being one of the advantages of a learners' dictionary. In fact, formal/informal indications were given in all the learners' dictionaries for the word *paucity* and in the Cambridge dictionaries for *elaborate*. Other words, such as *euphemism*, were not marked, as they are more neutral in register. It could be that the students had not understood that a word could be neither formal nor informal, suggesting that further teaching on register is necessary.

At the end of the questionnaire, space was left for participants to write comments on whether the exercise had changed their view of dictionaries. Of the 42 students who had participated, 16 replied affirmatively and 11 replied negatively. Of the negative comments, one student had already been using a learners' dictionary for five years and had found it helpful. Two students commented that they would continue to use the dictionary they already had, since they were more comfortable with it. Only one student was disappointed, commenting:

I expected that a learners' dictionary was more complete, with the same details in all words, not just in some words.

Four students felt that a learners' dictionary could enhance their English skills:

Learner's dictionary is a powerful tool during English study in that it force you to forget your native language and go through it totally in English background.

I need a learner's dictionary. It is useful not only in look up words but also helps your reading.

> *Learner's dictionary is very helpful if I write a report or essay.*
> *I think I should spend more time on paper dictionary and I find it is very useful for writing in the right way.*

Some students thus related the dictionary to the core skills of decoding and encoding, and at least one person realized the importance of working totally in their target language.

Six students thought that the learners' dictionary could give them more information than their bilingual dictionary:

> *The dictionary shows the context besides word class and pronunciation.*
> *I think have a learning dictionary can help you to understand the words, to know the usage more thoroughly while you can only learn the meaning of the words in elecernic [sic] one which is suit for quick search.*
> *Yes, it tells me using the dictionary is not only just know what the meaning is, but also we should know how to use and explain them in English. Furthermore, the example sentence could help me to understand the different use.*
> *Yes, I might need to have a learner's dictionary if it helps me more than the electronic dictionary.*
> *Yes, more details and information, better than my electronic dictionary.*
> *Personally, I used to use electronic dictionary. It's faster, but I find the learner's dictionary can help me a lot by providing details about the use of words.*

These students had progressed from seeing the dictionary purely as a decoding device and had realized the importance of contextual information and the usefulness of providing example sentences and collocations.

Five students commented that the exercise had changed their view of dictionaries in general. Student comments included:

> *Yes. I can't really tell what is a learner's dictionary before.*
> *Yes, dictionary is more useful than I think about it before.*
> *Yes, before I did not take note of the context of the word (formal, informal, scientific etc.). However, after doing this exercise I am made aware of this.*
> *As some dictionaries provide more information as well as the meaning of a particular word, it is probably better for people who are not only seeking the meaning of a word but also seeking the use of the word. It changed my view of dictionaries as before all the dictionaries are same.*

These students now saw that the dictionary was a wider resource than they had thought.

In an overall comparison of the two types of dictionary, learners' dictionaries were ranked more favourably in every category (see Table 2).

Table 2 Mean student responses to items regarding information provided in bilingual (BLD) or learners' (LD) dictionaries (1=strongly agree; 7=strongly disagree)

The dictionary allowed me to:	BLD (n=10)	LD (n=12)
Understand items in context	3.4	2.6
Use the words in speech or writing	4.6	3.0
Know which words to use before or after (eg prepositions, participles)	4.0	3.1
Know contexts for words (eg scientific, formal, informal)	4.1	3.6
Know how the word is pronounced	3.8	2.3

The biggest differences in scores were in relation to using words in speech or writing, and in knowing the pronunciation of a word. The responses given by the users of learners' dictionaries indicated that the information they had found had given them greater confidence for encoding activities. Learners' dictionaries were also thought to provide more information on collocations and context than bilingual dictionaries. This may have been because the learners' dictionaries provided example sentences incorporating the look-up words and giving a clear indication of the words' productive use. Despite the spoken pronunciation given by electronic dictionaries, students felt that phonological information was better in learners' dictionaries. This finding is surprising, given that teacher experience indicates that many students have difficulty using the International Phonetic Alphabetic (see, for example, Reif 1987) and that these participants did not have access to the CD ROMs which provide spoken pronunciation in all the latest editions of the learners' dictionaries. In general, however, these results indicate that the students were beginning to see that a learners' dictionary could contribute not just to the decoding of unfamiliar words, but to their productive use in encoding and their correct use in terms of register and context.

6. Limitations

The main limitations to this study are the small sample size (n=42) and the fact that sixteen students did not fill in the questionnaire correctly, completing answers for both bilingual and learners' dictionaries, rather than only for the dictionary they had used for the exercise. In addition, most students were not familiar with English learners' dictionaries, and needed more time to understand in detail how the dictionaries and their coding systems worked. Another lesson learned from this pilot administration of the questionnaire related to the wording of items. The question 'Did [the dictionary] explain all the words in the exercise correctly?' raised the issue of the meaning of '*correctly*', and a better wording for future use would be 'Did [the dictionary] explain all the words in the exercise adequately?'

7. Recommendations

Since the literature reveals that students require training in dictionary use (see, for example, Atkins & Varantola 1998b), a future study would include more explicit guidance in using dictionaries. Larger numbers of students from a wider variety of language and cultural groups could participate, and a different questionnaire could be administered for each dictionary type.

8. Conclusion

The students in this exercise had little detailed knowledge of learners' dictionaries before the session, but recognized that learners' dictionaries have potential to improve their academic writing skills by providing accurate grammatical and contextual information. However, even when students possess a learners' dictionary, their own lack of grammatical knowledge may frustrate their search (Nesi and Haill 2002: 300). It then becomes a chicken and egg situation. Can dictionary skills help students to improve their grammar, or is a good knowledge of grammar needed before dictionary skills can be gained? The two are probably complementary. The fact that four users of learners' dictionaries failed to find the obvious information on a word's formal/informal status confirms the conclusion of Béjoint (1981) and Atkins and Varantola (1998b) that students need training in the use of learners' dictionaries. Students also need to be shown or reminded of how the forms of a word can be built. In this way they will be able to distinguish nouns, adjectives and adverbs, so that words such as *euphemism*, *euphemistic* and *euphemistically* can be more easily recognized and found. They could also be made more aware of the importance of, for example, countability, in determining article use, or the irregular forms of English verbs, and look for these details in their dictionary searches.

Two vital questions remain. Will students use a heavy, hard copy learners' dictionary when an electronic bilingual dictionary is readily available? And, if the learners' dictionary is added to their electronic dictionary, will they use it in preference to the bilingual dictionary? Although participants in this study indicated that they appreciated the advantages of learners' dictionaries, actual future use of learners' dictionaries would need to be verified by further research. It remains clear, however, that the students benefited from their exposure to learners' dictionaries, ranking them more highly than bilingual dictionaries with regard to the usefulness of the grammatical, contextual and phonological information provided and, by implication, to their usefulness for encoding activities. What was true for the students in Béjoint's 1981 French study appears to be true for students in the current Australian study: learners' dictionaries obviously have the potential to play a key role in enhancing students' academic writing skills. It now lies with the teachers to recognize this potential and incorporate dictionary training skills in their ESL curricula.

Acknowledgement
This study was previously published in *TESOL in Context* 2005, (15) 2:30-37 and is used here with permission.

Appendix 1
Vocabulary exercise using dictionaries
(Answers have been supplied here. The original exercise contained gaps in place of the words in italics.)

Choose from the following words to complete the exercise below, remembering to make the words fit grammatically in the sentences.

    accentuate discrepancy   elaborate   elucidate
    epitome   euphemistically   idiosyncratically myriad
    panacea   paucity

1. I did not notice all those details in the plan, and now I do not understand. Please could you *elaborate*.
2. No one else had pronunciation like his; he spoke *idiosyncratically*.
3. There are *myriads* of so-called remedies for the common cold, but none of them work.
4. The two reports showed *discrepancies* and failed to corroborate each other.
5. The essay is not clear because the main points are not strong enough. You should *accentuate* them by using topic sentences.
6. The chef cooked a wonderful meal. In fact, you could say it was the *epitome* of a successful banquet.
7. The results of the study showed that the researchers needed to *elucidate* the main points by making them clearer.
8. No one has yet discovered a *panacea* for computer viruses, although there are many anti-virus programmes.
9. There is a *paucity* of information regarding the participants in the study.
10. There is a shortage of restrooms here, which means, speaking *euphemistically*, that there is a lack of toilets.

Appendix 2
Dictionary use chart

Dictionary used:				
Word	Word class (adjective/ adverb/ noun/ verb)	Context (formal/ informal/ scientific)	Other words given (eg prepositions)?	Pronunciation given?
accentuate				
discrepancy				
elaborate				
elucidate				
epitome				
euphemistically				
idiosyncratic				
myriad				
panacea				
paucity				

Appendix 3
Questionnaire on dictionary usage

1. How many dictionaries do you own?
2. What are their names (and dates of publication, if you know them)?
3. Have you ever used an English learners' dictionary?
4. If so, which one?
5. If you have used an English learners' dictionary, is it part of an electronic dictionary?
6. What dictionary did you use to do this exercise?
7. Please answer the following questions. Fill in one column only.

Bilingual dictionary		Learners' dictionary	
a) Did it explain all the words in the exercise correctly?	Yes / No	a) Did it explain all the words in the exercise correctly?	Yes / No
b) Which words were not explained?		b) Which words were not explained?	
c) What was not clear in the explanation?		c) What was not clear in the explanation?	

8. Did the dictionary give you enough information? Please agree or disagree with the following statements, giving details if you can.

The information in the dictionary allowed me to:	Bilingual dictionary	Learners' dictionary
a) Understand the items in context		
b) Use the words – if I had to – in speech or writing		
c) Know which words to use before or after (eg prepositions, participles)		
d) Know the kinds of contexts (eg scientific, formal, informal) in which the words are used		
e) Know how the word is pronounced		

9. Has this exercise changed your view of dictionaries? Give details.

Multiple word class entries in advanced learner's dictionaries of English

Sadayuki Nakane
University of Fukui
nakane@f-edu.fukui-u.ac.jp

1. Introduction

It has been one of the traditions of English lexicography to label each entry word in terms of grammatical categorization. In other words, dictionaries assign their headword lexemes to one or more word classes. This is perhaps because lexicographers believe that word class labelling is necessary to indicate the properties of a lexeme and of practical use to dictionary users in that it helps them predict its linguistic behaviour.

The problem here is that there are overlapping criteria for demarcating word classes, and that they produce borderline cases of lexical word class membership. 'There are plenty of linguistic parallels to the duck-billed platypus' (Leech et al. 2006: 36), but lexicographers must nevertheless assign every headword to a single or a mixed word class. The present chapter takes up some such borderline cases and shows how lexicographers agree or differ in their assignments of these words. Lexicographers' disagreements bring about confusion among dictionary users, and it should be part of their responsibility to minimize such confusion and promote better understanding of a generally serviceable pedagogical grammar.

The number of identified word classes differs among grammarians, although nine categories are generally recognized now, as Blake (1988: 14) observes: nouns, verbs, adjectives, adverbs, pronouns, prepositions, conjunctions, articles, and interjections. This kind of classification has a long tradition, traceable to the *partes orationis* of Latin grammar, and the article class that Latin lacked was added to adapt the Latin system to the modern European vernaculars. In the early seventeenth century, the term *article* was introduced by Elizabethans such as Thomas Tomkin and Ben Jonson in their grammars of English. The diversity of early classification of parts of speech or word classes in English is thoroughly examined by Michael (1970: 201-80).

Most modern grammar books designed for university students and advanced learners of English basically retain the same categories, though with some modifications. It should be noted, first of all, that they subsume the article under the broader class of 'determiners', while still keeping the conventional names, the 'definite article' and the 'indefinite article'.

The word classes of English are further divided into two broad categories, 'open' and 'closed'. Many grammarians seem to agree that the open category comprises four classes: noun, (full) verb, adjective, and adverb, while the rest are closed, so named because they are not usually open to new members. The closed word classes may be classified in different ways. However, present-day grammarians agree in recognizing at least four such classes: pronoun, preposition, conjunction, and determiner, the last two of which may also be named differently. Huddleston and Pullum (2005) and Biber et al. (2002) divide the traditional conjunction class into two new classes. They recognize coordinators and subordinators as distinct classes. Huddleston and Pullum (2005: 90-93) distinguish between a determinative and a determiner, and use the former as a term for a word class and the latter as a term for a function. Most modern grammarians think it worthwhile to recognize a class of auxiliaries as distinct from full or lexical verbs. Interjections and numerals or enumerators are normally considered members of the closed class and may be ignored as peripheral, because they are not essential elements in grammar. We should remember, however, that 'in some ways interjections and enumerators are like open classes' (Leech et al. 2006: 50), although they are usually classified as closed.

The criteria for word class identification may be morphological, syntactic, or semantic, but a combined consideration of form, function, and meaning is necessary for defining classes. Leech et al. (2006: 51) remark in this connection that function is most important, form next most important, and meaning least important. If so, function should be prioritized, but meaning may still play an important role.

As might be expected, the task of word class identification is not as easy as it seems, for many lexemes overlap across word classes. There are indeed borderline cases of word class membership, and yet lexicographers are obliged to favour one classification over another by employing the criteria that may be regarded most appropriate by as many grammarians as possible so as to help dictionary users understand how a word actually does or could behave.

2. Analysis

Let us examine some cases, and see how they are treated in dictionaries. *Grey/gray*, for example, is usually labelled as adjective, noun, and verb by learner's dictionaries, and there is no serious problem about this. However, COBUILD5 and LDOCE4 give an independent entry to *greying*, the former labelling it as an adjective and the latter as a noun. CALD2 lists it under the main entry *grey* and labels it as an adjective, while OALD7 and MED list it under the verb *grey* as one of the verb's inflected forms. CALD2 gives this illustrative *example*: 'He is greying now but still elegant.' Some might feel that it is more like an adjective than a verb, standing parallel to 'elegant', which is clearly an adjective. If we take 'is' for an auxiliary verb followed by a participle, there is no relevant verb for 'elegant', which needs a linking verb. Others may judge that the sentence is a sylleptic one where the verb functions in two different ways and argue that the *greying* here is still a verb form. In cases, admittedly few, where *greying* occurs with the verb *be*, the adverb *slightly* may precede or follow it; hence, it is not clear morphologically and syntactically whether *greying* is an adjective or a verb.

Quirk et al. (1985: 402-04) set up four criteria for adjectives: (a) occurrence in attributive function; (b) occurrence in predicative function (esp. after the linking verb *seem*); (c) acceptance of premodification by *very*; and (d) ability to take comparison. *Greying* is often used attributively, sometimes combined with an adjective, as in 'her long and greying hair' or 'the greying baby-boomers'. A majority of the 111 occurrences of *greying* in the British National Corpus (henceforth, BNC) are attributes. However, the BNC has no occurrence of this form as a complement after *seem*. 'His hair seemed to be greying' sounds natural, though, and people will agree that this *greying* is more verb than adjective. '*Very greying' is impossible. '?Tom's hair is more greying than Bill's' is implausible, but 'Tom is greying more than Bill' will be acceptable. Except for its occurrence in attributive function, *greying* seems to work as a participle of the verb *grey*.

Thus, to which word class should *greying* be allotted? The answer cannot be straightforward. If one encounters such a sentence as 'His hair was greying at the sides' (OALD7), one might think (a) that 'his hair' is in the process of becoming grey, or (b) that it is in the state of having a lot of grey hair at the sides. Interpretation (a) tends to shift to (b), because, except where a comparison with the past is being implied, the physical process of hair greying cannot be observed at the time the utterance has occurred. *Greying* in attributive function might legitimately be called an adjective, but the *greying* that comes after *be* may be said to be on its way to adjectivehood, in light of the other evidence given above.

LDOCE4 enters the same form *greying* only as a noun (e.g. 'the greying of classical music audiences', where the *-ing* form is preceded by a determiner and followed by a postmodifier in the form of a prepositional phrase, a typical noun phrase structure). This is a nominal use of the *-ing* form of the verb *grey*, and there are five similar uses of *greying* in BNC, but it may not be immediately clear that we have the noun *greying*, because *-ing* forms derived from verbs have the potential of being used as nouns. Classification of *greying* or any *-ing* form as belonging to any other word class than the verb should depend upon its frequency, syntactic behaviour, and perhaps semantic change. As the example in LDOCE4 indicates, the nominal *greying* has developed a figurative meaning of 'ageing' as well as the literal 'becoming grey'. FAV, LUM2, and WIS2 list the form as a noun with an extended metaphorical meaning equivalent to 'ageing', while G4 and NCol7 label *greying* both as a noun and an adjective.

It is difficult to say in some cases whether a word that comes in the premodifying position in a noun phrase is an adjective or a noun. It is a position that people tend to associate with adjectives because of their frequent occurrence there, but a noun may also appear in the same position. Crystal (1995: 211) analyses 'the garden party' and, by pointing out that it shows the morphological properties of a noun and an adjective, argues that *garden* should belong to 'a "mixed" word class'. However, Bauer (1998) and Giegerich (2004) would not doubt that it is a noun, and dictionaries do not assign *garden* to the adjective but to the noun class. This word appears in such combinations as *a garden chair, garden tools, a garden shed, a garden apartment/flat, a garden centre, a garden city*. We may divide these combinations into two groups: noun phrases or composite nominals (the first three) and compound nouns (the last three). A *garden chair* refers to any type of chair used in a garden, but a *garden party* is a formal social party held in a large garden, not any private party in a garden, and hence is now considered a compound noun. Generally speaking, compound nouns have a primary stress on the first constituent: *a gárden pàrty*, whereas in noun phrases a primary stress usually falls on the head: *a gàrden cháir*. This is not an absolute test for the distinction, though. *Garden* in *garden party* must have been a nominal premodifier in origin, but is now felt a base, which together with *party* forms a compound noun. It would be absurd to conclude that any instance of *garden* that appears in the position just before a noun is an adjective merely because it is a position often occupied by adjectives.

Garden-variety (e.g. *garden-variety science, musical, criminals, cases of fraud*) makes an interesting case for comparison. It is labelled as an adjective by all dictionaries I have consulted, although its form might suggest that it may be a compound noun, and indeed, *variety* in *a variety show* or *a variety store* is considered by some dictionaries to be a noun. The difference between *garden-variety* 'commonplace' and *variety* 'a form of theatre or TV entertainment' is that the latter may be used as a noun in various functions, but the former is used only as a premodifier having a sense equivalent to the adjective 'ordinary' or 'commonplace'. The original sense of *garden-variety* seems to be 'a variety (of flower, plant, etc.) that is found in an ordinary garden', which would suggest its nounhood, but as it is used metaphorically only in attributive function, it may be judged to be an adjective.

Concrete is also a multiple word class word, being an adjective, a noun, and a verb. It has been used for centuries as an adjective semantically opposite to *abstract*, but upon gaining the noun sense 'building material' in the mid nineteenth century, it went on to become an adjective with the related sense 'made of concrete'. In *a concrete building/floor/wall/pavement*, *concrete* may apparently be interpreted either as a noun or an adjective. It may be coordinated with a noun in the premodifying position, as in *concrete and clay products*, where *clay* is not normally recognized as an adjective by dictionaries. On the other hand, it may be coordinated with an adjective-equivalent, as in *a concrete or tiled floor*. Then, to which word class should it be assigned? One of the secure tests of determining membership of the adjective category is to check whether the target word occurs in predicative as well as in attributive function, although this will not apply to all adjectives. 'The floor is concrete' and 'These products are concrete' are acceptable, and the meaning of *concrete* here is 'made of concrete'; hence, concrete in *a concrete building* is an adjective. Note that concrete in *a cóncrete mìxer* is a noun base. A *concrete mixer* is a mixer of sand, water and cement to make concrete, not one made of concrete.

How about *night* as used in *a night train*? Determining the word class of this kind of *night* is not as easy as it may appear to be. *Night* may occur freely in attributive position (e.g. *night air, night light, night nurse*), but unlike *concrete* it hardly ever occurs in predicative position (**Our train was night, *The nurse was night*, etc.). *Night* in these examples is treated as an adjective by MED, LEXIS, and NCol7. *Day* may also be used in a similar way, as in *day job, a day game, day temperatures*, but *day* in this use is labelled as an adjective only by LEXIS, while MED and *NCol7* treat it as a noun, not an adjective. Japanese bilingual dictionaries other than LEXIS and NCol7 include this *night* under the noun entry, as seems more appropriate for both *night* and *day*, and interestingly they all add the explanation that it may be used 'adjectivally'. However, 'attributively' would be a more appropriate term, because the explanation actually refers to function, not word class. As with many nouns in attributive function, the premodifier *night* is semantically very variable, its senses being freely determined according to which noun it premodifies. *Night train* is one of the 'attribute–head NNs' (Giegerich 2004: 12), and the general semantic relation between the two nouns is 'associated with'. MED defines the adjective *night* as 'happening or existing at night', followed by four sub-senses: 'used at night', 'travelling at night', 'working at night', and 'active during the night'. None of these senses seems to apply exactly to the *night* in 'I've spent half my windswept life recently on night roads' (Wordbank). Theoretically, there can be as many associative senses as pragmatically required between the attribute *night* and the head noun.

The question about *a night out*, which may appear to be structurally similar to *a night train*, is different: which is the modifier, *night* or *out*? In other words, what is the head of the noun phrase? Deletion of *night* from *a night out* leaves an out, but the nominal *out* usually means 'an excuse or reason for avoiding an unpleasant situation' (CALD2), which is different from the meaning of *a night out*, where *out* means 'not at home'. *Out* in this sense is frequently used as an adverb: 'Let's eat out tonight,' which usually means 'Let's eat at a restaurant tonight.' The *out* in *a night out* and that in 'let's eat out' are semantically identical. Originally *a night out* seems to have referred to a night spent 'out' (i.e., not at home) at a restaurant, theatre, etc., in which case the noun head is *night* and the adverb *out* functions as a postmodifier, just as in the case of *a way out*. But whatever the original word formation of *a night out* might have been, *night out* is now considered a compound noun rather than a noun phrase. People would generally agree that the prepositional complement of *on* in 'Marla Maples wore it on a night out with Donald Trump in New York' (*The Times*, Jan. 1995) is not 'a night' but 'a night out'. There is also phonological evidence for this: an open juncture exists between *night* and *out*. We should be aware, however, that its plural form is *nights out* (not *night outs*), as in 'It's one of the many nights out organised by Flint' (*The Times*, Jan. 1995). This type of plural form is modelled on *way out/ways out* or *passerby/passersby*, where *out* and *by* are originally adverbial. As these examples show, *night out* has been fully lexicalized as a noun, and may occur in functions other than as a direct object, but four (FAV, G4, NCol7, and SA3) of the Japanese bilingual dictionaries I have used list it as part of the idiomatic or fixed expression 'have a níght óut'. LUM2 and WIS2 list *a night out* as a noun under the noun entry *night*. Given the noun status of *night out*, it is more appropriate and consistent to enter it as an independent headword just like *way out*, which is independently entered by FAV, G4, LEXIS, LUM2, NCol7, and SA3.

Out is usually used as an adverb or an adverbial particle, as in 'Did you take that out or did I?', but is it an adverb or an adjective if it appears after a linking verb, as in 'It was already out actually'? MED treats *out* as a 'function word', and gives the information that it may be used 'after the verb "to be": *You were out when I called*' (s.v. *out*), but the dictionary is silent about the word class to which it belongs. COBUILD5, LDOCE4, and OALD7 label *out* in the same use as an adverb, but CALD2 regards it as an adjective. This *out* does not immediately follow the linking verb seem, but is normally used with the infinitive 'to be', as in 'she seems to be out, I suppose they'll be playing bowls or something' (BNC: KP8). This is an indication that this *out* is not an adjective.

In the predicative position after a linking verb an adverb (esp. of space) may occur, functioning as an 'adverbial complement' (Greenbaum and Nelson, 2002: 29). Quirk et al. (1985: 730-32) call this an 'obligatory adverbial', and there is no well-grounded reason for deciding that such an *out* is an adjective, as this word normally functions as an adverbial. LUM2 is the only Japanese dictionary that claims adjective status for this use of *out*. However, NCol2 enters *out* as an adverb, but it notes that the word may be considered an adjective if it combines with *be* (s.v. *out*, adv.). In such an illustrative example as 'Our dog is out (there) in the garden' (LUM2, s.v. *out*, adj. 2), however, it would seem that 'out' is an adverbial of place and that the prepositional phrase 'in the garden' is an adverbial complement.

OALD7 does not recognize *out* as an adjective, but some *out*'s (e.g. 'Maxi skirts are out now', 'The machine is out again') are labelled as adjective by most dictionaries, usually with the usage note 'not before noun'. The *out*'s in these examples seem to be shortenings of out of fashion and out *of order* respectively. Prepositional phrases are known to work as adverbial complements or 'subject predicates' (Biber et al. 2002: 142). And in the sentence 'The thought of asking one of the Royal family for money to breed owls seemed a bit out of order' (BNC: CHE), the phrasal *out of order* is adjectival as is indicated by its collocation with the verb *seem* without 'to be'. *Out* in the slangy sense of 'unconscious' may be felt as adjectival, as its use in the following example might show, 'Jock seemed out on his feet, his head kept jerking forward and his eyes were continually closing' (BNC A61). These *out*'s may be labelled as adjective, even if they have no use in attributive function.

Out in the sense 'open about one's homosexuality' (COD11), however, is known to work attributively as well as predicatively: 'an out lesbian politician' / 'Are you out to your parents?' (MED, s.v. *out*, adj.). LDOCE4 and LUM2 mention this sense under the adverb *out*, with no example. *Out* in this connection seems to have come from some such expression as 'Their eldest son had "come out"' (NDAS, *come out*), where *out* is undoubtedly an adverb and 'He came out of the closet last year and his parents damn near died' (NDAS, *come out of the closet*), where *out of* may now be called a complex preposition, but originally out was an adverb and *of* a preposition meaning 'from'. This slangy *out* is undoubtedly adverbial in origin, but it has now come to be used not only in predicative but also in attributive function. Though the attributive use of *out* in this sense seems still pretty rare, BNC has an interesting example: 'I was living with the most out gay man I know' (CF4). One may choose to label it as an adjective, since the ability of functioning both attributively and predicatively may well be considered 'a central feature of adjectives' (Quirk et al. 1985: 404).

Apart is also a difficult case to handle. LDOCE4, CALD2, and COBUILD5 label this word as an adverb and adjective and OALD7 as an adverb only. MED broadly classifies it as a function word, and gives illustrative examples. When it occurs as a complement after the linking verb *be*, as in 'I'm never happy when we're apart', it is an adverb according to MED and COBUILD5, while CALD2 explicitly calls it an adjective. It is not clear to which word class LDOCE4 wants to allot this *apart*, as the dictionary only gives two parallel labels: 'adverb, adjective'. G4 and WIS2 give examples of *apart* after a linking verb, labelling it as an adverb.

The attributive *apart* in 'Madagascar is a world apart' is an adjective, MED explains, giving a parenthetical note 'only after a noun'. A few phrases with a similar structure are found: *a class apart*, *a breed apart*, or *a species apart*. The *apart* in these has a sense equivalent to 'removed from the common range' and may be felt to be adjectival owing to its extended meaning. This postnominal use of *apart* is restricted to this small group of fixed expressions, and does not necessarily justify a claim of adjectivehood for the word as such. In English, adverbs may function as postmodifier, as in 'the stars above', and the English *apart*, now lexicalised as an adverb, may be considered as functioning the same way as above. LEXIS, LUM2, and NCol7 include this sub-sense of *apart*.

LEXIS labels it as an adverb, but LUM2 and NCol7 regard it as an adjective.

3. Conclusion
Borderline cases of multiple word class membership sometimes defy clear-cut classification, but lexicographers should not adopt an overly simplified set of criteria for assigning the entry lexemes to their word classes when editing a dictionary, especially one designed for advanced learners. Such criteria have to be based on the grammar in which the lexicographers believe, even when this is not being formally set out. Crystal (2004: 191-92) aptly notes that 'word classes should not be taken as being in some way part of a terminological preamble to grammar, because in a real sense they assume a grammar before one can begin to talk about them.' Unfortunately, however, dictionaries used by learners do not usually provide enough information on what word classes are and how they are to be distinguished in the grammar on which they are based.

Lexicographers cannot be too careful in their precautions not to mislead dictionary users, who may be learning grammar from their inappropriate word class labelling. Several good grammars are accessible as university textbooks (e.g. Biber et al. 2002, Greenbaum and Quirk 1990, Nelson 2002, Huddleston and Pullum 2005, and Leech et al. 2006), and even if they use different terms for the same linguistic phenomenon, they have a lot in common with regard to word class demarcation, and this should be used as a basis for making more uniform criteria for word class assignment.

Appendix

Word class treatment of selected items in UK and Japanese dictionaries for advanced learners. Abbreviations: (adj.) = adjectival use; (v.) = mentioned with an example in the verb entry; (v.i.) = mentioned with no example in the intransitive verb sub-division; c.n. = entered as a compound noun; (idm) = treated as an idiom or collocaion; f.w. = function word.

Table 1 Treatment in UK monolingual dictionaries for learners

Entry	Example	CALD2	COBUILD5	LDOCE4	OALD7	MED
greying (1)	He is greying.	adj.	adj.	(v.)	(v.)	v.
greying (2)	the greying of...	–	–	n.	–	–
garden	a garden chair	n.	–	n.	n.	n.
garden-variety	garden-variety science	–	adj.	adj.	adj.	–
variety	a variety show	n.	–	c.n.	n.	n.
concrete (1)	a concrete wall	n.	n.	adj.	adj.	adj.
concrete (2)	a concrete mixer	c.n.	–	c.n.	c.n.	c.n.
night (1)	a night train	n.	–	n.	n.	adj.
night (2)	a night out	n.(idm)	–	–	n.(idm)	n.
out (1)	You were out.	adj.	adv.	adv.	adv.	f.w.
out (2)	Is he out?	–	–	adv.	adv.	adj.
apart (1)	We are apart.	adj.	adv.	adv./adj.	–	w.f./adv.
apart (2)	a world apart	–	–	–	–	f.w./adj.

Table 2 Treatment in Japanese bilingual dictionaries for learners

Entry	E-Gate	FAV	G4	LEXIS	LUM2	NCol7	SA3	WIS2
greying (1)	(v.i.)	(v.)	adj.	(v.)	(v.i.)	adj.	(v.i.)	(v.i.)
greying (2)	–	n.	n.	–	n.	n.	(v.i.)	n.
garden	n.(adj.)	n.(adj.)	n.(adj.)	n.(adj.)	n.(adj.)	n.	n.(adj.)	n.(adj.)
garden-variety	–	adj.	adj.	adj.	adj.	adj.	adj.	adj.
variety	c.n.	c.n.	c.n.	–	c.n.	c.n.	n.	n.
concrete (1)	adj.	adj.	adj.	adj.	adj.	adj.	adj.	adj.
concrete (2)	c.n.	c.n.	(c.n.)	c.n.	c.n.	c.n.	c.n.	n.(c.n.)
night (1)	n.(adj.)	n.(adj.)	n.	adj.	n.(adj.)	adj.	n.(adj.)	n.(adj.)
night (2)	–	n.(idm)	n.(idm)	–	n.(c.n.)	n.(idm)	n.(idm)	n.(idm)
out (1)	adv.	adv.	adv.	–	adv.	adv./adj.	adv.	adv.
out (2)	–	–	adj.	–	adj.	–	–	–
apart (1)	–	–	adv.	–	–	–	–	adv.
apart (2)	–	–	–	adv.	adj.	adj.	–	–

Representation of word combinations in illustrative examples in English learners' dictionaries

Hai Xu
Guangdong University of Foreign Studies
xuhai1101@yahoo.com.cn

1. Introduction

It is well recognized in the literature that one of the functions of dictionary examples is to show word combinations (Drysdale 1987, Cowie 1989). Yet it remains unclear what types of word combinations are generally represented in illustrative examples in English learners' dictionaries and what principles underlie the inclusion of word combinations in dictionary examples. This chapter attempts to address the issues by adopting a quantitative approach.

2. Types of word combinations

Before the investigation, it is worth considering the typology of word combinations. Howarth (1996) proposed a practical classification of word combinations. In his view, two principal criteria are central to the taxonomy: 'the semantic characteristics of the whole or parts and restrictions on commutability' (1996: 32). Word combinations (*composite units* in his term) are not discretely divided. Instead, they are on a continuum scale. The 'continuum model' as he called it is shown in Figure 1:

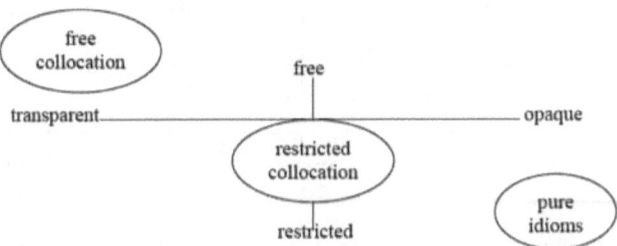

Figure 1 Howarth's classification of word combinations

Figure 1 demonstrates that horizontally, the factor of semantic transparency determines the types of word combinations, and vertically, the variable of structural invariability plays a role. At one end stand free collocations, which are semantically transparent and structurally free; at the other end are pure idioms, which are semantically opaque and structurally restricted. And straddled in between are restricted collocations. No sharply-cut boundaries exist in the three categories of word combinations. Howarth argued that in empirical studies, the following four types of composite units deserve special attention: *free collocation*, *restricted collocation*, *figurative idiom* and *pure idiom*.

The present study integrates Howarth's model of word combinations with Benson et al.'s classification (1986), which differentiates lexical collocations from grammatical ones.

3. Method

To investigate the types of word combinations in dictionary examples, some entries from the Big Five English learners' dictionaries and the *New English-Chinese Dictionary* (NECD3) were sampled. All the illustrative examples in the sample entries were then extracted. Meanwhile, the data sampled from the Big Five and from NECD3 were compared with the corresponding data in *the BBI Combinatory Dictionary of English* (BBI2) and in the *Oxford Collocations Dictionary for Students of English* (OCDSE1). Finally, the implications of the results were discussed with particular reference to the combinatory patterns as observed in the British National Corpus (BNC) and in the Chinese Learner English Corpus (CLEC).

Two criteria were established in the sampling of entry words. First, the selected words should cover all the ranges of word frequency. Second, they should cover the major parts-of-speech. To meet the two criteria, a noun, a verb, and an adjective respectively ranking in the top 3,000 most frequent words, in the word frequency from No. 3,001 to No. 5,000 and in the word frequency beyond the 5,000th, were selected (see Table 1).

Table 1 Sample entry words for the study

frequency / part-of-speech	lemmas ranking the top 3,000 most frequent words	lemmas ranking from 3,001 to 5,000	lemmas ranking beyond the 5,000th
noun	history	glory	superiority
verb	save	cure	rally
adjective	available	dreadful	foremost

4. Results

The illustrative examples sampled from the Big Five show some general tendencies in the inclusion of word combinations.

Firstly, free collocations predominate in dictionary examples, and other types of fixed lexical combinations, such as restricted collocations, figurative idioms and pure idioms, are not common. In the sample, there are 421 illustrative examples, but only seventy-eight relatively fixed collocations or idioms can be found in the examples (see Table 2). And in the entry *dreadful*, all the lexical combinations shown in the examples are free ones.

Table 2 Fixed collocations and idioms in the sample examples in the Big Five

	OALD6	LDOCE4	COBUILD4	CALD2	MED1
The rest is <u>history</u>.			√		√
<u>History</u> repeated itself.	√				
go down in <u>history</u>		√	√		√
to <u>save</u> his own skin	√	√			
<u>save</u> up	√	√	√	√	√
<u>save</u> (up) for	√	√	√	√	√
<u>save</u> sb./sth. from sth.	√	√	√	√	√
<u>save</u> on (fares/costs/ preparation time/electricity, etc.)	√	√	√	√	√
<u>available</u> for comment (hire/ sale)	√	√	√	√	√
in one's <u>glory</u>/in the glory of	√	√	√	√	√
in a blaze of <u>glory</u>		√	√	√	
crowning <u>glory</u>	√	√		√	√
reflected <u>glory</u>				√	√
one's moment of <u>glory</u>	√	√	√		
bath/bask in the <u>glory</u> of			√	√	√
<u>cure</u> sb. of sth.	√	√	√	√	√
<u>superiority</u> over		√		√	
air (of) <u>superiority</u>	√	√	√	√	√
<u>rally</u> behind	√			√	√
<u>rally</u> round/around	√	√		√	√
<u>rally</u> to his support/defense/ assistance	√	√	√	√	√
first and <u>foremost</u>			√		

Secondly, as indicated in Table 3, the lexical collocations in the sample (185 in total) outnumber the grammatical collocations (39). In other words, examples in English learners' dictionaries frequently illustrate lexical collocations rather than grammatical ones.

Table 3 Frequencies of lexical and grammatical collocations in the sample examples in the Big Five

entry words	freq. of lexical collocations	freq. of grammatical collocations	total
history	47	5	52
save	38	11	49
available	32	5	37
glory	23	3	26
cure	9	1	10
dreadful	17	0	17
superiority	4	3	7
rally	9	9	18
foremost	6	2	8
Total	185	39	224

Thirdly, Table 3 shows that the number of collocations in illustrative example varies according to the frequency of an entry word. The result of one-way ANOVA test ($F(2, 6) = 18.915, p < .05$) confirms the observation. The reason might be that a high-frequency word is often a heavy-duty word, and hence is more likely to collocate with other words.

Fourthly, although Table 3 seems to indicate that the exemplification rate of collocations is higher with the sample noun entries (85 collocations in total) than with the verb entries (77) and with the adjective ones (62), the parts-of-speech have a weak correlation with the occurrences of collocations in the illustrative examples ($F(2, 6) = .118, p .05$).

Lastly, the number of identical collocations exemplified in each of the Big Five is not high. Of the 421 sample illustrative examples, only forty-seven collocations occur in over three dictionaries.

In comparison with the sample data of BBI2 and OCDSE1 (the two specialized combinatory dictionaries), the Big Five fail to list sixty-three collocations (see Table 4). Furthermore, it was found that the following eight collocations, which the Big Five do not list, enter both combinatory dictionaries: *military glory, win glory, bring glory to, achieve superiority, enjoy superiority, clear superiority, numerical superiority* and *(so-called) racial superiority*. One wonders whether the above collocations have a high frequency in the BNC. If the case is true, the Big Five should be criticized for failing to exemplify some frequent collocations. If not, one can argue that only specialized combinatory dictionaries have space to exemplify such collocations.

The Word Sketch Engine was utilized to concordance the collocations in the BNC. The results are shown in the last column in Table 4. The slash ('/') indicates that the salience of a collocation is unavailable because of its low frequency in the BNC.

As Table 4 indicates, in terms of salience, twenty (31.75%) of the sixty

Representation of word combinations 187

collocations which the Big Five do not exemplify are insignificant; twenty-six (41.27%) collocations' salience are lower than eight; and only seventeen (26.98%) are higher than eight. To put it another way, the sample examples in the Big Five fail to illustrate merely 26.98% of frequent collocations.

With regard to the eight collocations that are listed in the two combinatory dictionaries, only two highly-salient collocations (i.e. *numerical superiority* and (*so-called*) *racial superiority*) are not exemplified in the Big Five.

To recapitulate, although they have a smaller coverage of word combinations than the specialized combinatory dictionaries, the Big Five include most of the highly frequent collocations in their illustrative examples.

Table 4 Collocations listed in BBI2 and in OCDSE1 but not in the sample examples in the Big Five

	BBI2	OCDSE1	Salience in the BNC
a piece of history		√	/
pass into history		√	9.5
go back to history		√	/
during sth's history		√	/
a period of history		√	11.7
a slice of history		√	/
previous/subsequent history		√	/
employment/sexual history		√	/
a battle/bid to save sth		√	(battle) 10.7, (bid) 8.6
sound dreadful		√	1.9
taste dreadful		√	/
really, quite, truly/pretty, rather dreadful		√	(really) 3.0, (quite) 2.9, (truly) 5.6, (pretty) 6.2, (rather) 1.9
full glory		√	6.7
military glory	√	√	/
bring sth. with glory		√	4.7
achieve glory	√		/
win glory	√	√	/
bring glory to	√	√	4.7
personal glory		√	4.4
for the glory of		√	0.5
completely	miraculously cure		√	(completely) /, (miraculously) 9.2
achieve superiority	√	√	2.6
enjoy superiority	√	√	/
hold superiority	√		/
clear superiority	√	√	/
numerical superiority	√	√	14.8

	BBI2	OCDSE1	Salience in the BNC
(so-called) racial superiority	√	√	14.6
absolute, complete, overwhelming, total | effortless superiority		√	(absolute) 5.2, (complete)/, (total)/, (overwhelming) 6.7, (effortless) 9.8
inherent, innate, intrinsic, natural superiority		√	(inherent) 7.3, (innate) 12.4, (intrinsic) 5.8, (natural) /
academic, biological, cultural, moral, physical, social, technical, technological superiority		√	(academic) /, (biological) 7.2, (cultural) 8.0, (moral) 9.7, (physical) 3.7, (technical) 7.5, (technological) 12.1,
military superiority		√	7.1
confirm, convince sb of, prove, show, underline | maintain | assert, assume, claim, imply superiority		√	(confirm) 8.1, (convince) 5.1, (prove) 5.1, (show) 4.3, (underlie)/, (maintain) 3.8, (assert) 13.4, (assume) 2.2, (claim) 3.3, (imply) 9.3
acknowledge, bow to superiority		√	(acknowledge) 8.4, (bow to) /
rally troops		√	14.6

Do the collocations exemplified in the Big Five have a high frequency in the BNC as well? The concordance results indicate that about 70% of those collocations are salient in the BNC, and that only 30% of the collocations have salience lower than one. The results agree with the expectation that most of the collocations exemplified in the Big Five should have a high frequency in natural discourse.

Let us turn our attention to the word combinations represented in illustrative examples in NECD3 — an English dictionary specifically designed for Chinese speakers. The dictionary encompasses some word combinations that none of the five English learners' dictionaries have included (see Table 5). Do these combinations have a high frequency in natural discourse? The results listed in Table 5 indicate that except the first two combinations, all are statistically insignificant. To put it another way, NECD3 wastes its space by exemplifying quite a number of low-frequency word combinations.

Table 5 Word combinations listed in the sample examples in NECD3 but not in the Big Five

Word combinations not listed in the Big Five but in NECD3	Salience in the BNC
a case history	20.0
oral history	10.4
unprecedented in history	/
save one's eyes	/
save the post	/
save the game	/

available means	/
available candidate	/
available nitrogen/water	/
dreadful scene	/
dreadful disrepair	/
rally one's courage	/
rally one's energy	/

Learners' dictionaries are supposed to meet the needs of a specific group of dictionary users. One may wonder whether the Big Five and NECD3 have solved some particular collocational problems that Chinese EFL learners have encountered. Before addressing this issue, let us consider which word combinations are overused by Chinese learners and which are underused. Table 6 lists the CLEC-based concordance results.

Table 6 Overused and underused word combinations in CLEC

	Overused word combinations (freq.)	Underused word combinations (freq.)
history	~ of (73); [as a course] maths, etc., ~ (24); in ~ (19)	[modified by adj.] natural/chequered/social ~ (0); [modified by n.] case/art ~ (0); trace/rewrite/write ~ (0)
save	~ (the/much/fresh) water (127); ~ dying patients (7)	~ on cost/bill (0); ~ soul/marriage/forest (0); ~ from death/extinction/closure, etc. (0); God ~ (0)
available	~ water (3); ~war (2); ~ way (1)	[modified by adv.] readily/currently/widely/freely ~ (0); be made ~ (0); sb. ~ (0)
glory	one night's ~ (1)	~ of God/lord (0); moment/blaze of ~ (0); crowning ~ (0)
cure	~ environment (1)	~ sb. of (1); [modified by adv.] completely/miraculously ~ (0)
dreadful	[as modifier] ~ world (1) / strain (1) / reputation (1) / bouncing (1); how ~ (2)	~ mistake/thing/thought (0); absolutely ~ (0); look ~ (0)
superiority	man's ~ (3); great ~ of (1); sense of ~ (1); concepts of ~(1)	air ~(0); demonstrate ~ (0); belief in ~ (0); numerical/racial/innate, etc. assumption of ~ (0)
rally	/	~ support/troops (0); ~round (0); supporters ~(0)
foremost	first and ~ (3)	[as modifier] ~ scholar/exponent, etc. (0); ~amongst (0); ~ in mind (0)

Evidently, in using word combinations, Chinese EFL learners encountered at least three problems. Firstly, they often used some unacceptable expressions. Expressions as *available war, *one night's glory and *dreadful reputation would sound odd to a native speaker. The freely-constructed combinations might have resulted from the negative transfer of learners' mother tongue (i.e. Chinese). Secondly, Chinese learners of English were often not aware of the range of combinations that an entry word could occur in. For instance, when the word *history* refers to a course or when it occurs in such constructions as *in history* and *history of*, the students were familiar with the usage of the word combinations. But it was beyond their knowledge that the word history could collocate with some relatively formal words, such as *chequered* and *trace*. Thirdly, in comparison with the native speakers' writing, Chinese learners' compositions covered a far smaller number of recurrent collocations. Many idiomatic combinations had not entered their productive vocabulary. Therefore, as far as the exemplification of collocations is concerned, a dictionary for Chinese EFL learners should take into account these specific needs.

It has to be admitted that in terms of the exemplification of word combinations, the Big Five outperform NECD3. As mentioned above, most combinations listed in the illustrative examples in the Big Five are those that frequently occur in natural discourse, whereas a large number of the combinations included in the examples in NECD3 are untypical ones. Moreover, while NECD3 often includes phrasal examples and presents them ineptly, the Big Five use sentence examples and adopt some effective techniques, such as bold type and gloss, to highlight collocations.

However, none of the six dictionaries has worked out a satisfactory solution to remind users of their errors in collocation. Such kinds of cues are especially helpful for learners who are unaware of their errors, or who are unable to retrieve the information from illustrative examples.

5. Discussion

The frequent use of free and semi-fixed collocations instead of figurative or pure idioms in dictionary examples can be attributed to (a) the space constraints, (b) the dictionary format, and (c) the frequency of collocations in natural discourse. A figurative or pure idiom is always opaque and needs quite a lot of space to illuminate its meaning, and an illustrative example cannot afford such space. In addition, a learners' dictionary normally has, at the end of an entry, a section for phrases and idioms. Last but not least, in natural discourse, collocations occur more frequently than idioms (Cowie, 1998: 10). Therefore, figurative and pure idioms should be cautiously used in illustrative examples in learners' dictionaries.

In the Big Five, the exemplification rate of lexical collocations is usually higher than that of grammatical ones. This practice, however, can be challenged. EFL learners are often found to be unclear about the usage of a particle. They often wrongly use or mistakenly omit a particle in an expression. Thus, more attention should be paid to grammatical collocations. Their usage should be exemplified in a learners' dictionary. To correspond with users' regular look-up habit, such a grammatical collocation can be exemplified under a content word, viz. a main constituent of that collocation.

It is unlikely for a learners' dictionary to treat collocations as lengthily as a combinatory dictionary. But pedagogical lexicographers must ensure that highly-salient collocations are sufficiently represented in illustrative examples in a learners' dictionary.

In addition, collocations that a target group of English learners have a vague idea about should be exemplified. Such informative examples will supply learners with a model for imitation. But how do EFL lexicographers know which collocations are problematic to users? One possible solution is to compare a learner corpus with a corpus of native speakers, single out the overused and underused word combinations, and employ effective techniques to exemplify the problematic combinations. This kind of corpus-based comparison always helps lexicographers to specify the collocational errors committed by a particular group of learners.

Based on the above discussion, two principles concerning the exemplification of collocations in English learners' dictionaries can be formulated: *the Principle of Frequency* and *the Principle of User-friendliness*.

The first principle requires that combinations included in an illustrative example should have a high frequency in discourse. The availability of large and balanced corpora and efficient concordance tools will facilitate the selection of those recurrent word combinations. Another category of word combinations which deserves lexicographers' special attention is those that often cause problems to learners. The collocational errors committed by learners will transmit a clear message to lexicographers: the correct usage of problematic collocations should be exemplified.

In order to attract users' attention to some typical collocations, corresponding examples should be user-friendly and effectively presented. Such effective techniques as gloss, rubric and example of incorrect usage can be considered.

6. Conclusion

This chapter surveys the types of word combinations represented in illustrative examples in English learners' dictionaries. It was found that free and semi-fixed collocations are more often exemplified, and that lexical collocations predominate over grammatical ones in illustrative examples. Two principles governing the exemplification of collocations were then proposed: the Principle of Frequency and the Principle of User-friendliness.

Acknowledgement

This research was supported by the MOE Project (Project No. 06JJD740007) of Key Research Institute of Humanities and Social Sciences at Universities in P.R. China.

Not quite first language, not quite second language either: Dictionary entries for learners caught in between

Peter K.W. Tan
National University of Singapore
petertan@nus.edu.sg

1. Introduction

The genre of the monolingual learners' dictionary (MLD) has now become firmly established, and has moved apace since the pioneering days around the Second World War years when three expatriate Englishmen tried their hand in lexicology (Cowie 1999; Jackson 2002). Michael West, most well known for his work on vocabulary control was working in India and published the first MLD (with J. G. Endicott), *The New Method English Dictionary* in 1935. Harold Palmer and Albert Sydney Hornby, based in Japan, published *Thousand word English* two years later. *The Idiomatic and Syntactic Dictionary* by Hornby and his collaborators appeared in Japan during the Second World War and was subsequently republished by Oxford University Press as *A Learner's Dictionary of Current English* (1952). The format initiated by West, Palmer and Hornby is essentially the one found the modern MLDs such as *The Cambridge International Dictionary of English* (CIDE), *The Oxford Advanced Learners' Dictionary* (OALD), *The Longman Dictionary of Contemporary English* (LDCE) and *The Collins COBUILD English Dictionary* (CED).

In all, we see the common concern to limit the defining vocabulary; to show and exemplify grammar patterns; and to indicate collocations and idioms. A feature associated with modern MLDs is their basis on real texts based on various corpora; this would clearly affect the examples that are presented. Corpora would also be able to establish which uses are dominant and point towards which entries need expansion and which need curtailing. Another innovation is the bundling with electronic versions of the dictionaries in the form of CD-ROMs. The way the definitions are presented may be updated, and the coding of grammatical information might also be changed. Individual dictionaries might include features, such as the inclusion of boxes on 'false friends' or *faux amis* in CIDE, or graphs showing written and spoken frequency contrasts in LDCE. Through all of this, though, the structure of the entry remains the one established by West, Palmer and Hornby.

They therefore essentially laid the groundwork for MLDs to come and have come to be recognized as a sub-genre to be distinguished from the dictionaries that arose out of the Samuel Johnson tradition which has a strong literary emphasis. Osselton notes that 'One third of all Johnson's quotations come from just four writers: Shakespeare (15%), Dryden (11%), Milton (5%) and Addison (5%)' (1983: 19). The *Oxford English Dictionary* can trace its genealogical line back to Johnson's *Dictionary of the English Language* (1755). Across the Atlantic, the tradition is traced back to Webster (or Merriam-Webster), but this is closely allied to the Johnsonian tradition except for the inclusion of encyclopaedic entries. So it is that there is now an assumed division of labour between MLDs and traditional dictionaries. Secondary and tertiary students for whom English is a first language or native language might be recommended a version of a traditional dictionary whereas those for whom it is a foreign language are recommended a MLD or a bilingual dictionary. The situation becomes problematic when English is neither a straightforward 'native language' or a 'foreign language' to the person:

> Indeed, the best dictionary is undoubtedly a human dictionary, in the form of an encouraging and knowledgeable parent, teacher, or colleague. The reason for this is that a good human dictionary instinctively assess the situation and tailors the information to the knowledge and needs of the enquirer. (Hulstijn and Atkins 1998: 11)

In the absence of this encouraging and knowledgeable person, we need to rely on the next best thing: a good dictionary. This is the reason that it matters, and this chapter suggests that the users cannot always be easily categorized and that categories of dictionaries could also usefully undergo some blending (or 'hybridization', to use a more current term). For this purpose then, I will focus especially on the Singaporean educational context and the Singaporean learner and user and emphasize the features that will be relevant to the notion of a desirable dictionary for this Singaporean learner.

2. Divergent needs

Among the more recent developments in research in lexicography is to desire to get information about how real dictionary-users in various contexts make use of dictionaries. Crystal, the well-known British linguist, has, in his ideal world, a 'proposal for an experimental dimension to lexicography, within the tradition of applied psycholinguistic studies of performance' (Crystal 2003: 326). The current emphasis of focusing on the actual behaviour of dictionary users is also confirmed by Hulstijn and Atkins:

> Until now, empirical research on dictionary use has been rather haphazard. What is needed is a systematic study of the way in which various variables interact when dictionary users consult a dictionary which contains complex information. (Hulstijn and Atkins 1998: 16)

It is therefore taken for granted that the kinds of use to which a person puts the dictionary will depend very much on factors such as the task that has to

be accomplished (is it a task that requires vocabulary production or is it to do with processing a text?) and the level of linguistic competence of the user. The relevant questions to ask are therefore:
- What is the level of the user's English competence?
- What is the nature of the user's variety of English?
- What kinds of tasks does the user need to employ the dictionary for?

I mention this not because this chapter will focus on the actual behaviour of dictionary users but because I want to emphasize the importance of having dictionaries relevant and targeted at particular users. My particular focus is to illustrate how what we already know about the context and needs of a particular group of users must make us reconsider the form of a dictionary aimed at this group. I also suggest that it is possible to answer those three questions by referring to what we already know about the dictionary users. I will consider in particular users of dictionaries of English in Singapore because this illustrates some of their difficulties when using existing dictionaries which make clear distinctions between 'traditional' dictionaries and MLDs. I will answer the first question by referring to the position of English in the Singaporean context, the second question by referring to a feature of Singaporean English that has not always received prominence, and the third by referring to the educational context in Singapore.

3. What is the level of the user's English competence?

The main traditional categorization has been along the lines of whether English is a Native Language (ENL), or a Second Language (ESL) or Foreign Language (EFL). McArthur (1998) traces this tripartite model back to a description in 1970 by Barbara Strang, Professor of English Language and General Linguistics at the University of Newcastle upon Tyne. This basic distinction was maintained by the key figures in English-language studies at the time: Randolph Quirk and Sidney Greenbaum (both of University College, London), Geoffrey Leech (University of Lancaster) and Jan Svartvik (University of Lund) who went on to publish the 1,779-page *Comprehensive grammar of the English language*. It is no wonder that this categorization is frequently used and remains influential. A subsequent influential model is Braj Kachru's three-circle model of World Englishes – consisting of the 'Inner Circle', the 'Outer Circle' and the 'Expanding Circle'. The model is regional in orientation and assigns countries into the three circles. What is perhaps more significant is that the three categories map themselves fairly neatly into the traditional categories, so that some might contend that the change was largely in nomenclature. Other labels also map themselves neatly into those categories: 'Older Varieties' (Inner Circle), 'New Varieties' or 'New Englishes' (both Outer Circle).

Although the tripartite distinction is not perfect and fails to make distinctions within the national communities, it is interesting that in the world of monolingual lexicography, there are only two categories: the traditional one for the Inner Circle, and MLDs for the Expanding Circle – and presumably also the Outer Circle. Despite the publication of dictionaries such as the second edition of *Times-Chambers Essential English Dictionary* (1997), adapted from an MLD which incorporates Singaporeanisms and Malaysianisms, dictionaries that incorporate the New Englishes in a sustained, rather than cursory, fashion are still few and far between.

In today's postmodern world, the language-country mapping is not clear cut, if it ever was. Schneider (2007), for instance, when discussing postcolonial Englishes, makes an internal distinction between the settler strand and the indigenous strand within each nation. The settler strand refers to the English variety that was passed down naturally from generation to generation even as the community settles in a new place, whereas the indigenous strand refers to the English variety acquired by the local population whose forebears did not have English as part of their repertoire of languages. He suggests that through different phases, these strands can begin to homogenize and that further internal distinctions can develop.

In the Singaporean context, the focus of this chapter, the settler strand is minuscule in contrast to the situation in Australia or even South Africa. I will use Schneider's label 'indigenous strand' to include the settlers from non-English-speaking backgrounds, and will include the Chinese, Malay and Indian communities in the way they are commonly identified by the government. If we were to use 'indigenous' more strictly, we would only be able to include the Malay communities, as this was the only community inhabiting the island in the early 19th century:

> In 1811 a band of about one hundred Malays from Johor, led by the Temenggong who was an officer of the Sultan of Johor, migrated southwards and settled on the bank of the Singapore River. At that time, however, the country was already populated by a small group of natives, known as orang laut, or sea gypsies, who were fishermen and pirates, living exclusively in their boats along the small rivers. (Saw 1999: 7-8)

(The 'natives' have since been assimilated into the Malay community.) The population is regularly classified into the four categories: Chinese, Malay, Indian and Others.

If we fast-forward the clock to the year 2004, we encounter a situation where all state schools teach in the medium of English, a Bilingual Policy is in place which requires ethnic Chinese pupils to learn Mandarin Chinese, ethnic Malay pupils to learn Malay and ethnic Indian pupils to learn Tamil (or a range of other Indian languages); but the system is being tweaked because of the changing home language profile of Year 1 (P1 or 'Primary One') pupils entering primary school. In the speech given by Tharman Shanmugaratnam, the Acting Minister of Education: 'Today, English is the language most frequently spoken at home by half of our Chinese pupils in Primary One' (Ministry of Education, Singapore 2004a). Although the speech was delivered by the Minister, it is likely to have been drafted by officials in the Ministry of

Education. A footnote provided in the written copy of the speech also adds:
> Preliminary figures show that about 49.8% of P1 students in 2004 come from homes where English is the dominant language used by the pupils, marginally higher than Chinese (48.5%). 15 years ago, English was the dominant home language for 23.5% of P1 pupils, one third of the number using Chinese (69.2%). (Ministry of Education, Singapore 2004a)

In another speech by the same Minister, delivered later that year, he gives further figures about the Malay and Indian population. (We might note that EL refers to the English language; CL to Mandarin Chinese; ML to the Malay language and TL to the Tamil language.):
> This year, 58% of our Indian Primary 1 students came from homes that spoke predominantly EL. The initial feedback from Tamil parents suggests that the issues facing TL students are fundamentally not different from those encountered in learning CL. For ML students, the issues are less severe. The ML shares the same script as EL. The majority of Malay students entering Primary 1 still use ML as their dominant home language, with just 22% using EL. (Ministry of Education, Singapore 2004b)

The Department of Statistics informs us that:
> In 2007, the Chinese formed 75 per cent of the resident population. The Malays and Indians accounted for 14 per cent and 9 per cent respectively. (Singapore Department of Statistics 2007: 4)

Therefore, the Chinese, Malays and Indians account for 98% of the population; and if we put together these figures and those from the Ministry of Education, we could say that of the children starting school, at least 45.7% come from English-dominant homes. (The figure was obtained by totalling the figures in bold here: Chinese: 75% x 49.8% = 37.4%; Malays: 14% x 22% = 3.1%; Indians 9 x 58% = 5.2%. I also say 'at least' because the 2% beyond the Chinese, Malay and Indian population is left unaccounted for. With the passing of the Compulsory Education Act in 2000, education is compulsory up to the age of 15 and practically every child of the appropriate age will have been enrolled to start primary school.)

Of course, this does not tell us what *kind* of English is being spoken at home, although Gupta's (1994) *The Step-Tongue* suggests that for some this would be the informal variety of English in Singapore known as Singlish (in the book, Gupta called it SCE or Singapore Colloquial English). Regardless of the variety of English used, if it is the dominant language at home, English can certainly be seen as a native or first language in Singapore. And if it is going to be used by a significant proportion of the new generation (45.7% is by all accounts a significant figure), it is also a significant native or first language in Singapore.

However, we will still need to remember the other 52.3% (from our 98% of the population) – again this is a significant figure by all accounts – whose dominant home language is a non-English language (Chinese varieties, Malay, Tamil, etc.) who would acquire English as a second language. The 'native language' could be a range of different languages, so that there is potential for different acquisition varieties. Indeed, there has been research on ethnic differences in the English in Singapore (Deterding and Poejosoedarmo 2000; Lim 2000), and we can assume that ethnicity correlates with particular native languages.

All of this makes the status of English among Singaporean pupils unclear. For a significant number, it is a native language; for others, it is a second language. This clearly problematizes the tripartite categorization that slots Singaporean English as ESL or into the Outer Circle. If this is the case, what then is the appropriate kind of English dictionary for Singapore? I will return to this question later.

4. What is the nature of the user's variety of English?

There has been extensive treatment of the features of Singaporean English, and I need not rehearse them all here. There are obviously particularities of vocabulary, grammatical constructions especially for the colloquial variety or Singlish (Low and Brown (2005) and Brown (1999) include many of these in their volumes). Instead I will focus on *one* particular aspect of English that would bear a direct relevance to the kind of dictionary that might be useful for learners and which has not always received much attention.

The multilingual nature of Singaporean society can be easily deduced from the section above, and it is this multilingual nature that makes users of Singaporean English very conscious of lexical items that are or might be derived from languages of the region. This has led to some loan-words to be re-etymologized. For example, some words that are derived from Arabic are re-etymologized as being derived from Malay. Therefore, a word like *sharia* has been internationalized and is used in English-language newspapers worldwide and can be found in English-language dictionaries. For example, a headline in *The Telegraph* on 4 July 2008 asks: 'Does Britain have space for Sharia?'

In Singapore, though, this word is treated as if it is only a Malay loan-word and is given a Malay-style pronunciation /"Sarja(h)/ and spelt as in Standard Malay *syariah*. (See, for example, the Syariah Court website. In Malay, the <sy> digraph represents the /S/ phoneme.) The Malay word is obviously derived from Arabic, but has undergone naturalization or assimilation and is written and spelt in a Malay fashion. Other examples include *Aidil Fitri* and *Aidil Adha* in Singaporean English (as opposed to *Eid ul Fitr* and *Eid ul Adha*). The terms *sharia*, *Eid ul Fitr* and *Eid ul Adha* are used, for example, in the BBC Religion and Ethics website.

Other words derived from Malay that have undergone naturalization and assimilation in English are also given a more Malay form (in terms of pronunciation and spelling according to Standard Malay). Examples include *amok*, *batik*, *kampong*, *orang-utan* and *sarong*. The pronunciation is Malay style (therefore /"sarON/ rather than /s@"rQN/; and /"oraN "utan/ rather than /@r&N@"t&N/), and spelling as in Standard Malay can be used (therefore

Not quite first language, not quite second language either 199

kampung or *sarung* instead of *kampong* and *sarong*), and naturalized variants (such as *amuck*) avoided.

Similarly, items derived from Chinese varieties might be re-etymologized as being derived from Mandarin Chinese (the official variety of Chinese in Singapore) rather than other Chinese varieties such as Hokkien (Southern Min) Chinese or Cantonese Chinese. Items that have been strongly established in international varieties of English tend to escape this: examples include *tea* and *ketchup* (both derived from Hokkien) or *wok* (derived from Cantonese) – the Mandarin Chinese versions of those are *cha*, *qiezhi* and *guo* respectively and are not used in English. (These are the forms in the official Mandarin Romanization or *hanyu pinyin*.) However, *char siu/char siew*, *dim sum* and *kung fu* (all from Cantonese) can become *chashao*, *dianxin* and *gongfu* respectively. This has been noted by Lim in a comparison of Singaporean and Malaysian newspaper corpora. He notes:

> SE [Singaporean English] loanwords from Chinese are quite commonly pinyinized whereas in ME [Malaysian English] they retain their traditional forms in the so-called dialects like Hokkien, Cantonese, etc. Words like dianxin, guotiao, gongfu and hongbao are invariably dimsum, kway teow, kungfu, and angpow respectively in ME. (Lim 2001: 134)

In such a context, the dictionary user might be best served by having appropriate information about these variant forms in a dictionary.

5. What kind of tasks does the user need to employ the dictionary for?

Part of the answer to the question can be extrapolated from the earlier discussion about the status and competence of Singaporean users. Obviously, the kind of dictionary that is the best is one that addresses the needs of the users, to take them from where they are to a higher level of competence. This question can also be answered by considering the educational context, and specifically the kind of English required for the school context – the immediate aim of the pupil is to be successful in the school context before he or she joins the workforce.

Learners are now increasingly being required not only to be effective users of language but to have some knowledge of the language – to know something about the history of the language and to analyse its use as well.

At the time of writing, the English Language curriculum is undergoing revision, with a new curriculum being developed for A levels (Advanced Level of the General Certificate of Education, used for university entry), available for pupils entering Year 11 (first year of junior college) in early 2009. Information garnered from press statements include the following:

> 'It is going to focus on language, linguistics and the use of language in different contexts, whether social or professional,' he [Lui Tuck Yew, Minister of State for Education] said. How the English language has changed over time will also be examined. (Ho 2007)

This suggests that at least some of the curriculum might be moving in the direction

of the English curriculum in England, Wales and Northern Ireland:
> At key stage 4 (for pupils aged 14 to 16), the programme of study calls for pupils to be taught about how language varies, including ... the **vocabulary and grammar** of standard English and dialectal variation; the **development of English**, including changes over time, borrowings from other languages, origins of words, and the impact of electronic communication on written language. (National Curriculum Online: English, key stage 4; emphasis original)

Knowledge about the language should also inform on language use. Indeed, Adamson (1989) suggests that the Romance-Germanic split in the English lexicon is something that could be usefully appreciated by students who need to manage registers that emphasize the formal and the intimate levels, the ideational and expressive functions of language. The Romance-Germanic split of course refers to how a very high proportion of vocabulary can be classified as having its origin in Romance languages (principally French and Latin) or in Germanic languages (principally Anglo-Saxon or Old English). Adamson quotes *Troilus and Cressida*: Cressida rather loftily ends her soliloquy on the problems of sexual fidelity with a couplet:

> O then *conclude*
> Minds sway'd by eyes are full of *turpitude*.
> (5.ii.111-112; author's emphasis)

The formality is emphasized by the choice of words (italicized above) with a Latin source. On hearing this, Thersites, the deformed and scurrilous Greek, translates this to more Germanic expressions:

> ... she could not publish more
> Unless she said, '*My mind is now turned whore.*'
> (5.ii.113-114; author's emphasis)

The vocabulary choice at once emphasizes the difference in status between the characters. Perhaps uniquely for English, therefore, is the fact that lexical source is correlated with the connotative texture of the item. Other Romance-Germanic pairings include *ascend* v. *go up* or *climb*, *extinguish* v. *put out*, *convivial* v. *jolly*, *sumptuous* v. *tasty*.

The source of the lexical items could therefore be seen to be significant not only from the point of view of a diachronic account of the English language but also signal particular connotative associations of particular lexical items through generations of use. English, perhaps more so than other languages, has elements of its linguistic history inscribed into its vocabulary.

6. Conclusion

To summarize the concerns raised in the previous sections, we could therefore say that in the context of Singapore, and in particular in the context of the needs of secondary school learners, the English dictionary, if it is a monolingual one, should:

1. contain grammatical information such as the plural and inflected forms of

words or the clause structure (because of its mixed status as both first and second language);
2. acknowledge features of Singaporean English, including vocabulary items or constructions particular to the variety or to the region (because the Singaporean learner has to be sensitized to variation and be made aware that Singaporean features are appropriate in some contexts and inappropriate in others); and
3. provide some information about etymology (because a maturity in the handling of the English language includes some sense of its origins, which in turn leads to a more sophisticated use of the language; and also because of the re-etymologizing tendencies in Singaporean English).

The first feature is an acknowledged strength of MLDs. The second feature is not found in most dictionaries (for reasons that are not surprising, considering the size of the Singapore market in the context of international sales of dictionaries), although it is beginning to appear (the second edition of *Times-Chambers, TCEED2*, and, in a minimal and cursory way, in some newer dictionaries by Oxford and Macquarie). The third feature is an acknowledged strength of the traditional historical dictionaries by Oxford and others inheriting that tradition. What would be welcomed, therefore, is a dictionary that could combine the strengths of MLDs and historical-literary dictionaries whilst incorporating features of Singaporean English. Obviously, one solution is to have one dictionary for each of these foci; given that learners are generally reluctant to do that, the best solution might be to have a blended dictionary that might indeed be seen as being the most appropriate for speakers of the New Englishes. Any takers then to compile such a dictionary?

Interlingual lexicography, with special reference to research priorities

R.R.K. Hartmann
r.r.k.hartmann@exeter.ac.uk

1. Introduction

My aim is to survey several important current issues in interlingual lexicography, in order to see what has been done and how much more needs to be done until we have a more complete understanding of what is involved, in terms of the six main perspectives of metalexicography. Questions will be asked about what the implications are for dictionary research.

2. On the status of interlingual lexicography

I define 'interlingual lexicography' as "a complex of activities concerned with the design, compilation, use and evaluation of interlingual dictionaries"; the 'interlingual dictionary' is in turn defined (in the DoL 1998/2001: 75) as "(a) type of reference work with information on more than one language". It is a term particularly needed either "when the contrast with 'monolingual dictionary' is stressed or when the distinction between 'bilingual dictionary' and 'multilingual dictionary' is considered irrelevant ...".

In the last two decades, we have all experienced the rapid rise of our specialization in an ever-widening range of topics and dimensions. These include, above all, the status of our field as a professional activity, and what this involves in terms of compilation activities along several stages (from recording or data-collection via editing or description to publishing or presentation). However, when we think of the prototypical lexicographer working on the prototypical dictionary, it tends to be the famous Johnson, Webster, Grimm and Littré associated with the monolingual general or historical dictionary rather than the anonymous band of dictionary makers working on a bilingual or multilingual project that few have written or even heard about.

Closely linked with professional approaches is the academic status of the discipline we recognize lexicography as being. Is it a scholarly activity that forms part of the university syllabus, together perhaps with such subjects as linguistics or education (linked to problems of multilingualism, language planning, language standardization, literacy, etc.), or is it a minority field struggling (like translation studies, terminology studies and the like) to establish itself in higher education?

For this interdisciplinary field of (meta-)lexicography, there are now many more textbooks available than ever before, although interlingual aspects are often ignored in them. We also do not know much about where and how lexicography is taught, how it relates to practical training provided by publishers, and how the development of national and international associations (and the meetings sponsored by them) has helped to consolidate it.

For monolingual lexicography, all this has been difficult enough to strive for (and sometimes to achieve), but for interlingual lexicography, which involves two or more languages, there are almost insurmountable hurdles. For a start, dealing with language pairs is bound to be harder than with single languages. Interlingual activities are also more intricate, involving degrees of bilingualism, language acquisition and translation (and consequently requiring more intercultural and interdisciplinary collaboration).

It is not surprising, then, that fewer experts have dedicated themselves to the task, less research has been done, and less literature is available on these topics. Although (paradoxically) foreign language learners are often observed to prefer bilingual to monolingual dictionaries, less attention has been given to, and much less is known about, their purpose, their design and their consultation. The result may well be the relatively low status that seems to be attached to interlingual dictionary-making, and even prejudices against it, as demonstrated by Piotrowski's (1989: 72) sarcastic comment, in an anthology published in Singapore, on the opinions of two eminent British linguists implying that students should be 'weaned away' from bilingual dictionaries, as they tend to 'perpetuate translation' and prevent 'free creative expression' in the target language. An additional problem is lack of familiarity with the literature in languages other than the scholars' own, with the regrettable result that, as Zgusta (1984: 275) has pointed out, "... lexicography still is largely compartmentalized by languages and that the flow of information from one centre of work to another is not yet what would be desirable."

The rest of this chapter will explore how progress can be and has been achieved by various means.

3. Research perspectives

Wherever lexicography has managed to become established, and whenever it has developed elements of self-reflection, sets of principles and codes of practice, we now speak of 'metalexicography' or 'dictionary research', for which about half a dozen 'perspectives' have been distinguished in the literature, notably dictionary history, dictionary criticism, dictionary typology, dictionary structure, dictionary use, and dictionary IT (Hartmann 2001, 2003). However, it must be admitted that most of the time these tend to focus on the traditions and practices of unilingual rather than interlingual lexicography. And, unfortunately, we do not know enough about whether and how these developments differ by language, country, and culture, as there are practically no comparative studies available; one exception is the paper by

Huang (1994), a contrastive account of what distinguishes metalexicography in China from that in the West. However, the last few years have seen improvements, in terms of conferences, research dissertations and textbooks devoted to interlingual issues.

I cannot devote equal amounts of attention to each of the six perspectives that can bring innovation. In the first, **dictionary history**, there is no general pattern for the treatment of dictionary traditions across language pairs. What several of the relevant authors share is their emphasis on 'plagiarism' (Hayakawa 2001). In some of these historical studies, the claim is made that the bilingual dictionary preceded the monolingual one. Certainly there has been a point of view, although it has been challenged, that this was the case for many languages of Europe at the time when they broke free from the domination of Latin.

What points can we generalize from some of the tendencies that have been diagnosed? Most studies have concentrated on the 'general' bilingual dictionary (which usually comes in two separate parts, although I know of one or two dictionaries that have combined the two parts into a single alphabetic sequence). Other interlingual genres are occasionally mentioned, such as the special-purpose or technical bilingual dictionary, the bilingual dictionary of idiomatic phrases, and the bilingual pronouncing dictionary. Directionality must also be an important consideration, depending on the status of the languages in question and the needs of the potential users. Thus, the beginning of a tradition is typically dominated by the major language (such as Latin in medieval Europe, and English today in most parts of the world), so bilingual dictionaries are designed initially and predominantly for reception and interpretation (reading, or decoding, or 'version' in French), while later on the productive uses become more important (writing, or encoding, or 'thème' in French). The overriding impression is that there are enormous divergences between the lexicographic traditions of various language pairs, such as English-French vs. English-German, or English-Chinese vs. English-Japanese.

To turn to the second perspective, **dictionary criticism**, we note that although there is a relatively long tradition, and several different approaches can be distinguished, the problem is that no-one knows for sure exactly how good (i.e. positive as well as negative) dictionary criticism should be carried out, least of all for interlingual dictionaries. Several criteria or sets of standards for evaluating and assessing dictionaries have been proposed, but only rarely are they applied to interlingual dictionaries. The comparative approach pioneered by Heuberger (2000) for the critical analysis of monolingual English-language dictionaries – five printed and four electronic, such as the OALD, with many editions since 1948 – has not yet been adapted to the needs of interlingual lexicography. The closest anyone has ever got to this was Iannucci's (1962) critical account of the less than satisfactory treatment of meaning discrimination in bilingual dictionaries, but it is limited to just that: 75 specimen entries in 32 dictionaries with English.

So what we can gather from all this is that we have very few guidelines for reviewing bilingual dictionaries, and those that are available, such as Steiner's (1984) checklist under three headings, 'inclusiveness', 'content' (including directionality and equivalence), and 'organization', are not widely known among dictionary critics, and comparative critical accounts of different interlingual traditions are practically non-existent.

The third perspective, **dictionary typology**, deals with the problem of classifying the ever-growing range of reference works. All monolingual dictionaries are potentially useful for interlingual purposes (such as the pioneering dictionary of German regionalisms, the VWBD 2004). Often they contain inherently interlingual information, as in thesauruses and dictionaries of synonyms, where there is a close parallel between explaining the meanings for words in terms of their (intralingual) near-synonyms or finding corresponding words in terms of their (interlingual) translation equivalents in another language. This is why they are often subjected to translation, as in the sub-genres that have been subjected to 'hybridization' in the form of so-called bilingualized dictionaries (Hartmann 2005a) for languages such as Chinese and/or Japanese, e.g. the NODE 1998/2007 or the DoL 1998/2003. The so-called general bilingual dictionary, such as the NACED (1978/2000), is the most well-known interlingual type, but it can be contrasted with more specialized formats (note that the directionality can go either way, or both ways, as happens in many dictionaries that have two parts addressing users from two languages, cultures, countries and markets).

Sometimes more than two languages can be involved, as in polyglot or multilingual dictionaries which have a long-established tradition in subject fields like law, music, medicine, science and technology. Contrary to general belief, it is not always easier to correlate technical terms across language barriers than it is to find translation equivalents for non-technical general and conversational words and phrases.

Finally, elements of all of these sub-genres can be presented in electronic form, or even combined, in a number of different ways. Two recent survey papers are relevant in this context, one written from the Japanese point of view in relation to foreign-language learning, and the other from the Chinese standpoint in relation to translation. Tono (2006) shows us that the typology of various reference materials (from the chip-operated pocket calculator and the CD-ROM-fed computer terminal to various online weblinks and parallel-database translation software) is confusingly challenging, while Zhang (2004) demonstrates that the quality of electronic dictionaries is surprisingly deficient, especially in terms of the often inadequate translation equivalents offered in such products.

What can we generalize about dictionary typology in relation to interlingual lexicography? It seems to me that we would be justified in saying that almost anything is possible, and therefore we need to keep an open mind on diverse new reference works, provided that we are confident they appeal and make sense to the average user.

The fourth perspective, **dictionary structure**, is a notoriously difficult and under-researched problem area. Since the classic paper by Haas (1962), compilers have struggled to supply the kinds of information categories that the 'ideal' bilingual dictionary should include, from all the lexical and grammatical details, levels of usage and personal names to specialized terminology, spelling, and pronunciation.

The most important information category is of course Haas's No. 1, 'just the right translation in the target language'. How are such lexical equivalents found and codified, how are all their occurrences in real contexts actually illustrated, and how are their various senses properly explained and discriminated? Most of us are fully aware of the fact that we can distinguish several types or levels of equivalence, from 'complete' (or full or exact or absolute) equivalence via 'partial' equivalence and 'false' equivalence to 'nil' or non-equivalence. Some of us may even know how some of these are covered in the dictionaries for a particular language pair, but the considerable variation between different language pairs has not been systematically catalogued, part of the mutual neglect and distrust between the two fields of lexicography and translation studies (Hartmann 2004).

I have space here just for one example from a bilingual dictionary compiled at Exeter, the CEDIP (1988), in which the translation equivalents are ingeniously arranged in a three-step sequence; thus for the Chinese idiom *bu ju li jie*, the three levels of equivalence are:
- 'literal' translation: *not stick to usual social rules*,
- 'free' translation: *pay no attention to convention*, and
- 'full' English equivalent: *do not stand on ceremony*, this being marked with the register labels 'literary' and 'colloquial'.

So, to generalize on dictionary structure today, more than 40 years after Haas's demands, we no longer regard them as unreasonably optimistic, especially with the means IT has put at our disposal.

The fifth perspective is **dictionary use**, a specialization to which I and some of my former students have made substantial contributions. First, a few comments are in order on some of the variables within the so-called user perspective. Many publications on the topic of observing and surveying dictionary users start with a reference to the famous American lexicographer Barnhart (1962), whose influential questionnaire survey had established that meaning and spelling outrank grammar and etymology, and may well have contributed substantially to the removal of historical facts from general and learners' dictionaries, in favour of stressing semantic and orthographic information.

The trend since the 1980s and '90s has been for more direct (rather than indirect) observation, from the relatively large-scale questionnaire survey to the relatively limited direct observation by test or protocol (although large numbers by themselves are no guarantee for reliability, and small numbers can still be useful if they reveal typical behaviour patterns of typical dictionary users). From Barnhart's survey of native-speaker students at American colleges we have moved on to the observation of learners of English as a Foreign Language and English as a Second Language, even English for Specific Purposes, and on to British learners of German (Hartmann 1982) and many other language learners around the world.

What can we abstract from these studies? The earlier research efforts were concerned with more general notions of dictionary 'reference needs', but gradually they have tended to focus on more specific instances of dictionary 'reference skills' associated with particular activity contexts. But practically no studies exist of the multifarious uses and users of technical dictionary genres, such as LSP experts. Even less is known about translators as dictionary users, as most studies devoted to dictionary use while translating are based on students of translation rather than professional translators. Let us hope that the trend towards more empirical research methods such as thinking-aloud protocols and experiments, as documented by Tono (2001), will continue and result in our wider awareness of all relevant factors.

The sixth branch or perspective of dictionary research is **dictionary IT**, or computational lexicography. I have already hinted at the fact that IT has made it possible not only to mechanize many lexicographic processes (e.g. word-processing and corpus technology), but also that many new types of reference works have been developed, under such names as 'electronic dictionary', 'online lexicon' and 'terminological database'. However, interlingual lexicography has not yet fully explored all the infinite possibilities, it also lags behind unilingual lexicography, and the literature often does not refer to bilingual dictionaries and translation at all, including the problem of how to treat (Haas's) multiple information categories.

4. Research priorities

We have seen that lexicography has matured, both in practice and in theory, in terms of more professional approaches to the discipline, more textbooks, more training facilities and more international associations. Some generalizations have resulted from the six perspectives of dictionary research: dictionary history, dictionary criticism, dictionary typology, dictionary structure, dictionary use, and dictionary IT. Now we need to ask about what sorts of desiderata remain.

Among the factors of interlingual dictionary use and dictionary production that need to be investigated more fully are the following 10 problem areas:

(1) What do we know about the varying levels of mother-tongue and foreign-language proficiency of the dictionary user, from beginner's to advanced level? We need more surveys of dictionary users, e.g. of the comparative sort that arose from the European-Union funded Thematic Network Project, which looked at problems of language

learning in higher education over a period of three years, and was published as a European Language Council report (Hartmann 1999). Specifically, its Sub-Project 9 concerned with dictionaries found that dictionary awareness among university students, at least in most European Union countries, is still much too limited, and also made a number of recommendations to counteract this deficiency, e.g. the development of a better 'dictionary culture' from primary school to university level and better 'dictionary provision' for all potential users.

(2) What are the types of activity engaged in by the typical user, while reading or writing or translating from one language to another? I have already referred to foreign-language learners and translators, but there are other user groups, such as scientists, writers and journalists about whose reference needs and reference skills we know hardly anything at all; some are mentioned in the collection of papers edited by Atkins (1998).

(3) What is the degree of knowledge sought, from general information to technical expertise? On linguistic as well as encyclopedic reference needs, there is only a limited literature available. The terminology of law could serve as an example here, especially legal translation, the topic of a recent book by Chromá (2004) who, from the vantage point of the Czech Republic, looked at the possibilities and requirements of a new bilingual dictionary of the language of law, to assist in this area of special-purpose communication.

(4) What genres of reference works are on offer, from general-purpose to special-terminological, or from monolingual to interlingual, or from print to electronic? IT has begun to widen the options, producing new types, and even hybrids of existing types, such as the bilingualized dictionary discussed by Thumb (2004) from the point of view of look-up strategies of Hong Kong learners of English. Still more information is desirable, however, for more dictionary types and pairs of languages (such as the database developed by San Vicente at Bologna for the bilingual dictionaries of Spanish and Italian: http://hesperia.cliro.unibo.it/).

(5) Which specific information categories are to be made available in the dictionary, from spelling and pronunciation to lexical meaning, usage and encyclopedic details? The only (comparative) treatment of the structure of bilingual dictionaries, Marello's textbook (1989), gives examples of various macrostructural and microstructural profiles in the bilingual dictionaries of the four language pairs covered, but this does not actually show all the ways in which all the information categories mentioned by Haas (1962) have been or should be presented. Among the neglected topics are pictorial illustrations (Hupka 1989) and typography/art/design (Luna 2004).

(6) Are we familiar with all the types and directionalities of the translation process, from mother tongue to foreign language, or vice versa, or from literal to free and idiomatic, including problems of sense discrimination and equivalence? I have mentioned some examples, and could add that Svensén's book (1993, especially its new Swedish 2nd edition 2004), is particularly helpful in giving many examples of partial equivalence, related to the problem of whether you are going from L1 to L2, or from L2 to L1. But more could be said about the subject of how lexical equivalents can be established by means of 'contrastive textology' or comparable parallel-text analysis (Hartmann 2005b), and what techniques have been employed for their treatment in particular language pairs (e.g. Adamska-Sałaciak 2006 for English and Polish).

(7) What is the sequence of operations in a typical consultation process, from choice of dictionary to search within the entry and integrating the result of the operation with the requirements of the activity? On the reference skills necessary to look up information in the dictionary, I can cite the paper by Nesi (1999), although it still neglects interlingual aspects.

(8) Which intradisciplinary methods are appropriate for carrying out research on the topics listed above? For all these we need to elaborate appropriate research techniques within lexicography and dictionary research (Hartmann 2001), although for each of its perspectives (dictionary history, dictionary criticism, dictionary use etc.) specific procedures may still need to be developed.

(9) What interdisciplinary methods can we draw on for such studies? One defining feature of all lexicography around the world is its so-called reference base. In our search for knowledge out of information, a basic human need, we all turn to reference books such as dictionaries, handbooks, directories and encyclopedias, monolingual and bilingual, general and technical, print and electronic. In the last few years, IT has indeed helped to strengthen these developments, so much so that there is now a good case for a so-called 'reference science', defined by McArthur (1998b: 218) as "... the study of all aspects of organizing data ...", recognizing at least 3 branches (traditional lexicography, 'encyclopedics', and a third that does not really have a name yet), each with many connections to other disciplines.

(10) What are the implications of all of this not only for lexicography, but also a number of other fields such as translation studies, technical terminology and foreign-language learning? The problem gets ever more complicated, as there we take on the role of responsible representatives of our discipline, which (almost like missionaries) we have to explain to others, in education (e.g. teacher training), in

media studies, even in politics. And this brings me back to the example I gave in point No. 1: what is the relevance of the observations and the recommendations we made under the banner of the European *Thematic Network Project* for the rest of the world, or what might be the relevance of what we do in English lexicography and dictionary research for other languages, and is what we know about interlingual dictionaries for one language pair – such as English and German – relevant to the lexicography of another language pair – such as English and Chinese?

To realize such research desiderata (Hartmann 2006), we need more and better training for lexicographers and dictionary researchers, better documentation (in the form of bibliographies, monographs and conference proceedings), more refined research methods, and a more complete coverage of all the above research topics within interdisciplinary settings. The evidence from my database of over 400 conferences gives me cause for optimism: the proportion of papers at such meetings devoted to interlingual topics is rising, e.g. in conferences run by EURALEX, NFL and ASIALEX, there are more individual conferences and even conference series covering such topics, e.g. San Vicente (2006), and there is more interdisciplinary contact, e.g. with subjects like translation, LSP terminology and corpus linguistics.

5. Conclusion

I have surveyed the scene of interlingual lexicography and metalexicography, and I hope I have managed to diagnose a few trends, such as professionalization, theory formation and research techniques. I trust you can agree that we need to do more in all these areas, and that these issues need to be more widely publicized to increase general dictionary awareness at all levels.

I recently acquired the LBCP (2001), a monolingual dictionary of Chinese proverbs presented through the medium of English, from which I finally quote the following by Han Fei Zi (Warring States Period) as a motto for the research programme advocated here: "Claiming certainty without corroborating evidence is stupid".

Internet-based communication and the ecology of dictionaries

Wengao Gong
National University of Singapore
g0402711@nus.edu.sg

1. Introduction

The worldwide flourishing of Internet-based communication over the past decade has not only changed our conceptions about human communication but also changed the environment for our language use. The emergence of Netspeak (Crystal 2001), a new linguistic dimension, has blurred the boundary between spoken language and written language and has become 'a whole new medium comparable to speech and writing in its distinctiveness and generality' (Crystal 2003: 426). What Crystal is referring to when he uses the term 'Netspeak' is actually the English language used in computer-mediated communication settings. In fact, if we take a wider perspective, we will find that Netspeak can take various linguistic forms such as Chinese, French, German, Russian, Japanese, Korean and Malay, just to name a few. The popularity of this new medium has brought about many interesting changes to our languages. One aspect of these changes is the rapid increase in lexis which is either generated in Internet-based communication settings or related to this form of communication. For example, the word *lol* (evolved from the English phrase 'laughing out loud') has become a very popular word in Internet-based communication settings (online chat, emails, BBS, and blogs) where English is the medium. Originally an acronym from a verb phrase, *lol* has recently acquired a whole range of different parts of speech. It can be used as a noun as it has a plural form of *lolz*; it can be used as a new verb and has its own past form *lolled*; it can be used as an adjective and has a comparative form of *loler* (there are disagreements over the part of speech of this new word: some people take it as another noun formed by adding *–er* to the verb *lol*); it can also be used as a very productive prefix for forming new nouns, for instance, *lolcats*. The emergence of *lol* as a word is a direct result of people's efforts to mimic laughing, an essential component of human communication in face-to-face settings in the early-day, text-only Internet-based communication environments. The phrase 'laughing out loud' has existed in the English language for ages but nobody came up with the acronym during the pre-Internet years. Of course, *lol* is not just an individual case; there are numerous other examples. What's more, English is not the only language which has witnessed the growth of such lexis. How to respond to the new linguistic developments has become an indicator of lexicographers' linguistic perspectives and their perspectives of dictionary-making.

The impact of Internet-based communication on dictionaries is not restricted to their contents, that is, whether to take in lexis generated in Internet-based language using environments. It is also exerting influence on the typology of dictionaries, the compiler-user relations, and even how dictionaries are compiled. The author will explore each of these aspects in turn, aiming at spelling out the new linguistic scenarios lexicographers are facing and their significance in dictionary-making practice.

2. Internet-based communication and the changing environment for language use

The advent of Internet technology has brought about many great changes to our daily life. Two aspects are worthy of particular mention here. One is the easier and quicker availability of information. For people who can get access to the Internet, information is just a mouse-click away. The other is the convenience of information exchange facilitated by Internet-based communication. Both aspects have directly contributed to the change of the overall environment for our language use. This change of environment will inevitably exert influence on the industry of lexicography.

The first influence comes from the enriched linguistic scenarios facilitated by the thriving of Internet-based communication and the consequent changes resulted in our language. Internet-based communication can be divided into different modes according to the specific medium used. Affected by the technological affordance of the medium or mode and the differences in situation and function, the language used in different modes takes on different linguistic features. Language in Internet-based communication environments can be roughly classified into four situations: language on webpages, language in asynchronous settings (such as emails and bulletin boards), language in synchronous settings, and language in blogs. One striking feature of Internet-mediated language is that the written form is being pushed to the extreme of performing the roles which used to be played by the spoken form, thus blurring the boundary between speech and writing. As Landau 2001 points out, 'the instantaneity of Internet communication gives it more of the quality of speech than of writing, though it is not speech. It is something in between' (Landau 2001: 242). This feature of Internet-based communication has led to the emergence of large numbers of innovative linguistic forms which were simply unimaginable during the pre-Internet age. The linguistic innovation in Internet-based communication settings has stimulated utterly different responses from different camps of scholars. The younger generation embraces these unconventional forms while the older generation finds these forms too innovative to make any sense. Purists call for campaigns to protect the standard language from the contamination of netspeak. In Shanghai, China,

Internet-based communication and the ecology of dictionaries 215

local laws have been passed to ban the so-called Internet Chinese language from the mainstream print and TV media and governmental documents, for instance. In Taiwan, the language which young people use in Internet-based communication settings is often referred to as 'huoxingwen' which means 'the language which only the Martians can understand'. Prejudiced conceptions of a similar nature about language in Internet-based communication settings might be one of the reasons for its nearly zero representation in large corpora. Gong (2005) has investigated the representation of computer-mediated English in four leading English corpora (namely, the British National Corpus (BNC), the Bank of English, the International Corpus of English, and the Cambridge International Corpus), and found that only the BNC included an approximately 240,000-word email component which consists solely of the email exchanges from the Leeds United email list. It is not known whether things have started to change over the past several years.

In order to get a rough idea about the current status of the treatment of Internet-mediated language in lexicography, the author carried out a small, informal investigation. As English and Chinese are the two languages used by a large population of Internet users, the author selected five established English words in Internet-based communication settings and five established Chinese words and looked them up in three recent English dictionaries and three Chinese dictionaries respectively. The English dictionaries are: the CD (*Chambers Dictionary*), the PED (*Penguin English Dictionary*), and CED (*Collins English Dictionary*). The Chinese dictionaries are: XHGC (*Xiandai Hanyu Guifan Cidian – Dictionary of Standard Modern Chinese*), DHXC (*Dangdai Hanyu Xinci Cidian – New Word Dictionary of Contemporary Chinese*), and XHXC (*Xinshiji Hanyu Xinci Cidian – Dictionary of Neologisms in New Century Chinese*). Tables 1 and 2 show the results:

Table 1 Results for English words

Lexis	Chambers Dictionary (03)	Penguin English Dictionary (03)	Collins English Dictionary (04)
online	√	√	√
offline	√	√	√
weblog or blog	X	√	√
chat	X	X	√
LOL	X	X	√

As can be observed from Table 1, all five words are found in *Collins English Dictionary*. As a general-purpose mainstream dictionary, *Collins Dictionary* is a pioneer to include lexical items that originated purely from computer-mediated language such as *lol* (laughing out loud). The *Penguin English Dictionary* is also quite responsive to the new lexical developments in the English language. It has included three out of the five words, although it does not go as far as *Collins* to include abbreviations specifically associated with chatroom English. The Chambers Dictionary seems to be less adventurous than the other two: it has only included the words 'online' and 'offline', which are more of a technical nature.

Table 2 Results for Chinese words

Lexis	Meaning	Xiandai Hanyu Guifan Cidian (04)	Dangdai Hanyu Xinci Cidian (04)	Xinshiji Hanyu Xinci Cidian (06)
zai4xian4	online	√	X	√
bo2ke4	weblog or blog	X	√	√
liao2tian1	chat	X	X	X
mei3mei2	pretty girls	X	X	√
shuai4ge1	cool boys	X	√	√

Table 2 presents the results for three Chinese dictionaries. The *Dictionary of Standard Modern Chinese* is the most authoritative among the three and it included only one of the words: the Chinese equivalent of the English word 'online', which might have been taken in as a technical term. That might be a reflection of its prescriptive nature, as its Chinese title (*gui1fan4*, meaning standard) suggests. The *New Word Dictionary of Contemporary Chinese* (a specialized dictionary) included two, and the *Dictionary of Neologisms in New Century Chinese* (the newest and a specialized dictionary) included four out of the five words. One thing worth noting here is that all the examples about the usage of those Internet-communication related Chinese words come from conventional media such as newspapers and magazines. Two inferences can be made from this phenomenon. One is that terms originated from Internet-based communication settings are actually spreading to conventional media or discourse. The other is that lexicographers in China tend to consider such terms as dictionary entry candidates (even for specialized dictionaries) only after they have made their way into conventional media.

The different practices in selecting words between the English and Chinese dictionaries may be attributed to the different statuses of the two languages. As the language of the Internet and a global lingua franca, English is the medium which carries most of the new lexical items which are related to the IT industry in general and Internet-based communication in particular. As a result, vocabulary related to Internet-based communication fits better with the English language itself. The impact of the Internet and computer-mediated communication on the Chinese language comes late but with great power. Associated with western technology and western culture, Internet-based communication in Chinese has generated large numbers of words and expressions which are often considered foreign, rebellious, and unconventional. This might have made Chinese lexicographers more cautious in deciding which words to include in their dictionaries.

Of course, whether to include a new word or expression in a mainstream general dictionary is mainly determined by the lexicographers' perspectives of language and their perspectives of lexicography. In both cases, if they hold a normative perspective, they will feel more comfortable to take the so-called conventional or established sources as the basis of lexis selection, thus being more cautious in absorbing new lexical developments into their dictionaries. If they adopt a descriptive (or informative) perspective, they will tend to be more open-minded and more responsive to the latest lexical developments. Starting from Samuel Johnson, dictionary-making has mainly been practised along the normative line. This practice has its own merits, which needs little explanation. However, it also has its limitations. The biggest problem with such practice is that dictionaries so compiled can only reflect the stable, established features of the lexis. They cannot adequately reflect the dynamics of lexical developments in time. Being responsive to current developments is a very basic expectation on the part of dictionary users. It would be too late if we only decide to include certain words into a dictionary after they have already become an established part of everybody's language. After all, one of the most practical reasons why people consult dictionaries is that they want to look up new or unknown words. Inadequate coverage and slow responses to recent linguistic developments will definitely undermine the authority of a dictionary even if its compilation is very professional.

Here we have touched upon two important issues in lexicography: representativeness and the attitude towards neologisms. For dictionaries to better reflect the reality of a language, we need a well-balanced corpus which can collectively represent the full repertoire of spoken and written performance across the broadest possible range of contexts and genres. Up till now, the language that dictionaries have described has been that of an edited copy (Landau 2001). Obviously, this cannot reflect the whole picture of a language, not even make a good snapshot. As was rightly predicted by Landau in 2001, more and more publications are now not in print, and varieties of usage that are typical of Internet-based communication are already there, waiting to be identified and characterized. With the growing use of language corpora in dictionary-making, the impact of the tightly edited text of mainstream publishers (on which most general dictionaries in the world have long been based) has developed signs of being diluted, as 'corpora take in a much greater variety of sources: offbeat and counter-culture publications; text made available electronically, which is often lightly edited or unedited; fiction; and speech, including the transcripts of radio and TV talk shows and unscripted political discussions' (Landau 2001: 272). Lexicographers at the time of having no computers and the Internet could not do much about the representation problem. Now the situation has changed. With better software and cheaper hardware, lexicographers are at a better position to ease the tension between being authoritative and being representative. The following quotation from Fitzgerald helps to illustrate my point:

It would be an ambitious pursuit, to say the least, for a dictionary to contain all of a language, but the elimination of spatial restrictions will enable dictionaries to more accurately and fully record a language. All manner of neologisms could be included, from the mainstream to the esoteric. This would be without paying the price of losing any of the historical nature of a dictionary, so that the digitized dictionary will be not only a more functional tool for the user, but also a better reflection of language (2000: 50). Maybe there is no such a thing as complete representativeness; it is always a matter of degree. Besides, lexicographers need to consider the tension between a dictionary's faithful representation of the lexicon of a language and the dictionary's usefulness from the perspective of the users, because many words considered to be important and useful by lexicographers are the ones which dictionary users are familiar with and seldom consult. That raises the issue of lexical coverage of a dictionary, which is closely related to the treatment of neologisms.

Proper treatment of neologisms seems to be another hard nut to crack in lexicography. Different lexicographers have different perspectives and different practices in this regard. Some scholars such as Landau (2001) seem to be suggesting that lexicographers should not be too rushed in taking in new words. He discourages the idea of dictionary compilers' trying to insert every new word to compete against each other in the market and to satisfy the curiosity of dictionary users for searching for the latest words, as implied by the following quote:

> Unfortunately, dictionary editors have everything to gain and nothing to lose by inserting every new word (or neologism), faddish or not, that comes along, since the popular view is that the ultimate test of every new dictionary is that it has the very latest words (Landau 2001: 204).

He is also concerned about the consequences of hasty inclusion of neologisms because these words may cause problems if they soon become obsolete. According to him, 'there is no reliable way to uncover the last few decades' *detritus* of new words, which will continue to take up space, like *weeds* hidden in the *luxuriant garden of vibrant flowers*' if there is no good corpus to help lexicographers to monitor which words are still popular and which ones are outdated (Landau 2001: 205, italics mine). Landau's concern makes sense to some extent, but the metaphors that he uses to refer to those words which have lost currency but yet still been kept in a dictionary imply too conservative an attitude towards neologisms. His attitude can be more clearly seen from the following quote:

> Even if a new word is used with great frequency over a short period of time, we want to know that it will not be obsolete by the time the dictionary is published. Fad words (or vogue words) may have enormous density of usage for a period of months and then disappear except for an occasional nostalgic use. For example, a number of new terms such as chat group which dictionaries will surely add to their next editions,

may be replaced in a few years by some newer terms, perhaps because of technological changes in the way chat groups operate. (Landau 2001: 204) Landau's worries would make more sense in situations where the capacity of dictionaries is limited and the duration for dictionary compilation is very long. With the availability of electronic dictionaries (Internet dictionaries included), we should hold a more open mind towards neologisms. Weeds and flowers are all members of an ecology, so are neologisms (of whatever kind) members of the true ecology of our language. Deliberately excluding new words just because we believe they may not last long or because they come from a communication setting which we believe to be unconventional or experimental (such as Internet-mediated language) sounds a bit arbitrary and may not be a well-grounded practice. This touches upon some very important issues in lexicography. For instance, how do we know for sure how long a new word is going to last? How long is long enough? How frequently should a new word be used and by whom before it can qualify itself as an official member of a dictionary? Who should have the final say? The answers to these questions will have a great deal to do with people's perspectives on dictionary making.

Some people may argue that we can always reduce the burden of general-purpose dictionaries by putting neologisms into specialized dictionaries. For instance, in China there are already two specialized dictionaries for Internet-mediated Chinese. Undoubtedly, specialized dictionaries are a possible way out, but they serve a much narrower range of users. Ordinary dictionary users may not like the idea of having several dictionaries at hand, each serving a different function. Normally, ordinary users will expect mainstream general-purpose dictionaries to include more words and cover a wider range (with a cheaper price, of course). It is high time for lexicographers to start thinking about how to better represent the already much-altered linguistic environment facilitated by the advancement in information processing technology and the popularity of Internet-based communication.

3. Internet-based communication and the typology of dictionaries

The ever-increasing availability of computers and the Internet has brought about revolutionary changes to the form of dictionaries. Nowadays, dictionaries are no longer in bulky print forms only; instead, many dictionaries are in the form of a portable electronic device or on the Internet where no tangible form of the dictionaries can be seen. In terms of information organisation structure, some electronic dictionaries just copy the macrostructure and microstructure of print dictionaries while others have their own unique features. For instance, some Internet dictionaries use hyperlinks for building links among related information or knowledge about its entries. As a result, cross-reference is just a mouse-click away. In print dictionaries, on the other hand, the effort required on the part of the users is much greater despite the fact that dictionary makers have long been working out ways to achieve cross-referencing of related words or information via indexing. Another feature which is associated with Internet dictionaries is that they can be used for free. We seldom hear about free print dictionaries unless we are using them in public libraries. Moreover, there are dictionaries developed by professional lexicographers and dictionaries collaboratively compiled by users. Again, the latter case simply doesn't happen in print dictionaries. Internet dictionaries are the only ones that have the potential of being used by anyone in the world for free, and some excellent dictionaries can indeed be found on the Internet (de Schryver 2003). Li (2005) gives a very good list of the free Internet dictionaries available, most of which are put online for public use by well-known professional dictionary publishers. Some of them need subscription to be used or used fully; others can be used for free but only with restricted functions. Many a time, these online dictionaries are there for the purpose of advertising themselves or promoting the sales of their print dictionary products. These dictionaries seldom say anything negative about themselves.

There is another type of free Internet dictionary which offers quite similar services as its commercial Internet dictionary counterparts yet seldom brags about its authority, scholarship, and precision as most print dictionaries do. Instead, it will remind their users of the incompleteness or potential inaccuracy of information and the potential risks of using the dictionary. TheFreeDictionary.com is an example of such a dictionary. When a user logs onto www.thefreedictionary.com and keys in a word, he or she will easily get the information about the word's meaning, pronunciation, part(s) of speech, collocations (if any), and synonyms by simply hitting the Enter key. By clicking on the 'about' hyperlink, the user will read a statement, a part of which is quoted below:

> The Content is provided 'as is' without warranty of any kind. Farlex does not make any warranty whatsoever as to the accuracy or completeness of the Content or the results to be obtained from using the Content and Farlex will not be responsible for any claims attributable to errors, omissions, or other inaccuracies in the information contained therein. The entire risk for the results and performance of the Content is assumed by you, the user. (http://www.thefreedictionary.com/about.htm)

This kind of statement is absolutely unimaginable for print dictionaries which are supposed to be authoritative and error-free. By taking the glory and responsibility away from the information provider, free Internet dictionaries are actually placing themselves under the scrutiny of their users. How strategies like this are going to work could be an interesting topic for serious research.

What we can observe from all these novel things is that Internet technology is enriching the typology of dictionaries while at the same time influencing dictionary users' perspectives about what dictionaries should be like and reshaping their dictionary consulting behaviours, especially dictionary users of the wired generation.

4. Internet-based communication and dictionary compilation

One more aspect of lexicography which is undergoing changes under the impact of Internet-based communication is the compiler-user relationship. According to Hartmann (2001), dictionary compilers do not normally communicate directly with their target users; they get feedback about their products from the indirect observations reported by teachers, reviewers, librarians or booksellers. With the popularity of Internet dictionaries, this situation seems to be changing. Many Internet dictionaries allow direct feedback from users via the feedback windows the website provides. Users can type their comments and feedback and send them directly to the compilers. Users can also give feedback via email. This new possibility gives users a chance to play a more active role in the process of dictionary compilation, improvement, and updating. Online dictionary users can even contribute their own entries. This is something which happens less frequently in the case of paper dictionary compilation. According to Quirk (1991), the Longman Dictionary editors once started a Longman Wordwatch campaign which attracted a large number of people in Britain to help them to keep watch on the new or unfamiliar words and uses of words in the language around them. They successfully obtained large numbers of citations from those volunteer 'wordwatchers' which provided greatly enriched resources for the Longman editors. It is not known how that was done, but one thing which can be inferred is that if the communication between those volunteer wordwatchers and editors was through normal correspondence like letters, that must have created a huge amount of work for the Longman editors. In other words, even if dictionary makers have the good intention of getting more users involved in their dictionary compilation, it would not be a technically inviting practice at a time when Internet-based communication was not as readily available as it is now. This also explains why most of the time dictionary users are just passive consumers.

Now this situation is changing. The popularity of Web technologies allows ordinary users of dictionaries who are not trained lexicographers to engage in dictionary-making (Damaso and Cotter 2007). One typical example is an Internet dictionary called UrbanDictionary.com (UD). UD is a slang dictionary with definitions written by its visitors. It allows users to create definitions for slang words and phrases and submit them for publication. Here, the user is the contributor and the Author-Editor (Damaso and Cotter 2007). UD is not meant to be used by all types of audience as its disclaimer on the website of this dictionary clearly states, because its content is frequently presented in a coarse and direct manner that some may find offensive. Users who may not like this style are advised not to visit their site (i.e. not to use the dictionary).

As a new species of dictionaries, UD is still in its infancy and has great room for improvement. What is of particular interest here is not how good or how bad UD is at its current status but rather how this dictionary is being compiled. This is probably the first free specialized dictionary (actually the first dictionary) ever compiled by dictionary users in human history. The birth of UD challenges the conventional practice of dictionary-making (or even reference information providing) which is typically 'top-down' (meaning from editors, through publishers, to readers) by offering an alternative of doing it the other way round, 'bottom-up' (Carr 1997). Perhaps 'bottom-up' is not an accurate description of the process involved in this new type of dictionary-making. Nevertheless, the concept of bottom-up lexicography is revolutionary. 'Bottom-up' editing may prove to be the most significant transformation of cyberlexicography (Carr 1997: 214). The foundation of this new type of dictionary is the Internet as a platform and Internet-based communication as a major means of information exchange and its content is about language phenomena in Internet-based communication settings.

UD's emergence poses certain challenges to a whole range of issues which are of fundamental importance to the industry of dictionary-making. It is already challenging our conventional conceptions about how dictionaries can be made, as mentioned earlier. It also provokes reflections about the authoritativeness of dictionaries and dictionary makers. Who should have the final say about the meaning (usage) of words of the language we are using? Professional lexicographers, ordinary language users, or both? What kind of relationship should it be between lexicographers and dictionary users? Who should define the quality of a dictionary? Which words should be included in what kind of dictionaries? Where does the future of conventional dictionaries lie? Considering the changed working environment for dictionary-making due to the advent of the Internet and Internet-based communication, the answers to these questions will not be straightforward.

New species of dictionaries such as UD may look unconventional, amateurish, or inconsistent and there might be a lot of problems with the 'bottom-up' editing practice of dictionary-making. Nevertheless, they have opened another possibility. It takes a bit of time to feel their impact. What we can learn from UD is that there is an alternative way of making dictionaries. Or at least, it shows that users can take a more active role in the process of dictionary-making than merely as a consumer or someone whose feedback may or may not be taken seriously by professional dictionary compilers. It is a new species which deserves more positive comments and a fairer treatment. It may look as unorthodox as its content, but it is an innovation. And this innovation is facilitated by Web technologies and Internet-based communication.

5. Conclusion

The working environment of dictionary-making is undergoing considerable changes due to the easy availability of the Internet and the popularity of Internet-based communication worldwide. Due to the language change triggered by the popularization of Web technologies and Internet-based communication, general-purpose dictionaries are facing some pressure to expand their coverage so as to better represent the changed linguistic scenario. The easy availability of the Internet is forcing dictionary publishers to develop online versions of their print dictionaries so as to cater to the changing habits of younger generation dictionary users. Meanwhile, due to the popularity of Internet-based communication, dictionary editors nowadays are able to get information regarding users' consulting needs and preferences and feedback about dictionary improvements directly from dictionary users. More importantly, the advancement in information processing technology together with the popularity of Internet-based communication is giving birth to new ways of compiling dictionaries and thus breeding new species in the ecology of dictionaries. It is high time for lexicographers to reconsider some of the fundamental issues such as linguistic perspectives in lexicography, representativeness, attitudes towards neologisms, and typology of dictionaries.

Relational network notation and the intelligent Web

Jonathan J. Webster
City University of Hong Kong
ctjjw@cityu.edu.hk

Ian C. Chow
City University of Hong Kong
ianchow@cityu.edu.hk

1. Relational network theory

Elaborating on the nature of language as an information system, Lamb (1974) describes it as 'a network of interrelationships'. This network is composed only of nodes and their connections. Lamb makes no distinction between linguistic information and non-linguistic information; all information is stored and processed the same way, as connections in a vast network. Information processing consists of (a) the transmission of activation along pathways defined by the network, and (b) changes in connection strengths. Mental networks (made up of nections) form the basis for our representation of reality. The model proposed by the theory is constantly being tested against the findings of neuroscience (Lamb 2004). We retrieve information by means of activation of networked nodes. Information does not exist in the nodes themselves but is instead retrieved via the connections between activated nodes.

Lamb's Relational Network Theory (Lamb & Webster 2004) provides the conceptual basis for implementing an interface ontology extending from the lexicogrammar as ground to meaning and context above. The boundary between lexicogrammar (wordings) and semantics (meanings) is a stratal one. Interface ontologies maintain this stratal distinction between conceptual and lexicogrammatical information while providing the means for mapping between them – 'an abstract semantic organization underlying our use of grammar and lexis that is motivated on essentially linguistic grounds and that acts as a complex interface between lexicogrammatical resources and higher-level strata in the linguistic system...' (Bateman 1991:31). On the one hand, the conceptual or sememic level provides the motivational covering or context for each choice that the grammar provides, while on the other hand, the lexicogrammar serves as a resource for both understanding and articulating semiotic constructs at higher strata of meaning and context.

2. Relational network notation

The focus of this chapter is on showing how relational networks can be represented using Relational Network Notation (RNN). RNN is based on Relational Network Theory, and offers a simple yet powerful means for representing lexicogrammatical, semantic and sememic information.

Figure 1 illustrates the network diagram for the lexeme *father*, in which there are multiple sememes represented by the same lexeme *father*. In other words, *father* can refer to the male parent or to a clergyman in the Roman Catholic or Anglican churches. This network diagram illustrates an OR node extending from a single lexemic unit upwards to several sememic units. Conversely, in the case of synonymy (e.g. father-daddy, big-large, hard-difficult) there is more than one lexeme connected to a single sememe via another node. The diagram also illustrates an AND node extending from several phonemic units to a single lexeme unit.

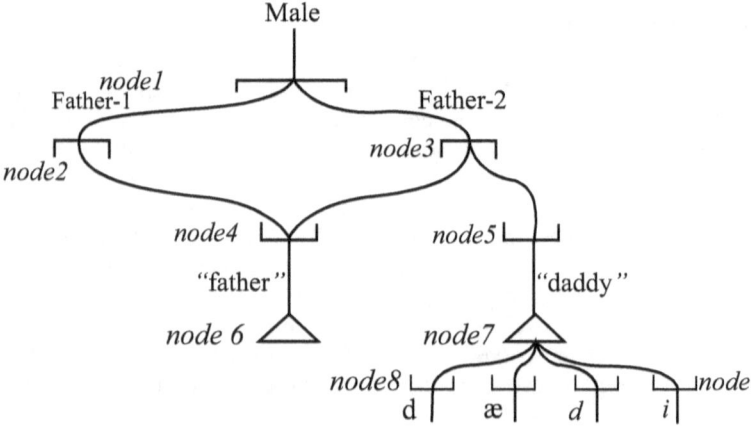

Figure 1 Relational network diagram for *daddy*

3. Ontology modelling of lexical information

We are using an ontology modelling language called Frame Logic (FLogic), along with various tools which together constitute a kind of ontology engineering environment to facilitate implementation of relational networks. FLogic is a database logic which 'accounts in a clear and declarative fashion for most of the structural aspects of object-oriented and frame-based languages', including such features as object identity, complex objects, inheritance, methods, etc. (Kifer 1995).

The first step in designing an ontology involves *conceptualizing* the problem

Relational network notation and the intelligent Web

domain in terms of concepts and relations. A *node*, the most basic concept, *points to other nodes*. The arcs between nodes are described by the *method to@*, which takes up to three parameters: a *threshold* value, an *identifier*, and a *sequence*. The threshold value is the number of arcs pointing from the node (where 1 = OR; > 1 = AND). The *identifier* is the parameter uniquely associated with that node. If the lines are Ordered, then a sequence value (1,2...n) is provided; if the lines are Unordered, then no sequence value is assigned. This is stated in FLogic with method overloading (Ontoprise 2003) as follows:
(1) node[to@(threshold, identifier)=>node].
(2) node[to@(threshold, identifier, sequence)=>node].

The parameterized method to@ describes the arc between nodes and takes either two or three parameters, depending on whether the arcs are ordered or not. Instances – the actual linguistic data – corresponding to the information shown in Figure 1, may be input into the knowledge base as the value for the parameter and identifier. This models the notion of information retrieved via activation of connected nodes; information is located in the link not at the node. Data in FLogic are as follows:
node1 [to@(1,Male)->>{node1,node2}].
node2 [to@(1,Father-1)->>{node4, node5}].
node3 [to@(1,Father-2)->>node4].
node4 [to@(1,"father")->>{node2,node3}].
node5 [to@(1,"daddy")->> node2].
node7 [to@(4,"daddy",1)->>node8;
 to@(4, "daddy",2)->>node9;
 to@(4, "daddy",3)->>node10;
 to@(4, "daddy",4)->>node11].
node8 [to@(1,d)->> node7].
node9 [to@(1,æ)->> node7].
node10 [to@(1,d)->> node7].
node11 [to@(1,i)->> node7].

Axioms allow one to infer new knowledge (and thereby increase the size of the knowledge base). One can write axioms, for example, which take the linguistic information about lexemes/words and sememes/concepts (both represented as a network of relationships) and further identify lexical relations such as synonymy, etc. This is illustrated in the following FLogic statements:
(3) FORALL X,Z,Y,A,B Z[sem_parent->>A] <- X[to@(1,Z)->>Y]
 AND Z:sememe AND Y:node[to@(1,A)->>X].

which may be re-stated as *Z is sememe-as-parent of A if node X has the value Y for the method* **to@** *with the parameter Z,* **AND** *Z is a sememe,* **AND** *Y is a node which has the value X for the method to@ with the parameter A.*
(4) FORALL X,Y,Z X[synonym->>Y] <- Z[sem_parent->>X]
 AND Z[sem_parent->>Y] AND
 Z: sememe AND X:lexeme AND Y:lexeme.

which may be re-stated as *X is a synonym of Y if Z is sememe-as-parent of X and Z is sememe-as-parent of Y.*

Finally, queries traverse the network to retrieve all the possible answers. In the following queries (see Figure 2), we retrieve all X and Y where X is sememe-as-parent of Y; the second query retrieves all X and Y where X and Y are related by synonymy. Note that in both instances, we are querying information not previously asserted in the knowledge base as facts, but rather inferred on the basis of the application of these axioms in the knowledge base. Figure 2 shows the results of the query in Ontobroker.

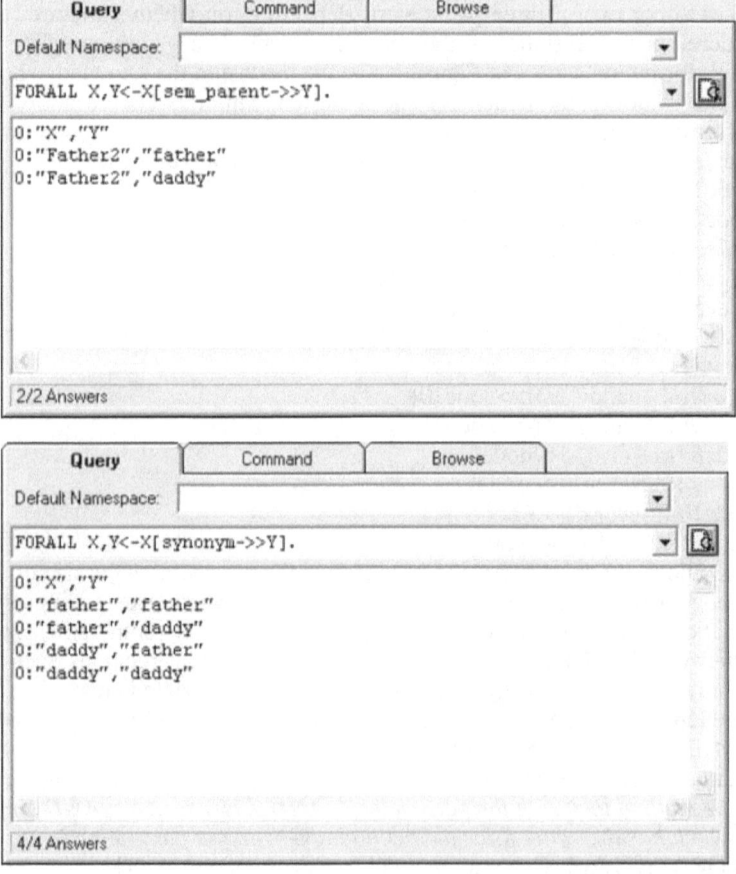

Figure 2 Displaying query results in Ontobroker

4. Populating RNN using WordNet lexical data

RNN is based on Relational Network Theory which offers a simple yet powerful means for representing lexicogrammatical, semantic and sememic information. Lexical entries are thus indispensable to our description of linguistic phenomena.

Lexical data in WordNet (Fellbaum 1998) is taken as a resource from which to populate the knowledge base. In WordNet, words (lemmas) are organized into synonym sets (synsets), each representing one concept, and there are different relations linking the synsets. This organization of lexical data provides a clear specification of lexical relations which makes it ideally suited to representation in RNN.

WordNet is implemented by means of RNN in an ontology engineering environment. WordNet lemmas with indication of linguistic properties and the relations between synsets are translated into Flogic formalism, facilitating reuse. New concepts are inferred in terms of the information represented in RNN. Simple mapping to RNN can be achieved by employing axioms.

Automatic mapping of lemmas into RNN involves the following steps: 1) unification of identical concepts, such as classes referring to the same concept should share the same object type. 2) application of mapping axioms to populate the relational network with instances from WordNet database. The axioms are illustrated in (5) and (6).

Provided that the schema of a synset is modelled in F-Logic as below:

synset[id-=> synset_id;
gloss=>synset_gloss;
haslemma=>> synset_lemmas].

(5) Unification of Identical concepts
(i) FORALL X,Y Y:sememe <- X:synset [gloss->Y].
which may be re-stated as *Y is a sememe if synset X (from WordNet) has the value Y as its gloss.*
(ii) FORALL X,Y Y:lexeme <- X:synset [haslemma->>Y].
which may be re-stated as *Y is a lexeme if synset X (from WordNet) has the value Y as its lemma(s).*
(6) Mapping Axioms for populating RNN and creation of connected nodes
(iii) FORALL A,B,S,L,G,O
 A:node[to@(1,G)->>(B:node)] <-
S:synset[id->O; gloss->G; haslemma->>L] AND G:sememe AND concat("node_",O,A) AND concat("node_",L,B).
which may be re-stated *as node A is connected to node B with method to@ with G as the information if G is the gloss, L the lemmas, O the id of Synset S; and G is a sememe; and A is created and named with the concatenation of "node_" and O while B is of "node_" and L.*
(iv) FORALL A,B,L,G
 B:node[to@(1,(L:lexeme))->>A] <-

A:node[to@(1,G)->>B] AND G:sememe
AND concat("node_",L,B).
which may be re-stated as *node B is connected to node A with method to@ with lexeme L as information if A is connected to B with method to@ with sememe G as information; and B is created and named with the concatenation of "node_" and L*.

Figures 3 and 4 depict the instantiation of the lemma *father* and its related information from WordNet to RNN and the query results through Ontobroker respectively. In Figure 3, concepts are labelled with a 'C' and lexical units are labelled with an 'L'.

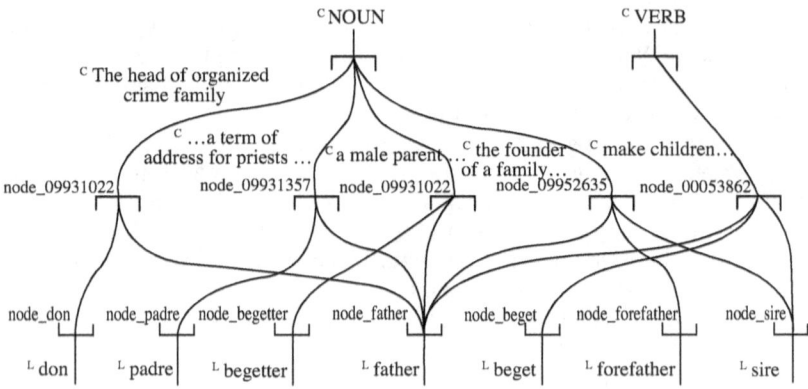

Figure 3 The concepts and synonyms of father in WordNet using RNN representation

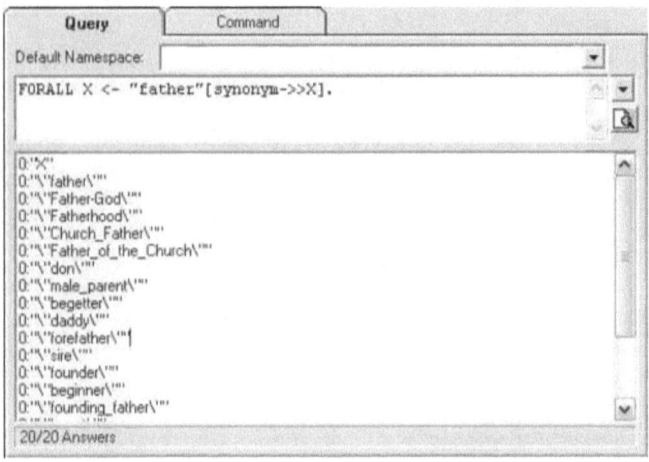

Relational network notation and the intelligent Web

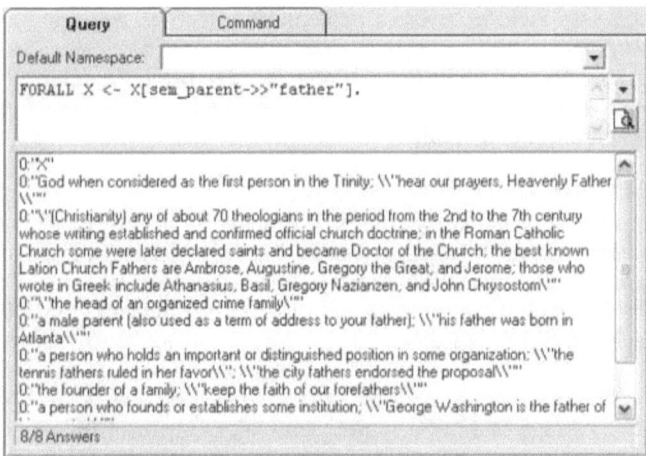

Figure 4 Displaying query results

5. Modelling meaning

Systemic Functional Linguistics (SFL) (Halliday 1999, 2004) proposes Ideational Meaning, Interpersonal Meaning and Textual Meaning as the three meta-functions of languages. Interpersonal Meaning explains how language enacts social relationships and serves as a tool in giving and demanding both information and 'goods and services'. Textual Meaning focuses on the organization and production of information into a cohesive and coherent text. Ideational Meaning refers to how experience is construed in language, in terms of three basic elements: PARTICIPANTS – the parties (abstract and/or concrete), normally realized as a noun or nominal group, involved in an event scenario. PROCESS, normally realized as a verb or verbal group, which is executed by a participant (actor) and may be directed at another participant (goal); CIRCUMSTANCE, normally realized as a prepositional phrase or adverbial group, which provides additional information, for instances, time, place and manner of the event. The configuration of PARTICIPANTS, PROCESS and CIRCUMSTANCE forms the transitivity of language, the structural realization of ideational meaning. In this chapter, we focus on transitivity, ontologically organizing the three elements.

PROCESS is the nucleus of ideational meaning. Basically, there are four types of PROCESSES: Material, Mental, Relational and Verbal. Each of them evokes different kinds of experience, such that there are four main categories of experience.

A Material PROCESS denotes an action event – 'doing' and 'happening'. PARTICIPANTS in this experience category can be labelled as *Actor*, *Goal*, and *Beneficiary*. *Actor* is the entity who/which does the action; *Goal* is the receiver of the action; *Beneficiary* is someone for whose benefit the action is carried out. Mental PROCESSES include verbs of perception, affection, cognition and volition. The PARTICIPANT who *thinks, sees, likes* or *wants* plays the *Sensor* role while the thing, idea, fact which is *thought, seen, liked* or *wanted* is referred to as *Phenomenon*. Similarly, Relational PROCESSES and Verbal PROCESSES denote other types of experience construal.

6. SFL PROCESS Verb Dictionary

The task of transitivity analysis requires a linguistic database with vast coverage of verbs annotated by PROCESS type. Taking WordNet as our linguistic resource, we are developing a SFL PROCESS verb dictionary facilitated by mapping of WordNet with various resources including SUMO and FrameNet. (Niles & Pease 2003, Shi & Mihalcea 2005, Chow & Wong 2006, Chow & Webster 2006)

The SFL PROCESS Verb Dictionary consists of verb entries from WordNet 2.1, which has a coverage of 13,650 synsets with 24,890 verbs. SFL PROCESS types are added to each synset entry. The identification of the process type is based on the knowledge acquired from the mapping of these three resources: WordNet, FrameNet and SUMO ontology.

Linkages between these three resources are extensively exploited and FrameNet frames are aligned with the four SFL PROCESS types. Taking a WordNet verb as an entry, the FrameNet frame mapped with the verb identifies the verb's SFL PROCESS type. The coverage of existing FrameNet WordNet verb mappings, although low, is resolved by using a statistical distribution analysis on SUMO-WordNet mapping to compute the connections between FrameNet Frame and SUMO; the result is then used to increase the verb mapping of FrameNet and WordNet (Chow and Webster 2007). The work both constructs the SFL verb dictionary and increases the interoperability of the three resources.

The SFL PROCESS type identification is further improved by clustering connected synsets with high semantic similarity. The clustering process utilizes WordNet relation links in addition with lexicographer file type and SUMO concept to recognize the semantic cluster boundary. Figure 5 shows the interface the SFL Verb-Process Search Tool under development

Relational network notation and the intelligent Web 233

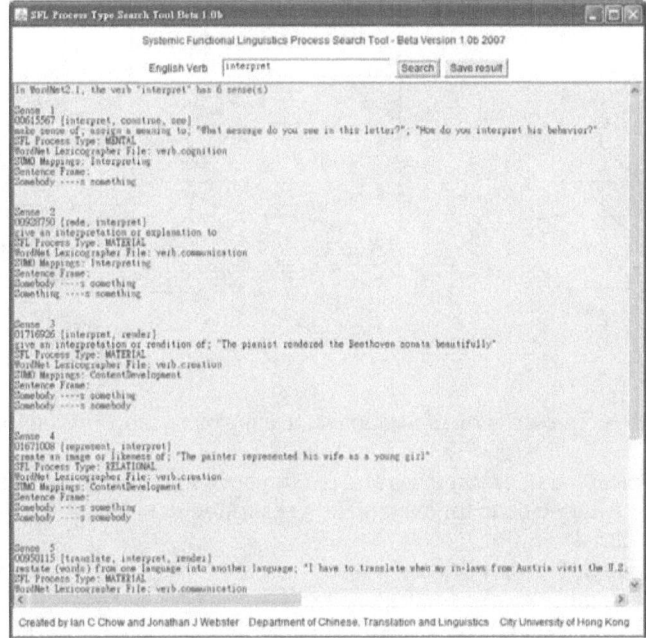

Figure 5 Screenshot of SFL Verb-Process Search Tool

7. Modelling ideational meaning

Modelling ideational meaning involves the identification of PROCESS and properly labelling the semantic role of each PARTICIPANT and reorganization of CIRCUMSTANCE. The correlation among the elements represents the ideational meaning. For example:

ACTOR MATERIAL GOAL CIRCUMSTANCE
(a) Tim bought a car last week.
SENSOR MENTAL PHENOMENON CIRCMSTANCE
(b) He likes it very much.

In example (a), the elements in terms of ideational meaning are:
   PROCESS: "bought"
   PARTICIPANTS: "Tim", "a car"
   CIRCUMSTANCE: "last week"
In example (b), the elements in terms of ideational meaning are:
   PROCESS: "likes"
   PARTICIPANTS: "He", "it"
   CIRCUMSTANCE: "very much"

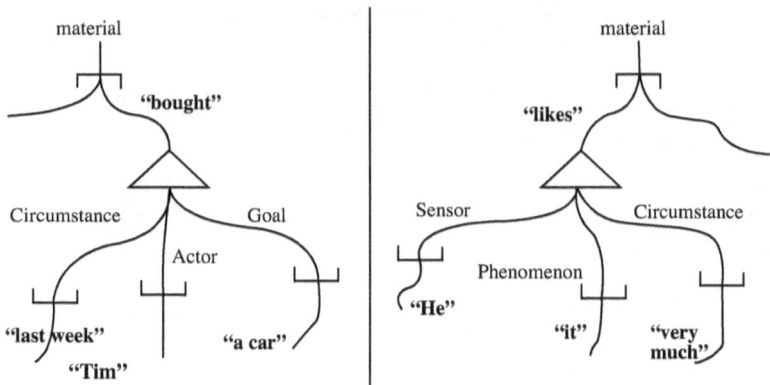

Figure 6 The RNN representation of ideational meaning of example (a) and (b)

The ideational meaning of example (a) and (b) can be represented in RNN as in Figure 6. The F-Logic code for example(a) is as follows:
n1[to@(1,material)->>n2].
n2[to@(3, "bought", circumstance)->>n3].
n2[to@(3, "bought", actor)->>n4].
n2[to@(3, "bought", goal)->>n5].
n3[to@(1, "last week")->>n2].
n4[to@(1, "Tim")->>n2].
n5[to@(1, "a car")->>n2].
A new parameter "sem_role" instead of "sequence" is defined as a new schema for AND nodes:
node[to@(threshold, identifier, sem_role)=>node].
The parameter "sem_role" holds the Semantic Role of the participants. PARTICIPANTS in an experience scenario behave differently from phonemic information in a lexeme. In both cases, conceptually, all links on the under side of an AND node have to be activated in order access the link on the top side of the AND node. When parsing phonemic information between lexemic information, a sequential constraint is also required.

Instances of language in use in daily life are texts, in which information about the PARTICIPANTS is not necessarily confined only to individual clauses, but rather may be spread across multiple clauses. Referring to examples (a) and (b) again but noting the fact that they are consecutive sentences from a text, Figure 7 shows the consolidated experience construed by example (a) and (b) in a relational network.

ACTOR MATERIAL GOAL CIRCUMSTANCE
(a) Tim bought *a car* last week.
SENSOR MENTAL PHENOMENON CIRCMSTANCE
(b) He likes *it* very much.

Relational network notation and the intelligent Web

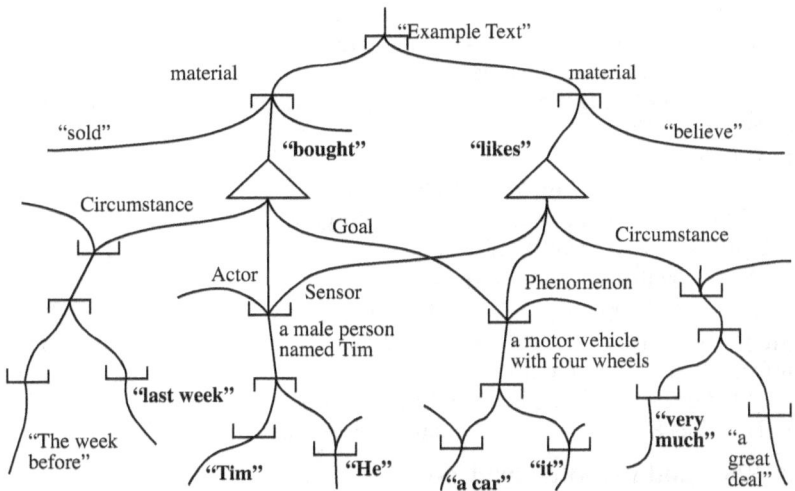

Figure 7 RNN representation of Ideational Meaning of example (a) and (b) consolidated

The OR node at the top relates the linguistic concept of PROCESS type Material and the lexical unit *bought*. The connection path then extends to an AND node linking another three nodes, each of which carries a linguistic concept: *Actor*, *Goal* and CIRCUMSTANCE. The three nodes then extend their links respectively, first to a semantic concept and then passing through another node down to its lexical representation. For example, focusing on the *Actor* concept, the activation passes through the upward-OR-node down to the semantic concept of 'a male person named Tim' and next through the downward-OR-node down to the lexical unit 'Tim'. In the next clause, the concept 'a male person named Tim' is linguistically realized by the lexeme 'He', and plays the role of *Sensor* in a mental event scenario evoked by the lexical unit 'likes'.

Figure 7 depicts how ideational meaning of a piece of text can be modelled in an ontology environment with the RNN. RNN is simple and powerful to conceptualize information of lexical stratum (word forms), semantic stratum (word meaning), conceptual stratum (SFL meta-concepts) and the whole network itself represents the entire experience construed by the relations among the strata.

Information in the network can be retrieved through activation of connected nodes. In terms of natural language, one can make queries such as the following:
- Who brought out the action mentioned in the text?

In F-Logic:

Axiom: FORALL W,T, X,Y,Z,P,Q, N,V,S T[hasActors@(S)->>W] <-

R[to@(1,T)->>X[to@(1,material)->>Y]] AND
Y[to@(N,V,actor)->>Z[to@(1,S:sememe)->>Y]] AND
S[sem_parent->>W:lexeme].
Query: FORALL Wrd,Sns <- "Example Text"[hasActor@(Sns)->>Wrd].
- What did Tim do ?
In F-Logic:
Query: FORALL Prc, Wrd, Role <-
"Example Text"[hasActors@(S:sememe)->>"Tim"] AND
Z[to@(1,S)->>Y[to@(N,Prc,Role)->>X]] AND
(NOT equal(Role,actor)) AND
X[to@(1,T:sememe)->>Y] AND T[sem_parent->>Wrd].

Similarly, axioms can be employed to facilitate queries for retrieving information such as the following:
- What does Tim think, believe, like or want?
- How has a particular event taken place, when? where? how?

8. RNN and the intelligent Web

The simplicity of RNN plus its applicability to all kinds of information storage suggests it may have a role to play in improving access to information on the Web. The Web provides a more general form of identifier indicating all kinds of information on the Web, called the Uniform Resource Identifier (URI). Uniform Resource Locators (URLs) are a particular kind of URI. All URIs share the property that different persons or organizations can independently create them, and use them to identify things. However, URIs are not limited to identifying things that have network locations, or use other computer access mechanisms. In fact, a URI can be created to refer to anything that needs to be referred to in a statement, including

- network-accessible things, such as an electronic document, an image, a service (e.g. today's weather report for Los Angeles), or a group of other resources.
- things that are not network-accessible, such as human beings, corporations, and bound books in a library.
- abstract concepts that do not exist physically, such as the concept of a creator.

We use RNN to model the Resource Description Framework (RDF), organizing information into a node-to-node environment following the RDF subject-predicate-object notion. The following Web information can be represented in RNN as shown in Figure 8:

1) The language of the webpage http://www.example.org/index.html is English (en).
2) The webpage http://www.example.org/index.html
is created by http://www.example.org/staffid/85740
3) The webpage http://www.example.org/index.html
is created on July 16.

Relational network notation and the intelligent Web

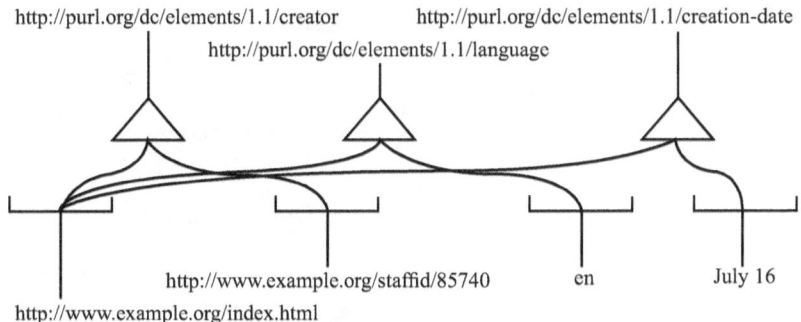

Figure 8 General Web information in RNN

The following query
>FORALL Z,W <-
>Y[to@(2,Z,1) ->> I[to@(1,"http://www.examples.org/index.html") ->>Y]] AND Y[to@(2,Z,2) ->>T[to@(1,W)->>Y]].

will obtain the following information about the web page in question:
"http://purl.org/dc/elements/1.1/creator", "http://www.examples.org/staffid/85740"

"http://purl.org/dc/elements/1.1/language", "en"

«http://examples.org/terms/creation-date», «July 16 «

Beyond the above general Web information, the ideational meaning construed by the text of a webpage can also be represented similarly. Linguistic information on a webpage is extracted by understanding the text in terms of PARTICIPANTS, PROCESS and CIRCUMSTANCE. RNN facilitates the consolidation of the semantic elements of different clauses and models a relational network representing the totality of the experience construed from the text. The whole *network of experience construal* is taken as the object of the predicate *ideational-meaning* by the subject *webpage*. See the following:

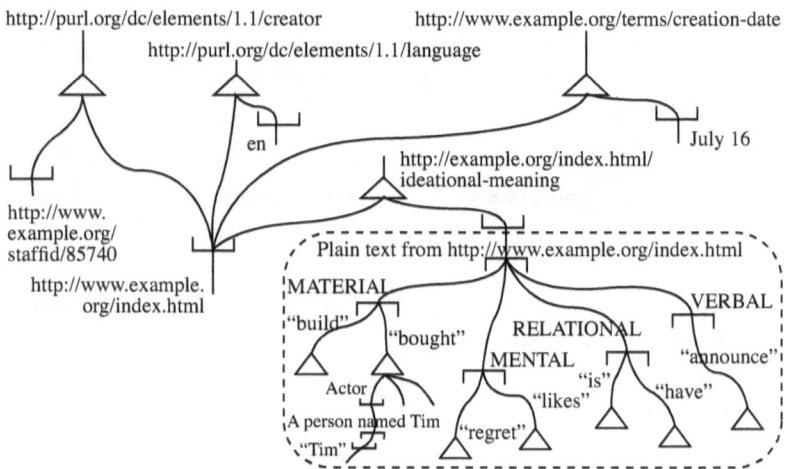

Figure 9 Web information in RNN including ideational-meaning from text

The following F-Logic query can be applied to access all **Actors** in MATERIAL EXPERIENCE construed from the text of the webpage.
    FORALL S,W <-

        Y[to@(2,Z,1)   ->>   I[to@(1,"http://www.examples.org/index.html") ->>Y]]

        AND Y[to@(2, " http://www.example.org/index.html/meaning",2)->>X]]

        AND X[to@(1,T)->>Y]

        T[hasActors@(S)->>W].

9. Conclusion

Ideational Meaning of a clause can be likened to a molecule, which typically consists of three elements. For a piece of text, its ideational meaning may be likened to a macromolecule instead of a number of molecules lined up one by one. Chemical reactions take place among molecules forming bonding between elements and thereby creating macromolecule. In the notion of knowledge base engineering, when new information is input, it does not stand alone individually or placed in a separate schema, rather, it bonds with old information to build the knowledge base. When one interprets a text, everything is taken into account. RNN makes it possible to represent the meaning conveyed by the text and facilitates access to this information.

Putting the corpus into the dictionary

Adam Kilgarriff
Lexical Computing Ltd.
adam@lexmasterclass.com

1. Introduction

A corpus is an arbitrary sample of language, whereas a dictionary aims to be a systematic account of the lexicon of a language. Children learn language through encountering arbitrary samples, and using them to build systematic representations. These banal observations suggest a relationship between corpus and dictionary in which the former is a provisional and dispensable resource used to develop the latter.

Let us review the Word Sense Disambiguation (WSD) research paradigm in this light. Consider SEMCOR, a hugely successful project and resource, very widely used and stimulating large amounts of WSD work. It is clearly a dynamic and important model, only exceeded in its take-up and impact by the WordNet database itself.

SEMCOR is a corpus where, for every instance of every open-class word, a person has inserted a WordNet sense number. It 'puts the dictionary (in the form of sense numbers) into the corpus'; like our title, but the other way round. We call this the PDIC model, in contrast with one which puts the corpus into the dictionary, the PCID model.

If one thinks of WSD as a task on the verge of hitting the marketplace and being widely used in applications, then PDIC is appropriate, as it represents the WSD task successfully done, and can be used as a model for what a system should do. However, it is widely acknowledged that WSD is not in any such near-to-market situation (as shown by discussions at the SENSEVAL-3 workshop (SENSEVAL-3 2004)) and we stand by our deep reservations about the nature of the WSD task (Kilgarriff 1997a, 1997b) which imply that this is unlikely to change. An alternative model, closer to the observations of the opening paragraph, is that the larger task is at a further remove from applications and is better seen as lexical acquisition. We are not yet (and probably never will be) at a stage at which a general–purpose WSD module is a relevant goal, but there are many language interpretation tasks which cannot be done without richer lexical representations. In the PCID model, the corpus serves to enrich the lexicon.

2. Levels of abstraction

The direct approach to corpus-dictionary linkage is to put pointers to dictionary senses into the corpus (in the PDIC model, as in SEMCOR) or to put pointers to corpus instances of words into the dictionary (in the PCID model). The direct approach has a number of drawbacks. The primary practical one is fragility. If the corpus (PCID model) or the dictionary (PDIC model) is edited or changed in any way, maintenance of the links is a headache. (This has been an ongoing issue for SEMCOR, as new versions of WordNet call for rebuilding SEMCOR in ways which cannot in general be fully and accurately automated (see Daudé et al 2000, 2001)). The theoretical one concerns levels of abstraction. A dictionary is an abstract representation of the language, in which we express differences of meaning but are not engaged with specifics of differences of form. The corpus is at the other end of the scale: the differences of form are immediately present but differences of meaning can only be inferred. What is needed is an intermediate level which links both to the meaning-differences in the dictionary and to the specific instances in the corpus.

Our candidate for this role is the grammatical-relation triple, comprising <grammatical-relation, word1, word2> (examples are <object, drink, beer> and <modifier, giant, friendly>). Tuples such as these have, of late, been very widely used in natural language processing (NLP), as focal objects for parsing and parse evaluation (e.g. Briscoe & Carroll 1998, Lin 1998), thesaurus-building (e.g. Grefenstette 1992) and for building multilingual resources from comparable corpora (e.g. Lű and Zhou 2004). Approaching from the other end, they are increasingly seen as core facts to be represented in dictionaries by lexicographers, who usually just call them 'collocations' (COBUILD 1987, and the OCDSE, Oxford Collocations Dictionary, 2003). In our own work, we compile sets of all the salient collocations of a word into 'word sketches', which then serve as a way of representing corpus evidence to the lexicographer (Kilgarriff & Tugwell 2001, Kilgarriff & Rundell 2002, Kilgarriff et al. 2004).

3. Aside: Parsing and lemmatizing

Few would dispute that collocations which incorporate grammatical information (and are thereby triples like <object, drink, beer>) are a more satisfactory form of lexical object than 'raw' collocates – those words occurring within a window of, say, three or five words to the right of, or to the left of, or on either side of the node word. Windowing approaches operate as a proxy for grammatical information and are appropriate only where there is no parser available, or it is too slow, or too often wrong. Historically, these factors have often applied and most older work uses windowing rather than grammar. As we are able to work with grammar, we do. We are repeatedly struck by how much cleaner the results we get are. We also find it preferable to work with lemmas rather than raw word forms, where a lemmatizer is available for a language.

4. Terminology

'Grammatical relation triples' being unwieldy, I shall call these objects simply 'collocations', or say that the one word is the other's 'collocate'. Strictly speaking, the items in the triples are lemmas which include a word class label (*noun, verb, adj* etc) as well as the base form; in examples, the word class labels will be omitted for readability. Naturally, some grammatical relations are duals (object, object-of) or symmetrical (and/or); for a full treatment, see Kilgarriff and Tugwell (2001).

5. The collocation database

In the proposed model, between the dictionary and the corpus sits a database. For each dictionary headword, there is a set of records in this database comprising
1) a collocate (including grammatical relation)
2) a pointer to the dictionary sense
3) a set of pointers to corpus instances of the headword in this collocation
The database is, in the first instance, generated from the corpus, so the corpus links are immediately available. To start with, the dictionary pointers are not filled in for polysemous words. (For single-sense words, the links can immediately be inserted.) A word sketch (see Figure 1) is an example of such a database. The corpus links are present, implemented as hyperlinks: for on-line readers, clicking on a number opens up a concordance window for the collocation (go to http://www.sketchengine.co.uk to register for an account).

goal BNC freq = 10631

and/or	1112	0.8	object_of	3430	3.1	subject_of	557	1.0
objective	57	32.86	score	797	75.31	come	78	28.4
try	30	32.67	achieve	363	48.14	give	34	14.57
goal	32	23.39	concede	126	47.79	win	13	14.32
penalty	20	22.75	disallow	26	34.87	help	10	10.69
target	22	20.1	pursue	75	33.13			
value	33	19.36	attain	34	29.34	**adj_subject_of**	**149**	**1.4**
conversion	12	18.92	net	18	26.7	important	10	15.32
aim	15	17.6	kick	36	26.2			
mission	11	16.29	grab	30	24.43			
priority	10	14.13	reach	78	23.81			
strategy	11	12.28	set	97	23.53			
point	19	12.21	notch	10	22.81			

a_modifier	2546	1.8
ultimate	83	42.22
away	25	32.56
winning	31	32.56
compact	34	31.79
stated	17	27.88
late	53	27.33
dropped	11	26.98
organisational	22	26.83
long-term	34	25.7
common	56	24.62
headed	11	24.48
organizational	18	24.45

n_modifier	1181	1.0	modifies	748	0.3	pp_after-p	58	7.1
drop	85	45.59	scorer	40	43.0	minute	37	39.18
penalty	100	45.27	difference	69	34.08			
league	90	37.36	scoring	17	29.24	particle	86	4.5
consolation	24	35.39	ace	18	28.33	back	32	28.93
opening	42	31.15	drought	14	26.56	down	32	28.62
second-half	13	30.46	post	34	25.55	up	14	15.44
first-half	12	30.04	kick	17	25.19			
minute	30	21.09	keeper	16	24.71	possessor	492	4.3
half	17	19.15	weight	21	21.01	England	12	13.95
policy	42	18.73	lead	16	20.29			
relationship	16	13.36	average	10	17.56	pp_from-p	275	4.1
development	22	13.22	setting	11	16.98	attempt	12	17.09

Figure 1 Word sketch for *goal* with data from the British National Corpus (BNC)

6. Limitations and potential extensions

The word sketch model is dependent on Yarowsky's 'One sense per collocation' (Yarowsky 1993): we assume that each collocation is, in itself, single-sense and can be mapped to just one dictionary sense. Of course this is not always true, and to the extent that it does not hold, the model will be inadequate and we will need to make the structure of the database record richer.

The triples formalism does not readily express some kinds of information which are known to be relevant to WSD. An intermediate database to link dictionary to corpus should have a place for all relevant facts. Two kinds of fact which do not obviously fit the triples model are grammatical constructions and domain preferences.

Many, possibly all, grammatical constructions can be viewed as grammatical relations (with the 'other word' field null). Thus a verb like found, when in the passive, means "set up" ('the company was founded in 1787'). In this case we associate the triple <passive, found, _> with the "set up" meaning. We have already implemented a range of 'unary relations' within the Sketch Engine, and believe this approach will support the description of all grammatical constructions.

As much recent work makes clear, domains are central to sense identification (e.g. Agirre et al 2001, Buitelaar & Sacaleanu 2001, McCarthy et al 2004). However, it is far from clear how domain information should be expressed:

hand-developed inventories of domains have many shortcomings, but data-driven approaches to domain induction are not yet mature and suffer from the arbitrariness of the corpora they use. The incorporation of domain information into the database model requires further work.

Whereas a collocate tends to be associated with one and only one sense, so can it be used to generate a Boolean rule of the form 'collocation X implies sense Y', where both grammatical constructions and domains provide preferences. Royalty (singular) usually means "kings and queens", whereas royalties (plural) usually means "payments to authors". However, a rule 'singular implies kings-and-queens' should not be Boolean: we often talk about, for example, royalty payments, which are payments to authors, not to (or from) kings and queens. The facts are preferences, or probabilistic, rather than categorical. Our current model does not incorporate preferences or probabilities, and they raise theoretical problems: are the probabilities not as arbitrary as the corpora they were drawn from? This, again, needs further work.

The formalism will allow Boolean combinations of triples and of senses, so it is possible to say, for example, 'triple X AND triple Y imply NOT sense Z'. We envisage that unary relations (e.g. grammatical constructions) will often be used to rule out senses, or in conjunction with collocates.

Once solutions to the domains issue are found, we will be able to view the database connecting corpus to dictionary as a database of collocations, constructions and domains: a CoCoDo database.

7. Linking collocations to senses

There are a number of ways in which the pointers to dictionary senses might be added. Over the last forty years the WSD community has developed a host of strategies for assigning collocates to dictionary senses (Ide & Véronis 1998, Kilgarriff & Palmer 2000, SENSEVAL-2 2001, SENSEVAL-3 2004, SENSEVAL-4 /SEMEVAL-1 2007). Many of them can be applied (depending, obviously, on the nature of the dictionary and the information it provides).

We have specified the problem as the disambiguation of collocates rather than corpus instances. In practice, collocates (more widely or narrowly construed) are the workhorse of almost all WSD. The core is of identifying a large set of collocates (or, more broadly, sentence patterns or text features) which are associated with just one of the word's senses, which then may be found in a sentence or text to be disambiguated. The task of assigning collocates is a large part of the task of assigning instances.

Other differences between the task as specified here and the traditional WSD task are as follows:

1) **Dictionary structure:** We can link to any substructure of the dictionary entry; if the entry has subsenses, or multiwords embedded within senses or *vice versa*, we can link to the appropriate element, and so need not make invidious choices about whether to use 'fine-grained' or 'coarse-grained' senses.

Putting the corpus into the dictionary 245

2) **Other dictionary information:** Since the larger goal is the enrichment of lexical resources, where a resource is already rich, the information it contains is given. It can be used in WSD, and does not need to be duplicated. One resource we have looked closely at, the database version of Oxford Dictionary of English (McCracken 2003), contains particularly full information on domain, taxonomy, multiwords, grammatical and phonological patterning etc., all sense-specific. This is all immediately available, both for disambiguation and, obviously, in the output resource.
3) **Precision-recall tradeoff:** There is no commitment to disambiguating all corpus instances (or all collocates). Like many NLP tasks, WSD exhibits a precision-recall tradeoff. If a system need not commit itself when the evidence is not clear, it can achieve high accuracy for those cases where it does present a verdict. WSD has usually been conceptualized as a task where a choice must be made for every instance (so precision = recall) and in the PDIC model this seems appropriate. But in the PCID model it is not necessary. What we would like is **some** corpus-based information about all dictionary senses, and it is immaterial if there are some corpus instances which do not contribute to any lexical entry. Once we view the WSD task in this light, we welcome high-precision, low-recall strategies (e.g. Magnini et al 2001, which achieved precision of 5% higher than the next highest-precision system in the SENSEVAL-2 English all-words task, with 35% recall). We can do WSD without the shadow of an apparent 60% precision ceiling (SENSEVAL-3 2004) hanging over us.
4) **Mixed-initiative methods:** Once WSD is seen as a step towards the enrichment of lexical resources, it becomes valid to ask how humans may be involved in the process. Kilgarriff and Tugwell (2001), and Kilgarriff, Koeling, Tugwell and Evans (2003) present a system in which a lexicographer assigns collocates to senses, and this then feeds Yarowsky's (1995) decision-list learning algorithm. In general, in the proposed architecture, both people and systems can identify collocate-to-sense mappings, with each potentially learning from evidence provided by the other and correcting the other's errors or omissions. (There will be a set of issues around permissions: which agents (human or computer) can add or edit which mappings.) Ideally, the process of identifying the mappings for a word is a mixed-initiative dialogue in which the lexicographer refines their analysis of the word's space of meaning in tandem with the system refining, in real time, the WSD program which allocates instances to senses and thereby provides the lexicographer with evidence.

8. Dictionary-free methods

While most WSD work to date has been based on a sense inventory from an existing resource, some (e.g. Schütze 1998) have used unsupervised methods to arrive, bottom-up, at its own senses inventory.

If the PCID model is being used to create a brand new dictionary, or if a fresh analysis of a word's meaning into senses is required, or if some dictionary-independent processing is required as a preliminary or complement to a dictionary-specific process, then dictionary-free methods are suitable. Methods such as Schütze's (1998) are based on clustering instances of words. Our strategy will be to cluster collocates. One method we have already implemented uses the thesaurus we have created from the same parsed corpus as was used to create the word sketches. Looking at the verbs that *goal* is object of, in Figure 1, we see a number of verbs with closely related meanings, and we would like to form them into two clusters, one for sporting *goal*s and one for life *goal*s (these being the two main meanings of *goal*). In the thesaurus entry for *disallow*, we find, within the top ten items, *concede* and *net*, thus providing evidence that these three items cluster together. The list below is a variant of the object_of list for *goal* in Figure 1, with the collocations clustered. With just one exception, each cluster indicates just one sense of *goal*: the clusters under *score* and *concede* all (except *reach*) imply sporting goals, whereas the clusters under *achieve* and *pursue* are all life goals.

object_of	3302	3.0
score 758	936	74.31
reach 78 hit 42 strike 21 miss 11 lose 15 collect 6 save 5		
achieve 360	644	48.29
define 30 share 26 identify 20 establish 21 specify 10 produce 27 manage 11 implement 6 claim 12 secure 7 develop 14 choose 10 need 20 promote 6 list 5 create 11 state 6 seek 7 support 7 allow 10 determine 5 express 5 include 8		
concede 114	120	46.87
yield 6		
disallow	26	35.42
pursue 73	146	33.22
attain 34 satisfy 11 realize 10 fulfil 8 realise 10		
net	17	26.79

Figure 2 Clustered word sketch

Another method depends on the observation that a single instance of a word may exemplify more than one collocation. The instance *score a drop goal* exemplifies both <*object, score, goal*> and <*modifier, goal, drop*>, and so provides evidence that these two collocations should be mapped to the same sense.

Collocate-clustering is best seen as a partial process, marking collocates as sharing the same sense only when there is strong evidence to do so and remaining silent elsewhere. It then provides good evidence for other processes, dictionary-based or manual, to build on.

9. The dispensable corpus

As mentioned in the opening paragraph, a corpus is an arbitrary sample. A person's mental lexicon, while developed from a set of language samples, has learnt from them and moved on. The corpus is dispensable. In a PDIC approach, this clearly does not apply: if the corpus is thrown away, all the evidence linking corpus to dictionary is lost too. Likewise for a PCID approach with direct corpus-dictionary linking. But in the model presented here, if the corpus is thrown away, the collocate-to-sense mappings are rich, free-standing lexical data in their own right (and could readily be used to find new corpus examples for each collocate or sense).

10. Conclusion

The chapter, when originally written in 2004, charted the way ahead. Some of the ideas had, as indicated, already been explored, using the Sketch Engine (http://www.sketchengine.co.uk) platform and its predecessor, the WASPbench. (The Sketch Engine identifies all items – collocations, triples, word instances – as URLs, thereby supporting distributed development, open access, and connectivity with other resources.)

We are working with the developers of a leading dictionary editing system, so that the editing software can be used for managing the CoCoDo database and associating collocations with senses. Collaborations with dictionary publishers, to enrich their existing dictionaries, are under discussion.

Towards a multimodal dictionary of narration

Ismail S. Talib
National University of Singapore
ellibst@nus.edu.sg

1. Some characteristics of specialist dictionaries

1.1. Specialist and general dictionaries

This chapter will deal with some of the characteristics and problems of specialist dictionaries in general and a dictionary of narrative in particular, such as the need to add multimodal clarifications or illustrations for some of the entries. It will not make wide-ranging comparisons between this type of dictionary with more general lexicographical projects involving the lexicon of particular languages. However, some specific comparisons or correlations may be relevant. The relevance may be correlative, but it may have a more direct connection.

Among the more direct correlations between these two types of dictionaries is the fact that some lexical items in certain disciplines do find their way into language in general. The problems in the definitions of some of these terms in the specialist dictionary may thus be carried over to the general dictionary. The possibility of a problematic counter-directional influence on the specialist lexicon may also be there. In this regard, Kate Burridge (2005: 16) notes:

> When everyday language swipes words from specialist languages the effect is usually a broadening of definition. The original narrow specification is lost and the term expands its meaning.

What the expansion of the meanings of some specialist terms does is to create new problems in the definitions of these terms in the specialist dictionary. In time, some specialist readers may perceive the terms as broader or looser than they originally were in the specialist lexicon. At least two of the narrative terms selected for discussion in this chapter, for example, have become part of the general English vocabulary, and are now no longer restricted to the specialist lexicon. Their appearance in the language in general however, makes their specialist definitions less specific. This may in turn create problems in the definitions of such terms in the specialist dictionary, especially if the dictionary is not limited to definitions that are based on expert advice, but aims to take the lack of specificity into account by looking at how they are actually used in the corpus (Norman 2002).

1.2. Translatability of specialist dictionaries

Specialist dictionaries have their own unique characteristics that are not shared by general dictionaries. Some specialist dictionaries can actually be translated into other languages, unlike general dictionaries, which cannot, almost by definition, be translated. However, there are some limitations in the translation of a specialist dictionary, and translatability may depend on the discipline involved. If it is a dictionary of a particular discipline in the humanities, such as narrative studies, there is good probability that many of the terms have a more intrinsic relationship to the language that it is written in. As a result, the translation of such a specialist dictionary is usually more difficult than that of a specialist dictionary of a scientific discipline.

Although, as indicated above, specialist dictionaries usually give more precise – or narrower – definitions than general dictionaries, some terms, especially those found in humanities dictionaries, may remain specific to the original language. These terms are not easily translated, partly because of what can be described as the 'opacity of the specialist lexicon in whichever language it was to be found' (MacConchie 1997: 51).

A related reason for the difficulty in the cross-linguistic transference or translation of terminology is the use of idiomatic expressions. Idiomatic expressions must be taken into account even in some scientific dictionaries (Wiseman and Feng 1998). These expressions are naturally more prevalent in the terminology of specialist humanities dictionaries, either by having a significant impact on some of the terms found in the discipline, or are themselves used as terms: a good example here is the term *point of view* in narrative studies.

The opacity of language and the prevalence of idiomatic expressions mean that if the specialist dictionary is eventually translated, there has to be some compromise. It is likely that the translated dictionary will comprise fewer terms than the original, or, some terms are simply borrowed, unchanged, from the source language. The price that may have to be paid for the translation of a specialist dictionary in the humanities is either the lack of comprehensiveness, or the selective non-translation of terminology, or both.

1.3. Multimodal illustrations and their limitations

Another characteristic of some specialist dictionaries is the difficulty of using only words in trying to proffer explanations of some terms. This is moving a step further away from non-translatability, as the words cannot be accurately or adequately 'explained' in any language by using other words in the language. This is a problem faced by some specialist dictionaries in both the humanities and the sciences. This problem is, of course, not only confined to specialist dictionaries. There is in fact an inherent philosophical difficulty in using words to explain anything, including the explanation of other words that do not have multimodal dimensions. For Patrick Hanks

(2003: 205), 'natural languages are not precise mathematical systems, and meaning statements, are not, literally, equations'.

If there are difficulties in using words to explain other words, as in general dictionaries, there are bound to be, in specialist dictionaries, even more difficulties in the use of words to explain some of the terms that refer to non-linguistic entities or processes. In fact, some of the terms in a dictionary of narrative cannot be adequately explained by using the conventional means of using only words; it can even be argued that such a method of explanation would mislead the reader. This is especially the case with some terms pertaining to cinematic narratives.

One way out in the explanation of terms that refer to non-linguistic entities or processes is the use of static graphics as an aid to explanation. Static graphics, of course, have been used for the explanation of some words in dictionaries – both general and specialized. However, static graphics can prove to be as misleading as, or even more misleading than, the use of only words for some of the terms used in the description or analysis of cinematic narrative. Even in a general dictionary, to extend an example given by Vincent Ooi (1998), the word *bell* may be 'explained' by resorting to a picture or drawing of a bell. But this is inadequate, and may even be misleading. More important than how the bell looks, is its sound. As Ooi (1998: 121) exclaims, 'it would be nice if the sound of a bell could be heard at the same time for those who have multimedia machines!' The definitions of some of the terms used in the description of certain non-linguistic processes found in cinematic narratives are even more complicated than the definition of a bell, and need multimodal illustrations for them to be adequately defined. Words alone are clearly inadequate.

For various reasons however, the use of the more conventional words-only method for lexicographical explanation is still around. In some cases, it may in fact be desirable for this approach to be sustained. There are virtues in word-only explanations in lexicography that more multimedia-dependent explanations have not quite superseded. Dictionaries that use multimedia content may become a little too complicated, and cannot be easily used. The Oxford-Duden dictionaries for example, at least as they were originally conceived, used graphics extensively and as comprehensively as possible, but not other multimedia content. However, these dictionaries have been criticized for being 'so packed and complicated, with every nook, cranny and micro-part labelled, that they are often difficult to use' (Frawley et al.: 10).

The attempt to comprehensively add other media, such as sound and video, may in fact result in further complications that make using a dictionary even more difficult. However, there is a saving grace when one looks at the lexicography of narrative, as the inadequacy or even falsity of word-only explanations seems to be largely confined, if not exclusively, to motion picture narratives with sound. The explanation of terms pertaining to written narratives does not appear to be beset with similar difficulties.

Trying to explain narrative terms by resorting to multimodal means may create an ostensible imbalance in the lexicographical project which may make the explanations of film narrative terms appear more generous than those pertaining to written narratives. A comparable variation in the need for multimodal explanations of terms is found in other specialist dictionaries, where the lexicographer needs to look for a sense of balance, so that the terms which may be quite sufficiently defined in words do not appear to be deceptively inadequate alongside those that use multimodal explanations or illustrations.

As indicated earlier, one of the difficulties of defining terminology pertaining to motion picture narratives with sound is the artificiality of such definitions to begin with: they seem to be poor, or at best, passable pegs on which some concepts that involve vision and sound are hung. Another difficulty is the confusion with how some terms used for written literature are used in cinema. The notion of *interior meaning* as it is used in *auteur theory* for example, has been described as 'ambiguous in any literary sense because part of it is imbedded in the stuff of the cinema and cannot be rendered in non-cinematic terms' (Sarris 2004: 31).

1.4. Discoursal contexts

A further difficulty has to do with discourse – the textual and sociocultural contexts that some of the terms are reliant on, and without which they become misleading or meaningless. However, in spite of the importance of discoursal meaning, dictionaries cannot comprehensively deal with all facets of meaning. If we look at the three broad ways that the study of meaning is traditionally understood: lexical, syntactic and discoursal, dictionaries, for various reasons, concentrate only on lexical meaning. But the concentration on lexical meaning is inadequate or biased (Benson 2001: 15-16). Moreover, even if the concentration is on lexical meaning, the most voluminous dictionaries cannot include all the lexical definitions in a language, or, for that matter, all the definitions in certain disciplines. Besides, the lexical meanings of the words that are included are not always sufficiently defined (Robinson 1954).

To add to the complication, these discoursal features go beyond written language, and involve what the film scholar Christian Metz (1974) has described as *image discourse*. In this context, we are looking at discourse from an extra-linguistic angle, and the difficulties in the definition of some multimodal narrative terms, as seen in their discoursal contexts, may not apply to the terms of written narratives, whose discoursal contexts are linguistically based, and less complicated.

Towards a multimodal dictionary of narration 253

2. Terms needing multimodal clarifications

2.1. Selected terms

Among the definitions of narrative terms that present us with difficulties if only written linguistic definitions are given, are the following:
- Flashback
- Voice-over narration
- Point-of-view shot

On the surface, the above terms may appear to be simple. However, their complexity, and hence the difficulty in explaining them in a dictionary, will come to the fore if we examine some actual examples in cinematic narratives.

2.2. Flashback

The term *flashback* is clearly part of English vocabulary today, and can be found in the Oxford English Dictionary [henceforth, OED]:

Cinemat. A scene which is a return to a previous action in the film, a CUT-BACK; hence, a revival of the memory of past events, as in a pictorial or written presentation. (See FLASH $n.^2$ 1e, and $v.^1$ 12b.)

The above definition however, is unsatisfactory. How does one 'return to a previous action' in a film? If the character in a cinematic narrative repeats or imitates an action that has been done previously, does that constitute a *flashback*? No, quite obviously one must move backwards in time as well. The repetition or imitation of action to the future of the earlier original action does not constitute a *flashback*. Now, the idea of moving backwards in time actually presents us with another can of worms. I have myself defined *flashback* in the draft of my dictionary of narrative in the following way:

An earlier **event** that is **narrate**d later in the **discourse**. Also called **analepsis** in **narrative theory**.

The above definition of course belongs to a specialist dictionary. Although all the words above, except for *analepsis*, can be found in English, and hence appear in any comprehensive dictionary of the language, the term is obviously defined in a rather specialized way.

However, the definition still falls short, as *flashbacks* do not merely arise arbitrarily. They are activated by certain motivating factors in the narrative, and these factors should be included for the definition to be more satisfying. But the question is how and to what extent they could or should be included. It is suffice to say that *flashback* should not be defined simply as moving backwards in time, or that it is necessarily the revival of the memory of past events, even if this is frequently the case. Another possibility is that it serves the function of explaining to the audience what happened in the past, so that the narrative would be better understood by the audience, even though the memory of any of the characters is not actually involved (see the illustration below, which of course, could be made clearer if the appropriate video clip is played). Also, a combination of these functions may be involved, even if one looks at a single cinematic narrative, or even, for that matter, at a single flashback.

Figure 1 Flashback in *The Godfather: Part II*

Fade-out–fade-in transition in Francis Ford Coppola's[1] *The Godfather: Part II* (1974), which signals a flashback, but which clearly does not involve the memory or storytelling of the character Michael Corleone (left) of what happened in the pre-gangster days of his father, Don Vito Corleone (right).

2.3. Voice-Over Narration

Unlike the term *flashback*, the term *voice-over narration* is not found as a whole term in the OED. Instead, there is the term *voice-over* in the dictionary:

voice-over, narration spoken by an unseen narrator on a film or television broadcast; also, the unseen person whose voice is heard; also *attrib*.

I have no problems with the OED's division of the term into two, with entries for *voice-over* above, and *narration* defined elsewhere in the dictionary. However, there are problems with the content of the definitions above.

In the first definition, narration seems to be assumed whenever the word 'voice-over' is used. However, this is not how we understand the term. Unless the full term *voice-over narration* is used, *narration* should not be assumed by default, as the voice-over need not be narrating, but may serve an argumentative or expository function. The second definition above seems to have got it right, but as a more general definition, it should have preceded the

Towards a multimodal dictionary of narration 255

earlier one. Nonetheless, both the definitions make the assumption that the personage involved in the *voice-over* is 'unseen'. This is unclear, and even misleading. What happens if the personage involved in the *voice-over* can be seen on the screen, in the sense that the audience could see the character while the voice-over narration – which presumably occurs some time to the future of the actions of the character on the screen – is heard? An example is shown below. Perhaps what is meant here – and what could be put more precisely – is that the character is *not seen uttering the words of the voice-over narration*. But it is not correct to say, without qualification, that the character who narrates is 'unseen' when the voice-over narration takes place. Again, looking at actual cinematic footage may prevent the lexicographer from stumbling into the pitfalls found in the OED entry, and a static picture, like the one below (which is perhaps helped by the subtitle), does not quite explain the possibilities and limitations of the term as well as the appropriate video clip.

Figure 2 Voice-Over narration in *Zamani Barayé Mast Asbha*

Voice-over narration where one of the voice-over narrators physically appears, with her voice-over telling us (and her unseen interlocutor) about what she does for a living. She is of course not seen uttering the Farsi words as translated in the subtitle above (which indeed validates what she says as *voice-over narration*). But she is not, at the same time, actually 'unseen', as we can clearly see her on the screen above. The example is taken from the Iranian movie, *Zamani Barayé Masti Asbha* (2000), directed by Bahman Ghobadi[2].

2.4. Point-of-View Shot

Like *voice-over narration*, the full term *point-of-view shot* is not found in the OED. As a contrast to both *flashback* and *voice-over narration*, it is a specialized term that has not found its way into the language in general. However, the first half of the term, *point of view*, is a common lexical item,

and hence, it can be found in the OED:
> **point of view** *n.* [after French *point de vue* (1689; earlier in technical senses: see *point of sight* n. at Phrases 4l)] the position from which something is seen or viewed; (*fig.*) the perspective from which a subject or event is perceived, or a story, etc., narrated; a mental position or attitude (now the usual sense); occas. *attrib.*

With the *point-of-view shot*, it is the physical notion of *point of view* above that is relevant; more specifically, 'the position from which something is seen or viewed'.

However, there needs to be a further specification to this definition. The position from which the stretch of the motion picture is taken should be from the physical perspective of one of the characters in the movie. Another specification needs to be added, although, on the face of it, it may be too obvious to mention, and that is, the camera must be positioned as if it is presenting the direct perspective of the eyes of one of the characters for the shot to be described as a *point-of-view shot*. On the surface, this may not seem problematic. Indeed, a static image will fulfil the explanatory task adequately (as illustrated by the first picture below), if a visual instrument is used by the character, and if
- the camera takes the shot through the visual instrument, or
- the camera takes a simulated shot as if the perspective is seen through the visual instrument, or
- the shot is masked through editing to make it look like it is seen through the visual instrument,

But problems arise when what is seen by the character is seen with the naked eye. In this case, the camera baldly simulates the character's vision without any striking or strong indicators that differentiate it from the 'neutral' or non-human perspective of the camera (see the second illustration below). Should this also be described as a *point-of-view shot*? Again, a static image does not quite 'define' it as a point-of-view shot. An appropriate video clip does a far better job in illustrating it as such.

Figure 3 Point-of-View Shot through a ViewFinder in *Traffic*

If the shot is seen through the perspective of a visual instrument, such as that of a rifle's viewfinder above, describing it as a *point-of-view shot* by using a static image might not be a problem. The example is taken from Steven Soderbergh's[3] *Traffic* (2000).

Figure 4 Point-of-View Shot through the Naked Eye in *Mystic River*

If the shot is seen through the naked eye, it is more difficult to use a static picture of part of the shot to explain that it is a *point-of-view shot*. The picture above, from Clint Eastwood's[4] *Mystic River* (2003), unlike the earlier picture, does not stand by itself. In order to justify it as a *point-of-view shot*, an explanation is needed that the shot is continuously taken from the back of a stationary car, where a character who is looking at the girl is hiding. The appropriate video clip, however, will be virtually self-explanatory, and will also clarify the shot as a *point-of-view shot* much better than the static image.

3. Conclusion

Compiling a dictionary with multimodal illustrations will of course solve some of the problems of defining lexical items that cannot be 'defined' by using only words, whether it be a specialist or general dictionary. Multimodal dictionaries are increasingly common as the years go by. In fact, one reason for putting dictionaries in CDs or DVDs, unless one is dealing with a voluminous word-only dictionary like the OED, is usually linked to the possibility of adding a multimedia dimension to the dictionary. Of course, everything else being equal, such dictionaries may get a better response from the public than conventional ones, or at least, they attractively widen the publication range of a dictionary publisher.

There are virtues and challenges of course in word-only specialist dictionaries, or, for that matter, in word-only definitions. This is an aspect of dictionary compiling which I have mentioned in passing in this chapter, preferring to focus on what are rather new but gradually more common problems in the definitions of the lexicon of some disciplines and in a dictionary of narrative in particular. These problems will become more prevalent in the future. What we can say in this connection is that the possibility is very real that some specialist dictionaries of the future may end up not consisting of words, but videos, pictures and non-linguistic sounds, and other videos, pictures and non-linguistic sounds will be used to 'define' them. Words may serve inadequate labelling functions in such dictionaries, as the videos, pictures and non-linguistic sounds that they label and define are more central.

Notes
1. Coppola, F. F. (director and producer). 1974. The Godfather: Part II. Hollywood: Paramount Pictures.
2. Ghobadi, B. (director and producer). 2000. Zamani Barayé Masti Asbha. Tehran: Bahman Ghobadi Films and Farabi Cinema Foundation.
3. Soderbergh, S. (director). 2000. Traffic. Universal City, CA: USA Films
4. Eastwood, C. (director and producer), Berman, B. (executive producer). 2003. Mystic River. Burbank, CA: Warner Bros. Pictures.

References

A. Dictionaries and other reference works

BBI: *The BBI Combinatory Dictionary of English.* 1997. M. Benson, E. Benson, and R. Ilson (eds.). Amsterdam: John Benjamins.

CD: *The Chambers Dictionary.* (9e) 2003. C. Gleeson, M. Munro, and M. Thomson (eds.). Edinburgh: Chambers Harrap.

CALD: *(The) Cambridge Advanced Learner's Dictionary.* [1e 2003 E. Walter and K. Woodford (eds.), 2e with CD-ROM 2005]. Cambridge: Cambridge University Press.

CALD-OL. http://dictionary.cambridge.org/.

CED: *Collins English Dictionary.* 2004. S. Anderson, J. Butterfield, J. Daintith, A. Holmes, A. Isaacs, and J. Law (eds.). Glasgow: HarperCollins.

CEDIP: *(A) Chinese-English Dictionary of Idioms and Proverbs.* 1988. X. Heng and X. Zhang (comp.) (Lexicographica Series Maior 24). Tübingen: Max Niemeyer Verlag.

CIDE: *Cambridge International Dictionary of English.* 1995. P. Procter (ed.). Cambridge: Cambridge University Press.

CIHAI: *Ci Hai (A Grand Dictionary of Chinese).* 1980. Shanghai: Shanghai Dictionary Press.

CLD: *Cambridge Learner's Dictionary.* 2004. P. Gillard and E. Walter. (eds.). Cambridge: Cambridge University Press.

CLD-SBV: *Cambridge Learner's Dictionary: Semi-Bilingual Version.* 2004. Y. Tono, and P. Guillard (eds.). Tokyo: Cambridge University Press and Shogakukan.

COBUILD: *Collins COBUILD (Advanced Learner's) English Dictionary.* J. Sinclair [1e 1987, 5e 2006] (ed.). London/Glasgow: HarperCollins.

COD11: *Concise Oxford English Dictionary.* (11e) 2004. C. Soanes, and A. Stevenson (eds.). Oxford: Oxford University Press.

DHXC: *Dangdai Hanyu Xinci Cidian (New Word Dictionary of Contemporary Chinese).* 2004. W. Qu and M.G. Han (eds.). Beijing: China Encyclopaedia Publishing House.

DoL: *Dictionary of Lexicography.* 1998/2001. R. Hartmann and G. James (comp.). London: Routledge. [Japanese translation *Jishugaku jiten.* S. Takebayashi et al. (eds.). Tokyo: Kenkyusha 2003].

E-GATE: *E-Gate English-Japanese Dictionary.* 2003. S. Tanaka, S. Takeda, and S. Kawade (eds.). Tokyo: Benesse.

FAV: *Advanced Favorite English-Japanese Dictionary.* 2002. H. Asano, H. Abe, and T. Makino (eds.). Tokyo: Tokyo-shoseki.

G4: *Taishukan's Genius English-Japanese Dictionary.* (4e) 2006. T. Konishi, and K Minamide (eds.). Tokyo: Taishukan.
LBCP: *The Little Book of Chinese Proverbs.* 2001/2004. J. Clements (comp.). Bath: Parragon.
LDOCE: *Longman Dictionary of Contemporary English.* [1e 1978 P. Procter (ed.), 4e 2003 D. Summers (ed.).] London: Pearson-Longman.
LDOCE-OL: *Longman Dictionary of Contemporary English Online.* http://www.ldoceonline.com/.
LEXIS: *Obunsha Lexis English-Japanese Dictionary.* 2003. K. Hanamoto, K. Nomura, and R. Hayashi (eds.). Tokyo: Obunsha.
LLA: *Longman Language Activator.* 1993. Harlow: Longman.
LUM2: *Kenkyusha's Luminous English-Japanese Dictionary.* (2e) 2005. S. Takebayashi, Y. Kojima, N. Higashi, and K. Akasu (eds.). Tokyo: Kenkyusha.
MECD: *A Modern English-Chinese Dictionary.* 2003. S. Guo (ed.). Beijing: Foreign Language Teaching and Research Press.
MED: *MacMillan English Dictionary for Advanced Learners.* 2002. M. Rundell et al. (ed.). Oxford: Macmillan Education.
NACED: *New Age Chinese-English Dictionary/Xinshidai Hanying Dacidian.* 1978/2000. J.R. Wu and Z.Q. Cheng (eds.). Beijing: The Commercial Press.
NCMFD: *New-Century Multi-Functional English-Chinese Dictionary.* 2003. W.D. Dai (ed.). Shanghai: Shanghai Foreign Language Education Press.
NCol7: *Kenkyusha's New College English-Japanese Dictionary.* (7e) 2003. S. Takebayashi, N. Higashi, H. Suwabe, and Y. Ichikawa (eds.). Tokyo: Kenkyusha.
NDAS: *New Dictionary of American Slang.* 1987. R.L. Chapman (ed.). London and Basingstoke: Macmillan.
NODE: *(The) New Oxford Dictionary of English.* 1998. J. Pearsall (ed.). Oxford: Oxford University Press. [Chinese bilingualization *Xin Niujin Yingyu Cidian* (*Yinghan Shuangjieben*). Shanghai: Foreign Language Education Press 2007].
OALD: *Oxford Advanced Learner's Dictionary of Current English.* Oxford: Oxford University Press [1e 1948, A.S. Hornby (ed.), 7e 2005 S. Wehmeier (ed.). CD-ROM 2000. Chinese bilingualizations, F.K. Cheung et al. (ed.). Taipei/Hong Kong 1966/1970/1984/1986/1994/1997].
OALD-OL: *Oxford Advanced Learner's Dictionary of Current English Online.* http://www.oup.com/oald-bin/Web_getald7index1a.pl/.
OCDSE: *Oxford Collocations Dictionary for Students of English.* 2003. D. Lea (ed.). Oxford: Oxford University Press.
OED: *The Oxford English Dictionary.* [1e 1888 A.H.J. Murray; current edition J. Simpson et al. (ed.).] Oxford: Oxford University Press.
OED-OL: *The Oxford English Dictionary Online.* http://www.ode.com/.
PED: *The Penguin English Dictionary.* 2003. R. Allen (ed.). London: Penguin.

SA3: *The Super Anchor English-Japanese Dictionary.* (3e) 2003. K. Yamagishi (ed.). Tokyo: Gakushu-Kenkyusha.
TCEED2: *Times-Chambers Essential English Dictionary.* (2e) 1997. E. Higgleton, and V.B.Y. Ooi (eds.). Singapore: Federal Publications/ Chambers-Harrap.
VWBD: *Variantenwörterbuch des Deutschen.* 2004. Die Standardsprache in Österreich, der Schweiz und Deutschland sowie in Liechtenstein, Luxemburg, Ostbelgien und Südtirol. U. Ammon et al. (eds.). Berlin: W. de Gruyter.
WIS2: *The Wisdom English-Japanese Dictionary.* (2e) 2007. N. Inoue, and I. Akano (eds.). Tokyo: Sanseido.
XHC: *Xiandai Hanyu Cidian: Bilingual Edition (A Dictionary of Modern Chinese).* 2002. Beijing: Foreign Language Teaching and Research Press.
XHGC: *Xiandai Hanyu Guifan Cidian (Standard Modern Chinese Dictionary).* 2004. X.J. Li (ed.). Beijing: Foreign Language Teaching and Research Press and Chinese Language Press.
XHXC: *Xinshiji Hanyu Xinci Cidian (Dictionary of Chinese Neologisms in the New Century).* 2006. J. Wang (ed.). Shanghai: Chinese Dictionary Press.
XYC: *Xin Yinghan Cidian (New English-Chinese Dictionary).* 2000. Y. Wu (ed.). Shanghai: Shanghai Translation Press.

B. Other literature

Aarts, B., Denison, D., Keizer, E. and Popova, G. (eds.). 2004. *Fuzzy Grammar: a Reader.* Oxford: Oxford University Press.
Abdullah, H. 1974. *The Morphology of Malay.* Kuala Lumpur: Dewan Bahasa dan Pustaka.
Adamska-Sałaciak, A. 2006. *Meaning and the Bilingual Dictionary* (Polish Studies in English Language and Literature 18). Frankfurt: P. Lang.
Adamson, S. 1989. 'With Double Tongue: Diglossia, Stylistics and the Teaching of English' in M. Short (ed.), *Reading, Analysing and Teaching Literature.* London: Longman, 204-240.
Agirre, E., Ansa, O., Martínez, D. and Hovy, E. 2001. 'Enriching WordNet Concepts with Topic Signatures' in *Proceedings of the North American Chapter of the Association for Computational Linguistics (NAACL) Workshop on 'WordNet and Other Lexical Resources: Applications, Extensions and Customizations.'* Pittsburgh, USA. Arxiv preprint cs/0109031.
Aitchison, J. 2002. *How Asia Advertises: the Most Successful Campaigns in Asia-Pacific and the Marketing Strategies behind them.* Singapore: John Wiley and Sons.
Al-Ali, M.N. 2004. 'How to Get Yourself on the Door of a Job: a Cross-cultural Contrastive Study of Arabic and English Job Application Letters.'

Journal of Multilingual and Multicultural Development 25(1): 1-23.
Allerton, D.J. 1973. *Valency and the English Verb*. New York: Academic Press.
Al-Kasimi, A.M. 1977. *Linguistics and Bilingual Dictionaries*. Leiden: Brill.
Ariffin K. and Anuar N. 2004. 'The Use of Superiority Claims in Advertisements' in I. Zubaidah, M.Z. Ainun Rozana, K. Fauziah, B. Lohanayahi and S.A. Rajeswary (eds.), *Language, Linguistics and the Real World – Vol. II: Language Practices in the Workplace*. Kuala Lumpur: University of Malaya, 135-162.
Atkins, B.T.S. (ed.) 1998. *Using Dictionaries: Studies of Dictionary Use by Language Learners and Translators* (Lexicographica Series Maior 88). Tübingen: Max Niemeyer Verlag.
Atkins, B.T.S. and Varantola, K. 1998a. 'Language Learners Using Dictionaries: the Final Report on the EURLEX/AILA Research Project on Dictionary Use' in B.T.S. Atkins, 21-81.
Atkins, B.T.S. and Varantola, K. 1998b. 'Monitoring Dictionary Use' in B.T.S. Atkins, 84-122.
Azhar M.S. 1988. *Discourse Syntax of 'YANG' in Malay*. Kuala Lumpur: Dewan Bahasa dan Pustaka.
BBC Religion and Ethics. http://www.bbc.co.uk/religion/index.shtml/.
Barnhart, C. 1962. 'Problems in Editing Commercial Monolingual Dictionaries' in Householder and Saporta, 161-181 [reprinted as Chapter 14 in Hartmann 2003, Vol. I: 285-301].
Bateman, J.A. 1990. 'Upper Modeling Organizing Knowledge for Natural Language Processing' in *Proceedings of the 5th International Workshop on Natural Language Generation*. Pittsburgh, PA, 54-61.
Bateman, J.A. 1991. 'The Theoretical Status of Ontologies in Natural Language Processing' in *Proceedings of the Workshop on 'Text Representation and Domain Modelling – Ideas from Linguistics and AI'*. Berlin.
Batey, I. 2002. *Asian Branding: a Great Way to Fly*. Singapore: Prentice Hall.
Bauer, L. 1998. 'When Is a Sequence of Two Nouns a Compound in English?' *English Language and Linguistics* 2(1): 65-86.
Bauer, R.S. 1995. 'Syllable and Word in Cantonese.' *Journal of Asian Pacific Communication* 6(4): 245-306.
Béjoint, H. 1981. 'The Foreign Student's Use of Monolingual English Dictionaries: a Study of Language Needs and Reference Skills.' *Applied Linguistics* 2(3): 207-222.
Béjoint, H. 1990. 'Culture-Specific Items in Bilingual Dictionaries of English.' *Dictionaries* 12: 43-54.
Béjoint, H. 1994. *Tradition and Innovation in Modern English Dictionaries*. Oxford: Oxford University Press.
Béjoint, H. 2001. *Modern Lexicography: An Introduction*. Oxford: Oxford University Press.

Benson, P. 2001. *Ethnocentrism and the English Dictionary*. London: Routledge.
Bensoussan, M., Sim, D. and Weiss, R. 1984. 'The Effect of Dictionary Usage on EFL Test Performance Compared with Student and Teacher Attitudes and Expectations.' *Reading in a Foreign Language* 2(2): 262-276.
Bhatia, T.K. 1987. 'English in Advertising: Multiple Mixing and the Media.' *World Englishes* 6(1): 33-48.
Bhatia, T.K. 1993. *Analysing Genre: Language Use in Professional Settings*. London: Longman.
Bhatia, T.K. and Moody A. (forthcoming). 'Asianness in Asian Advertising' in T.K. Bhatia and W. Ritchie (eds.), *English in Asian Advertising*. Asian Englishes Today Series. Hong Kong: Hong Kong University Press.
Biber, D., Conrad, S. and Leech, G. 2002. *Longman Student Grammar of Spoken and Written English*. Harlow: Longman/Pearson Education.
Blake, N.F. 1988. *Traditional English Grammar and Beyond*. Basingstoke and London: Macmillan.
Brians, P. *Common Errors in English*. http://www.wsu.ed.u/~brians/errors/.
Briscoe, E.J. and Carroll, J. 2002. 'Robust Accurate Statistical Annotation of General Text' in *Proceedings of the International Conference on Language Resources and Evaluation 2002*. Las Palmas, Gran Canaria, 1499-1504.
British National Corpus. http://scn02.corpora.jp/~sakura04/.
Brown, A. 1999. *Singapore English in a Nutshell: an Alphabetical Description of its Features*. Singapore: Times Academic.
Bruthiaux, P. 2000. 'In a Nutshell: Persuasion in the Spatially Constrained Language of Advertising.' *Language and Communication* 20(4): 297-310.
Buitelaar P. and Sacaleanu, B. 2001. 'Ranking and Selecting Synsets by Domain Relevance' in *Proceedings of the North American Chapter of the Association for Computational Linguistics (NAACL) Workshop on 'WordNet and Other Lexical Resources: Applications, Extensions and Customizations,' NAACL 2001*. Pittsburgh, USA. http://dfki.de/~paulb/lexrex.pdf/.
Burchardt, A., Erk, K. and Frank, A. 2005. 'A WordNet Detour to FrameNet' in H.-C.S.B. Fisseni, B. Schröder and P. Wagner (eds.), *Sprachtechnologie, mobile Kommunikation und linguistische Resource* (Computer Studies in Language and Speech 8). Frankfurt am Main: Peter Lang, 408-421.
Burridge, K. 2005. *Weeds in the Garden of Words: Further Observations on the Tangled History of the English Language*. Cambridge: Cambridge University Press.
Campoy, C. and Safont, P. (eds.) 2004. *Computer-Mediated Lexicography in the Foreign Language Learning Context*. Castello: Universitat Jaume I.
Carr, M. 1997. 'Internet Dictionaries and Lexicography.' *International Journal of Lexicography* 10(3): 209-230.
Chan, S.W. (ed.) 2004. *Translation and Bilingual Dictionaries* (Lexicographica Series Maior 119). Tübingen: Max Niemeyer Verlag.

Chang, H.H.L. and Moody, A. (forthcoming). *The Use of Written Cantonese in Hong Kong Magazine Advertising.*

Chen, P. 1999. *Modern Chinese: History and Sociolinguistics.* Cambridge: Cambridge University Press.

Cheung, Y.S. 1992. 'The Form and Meaning of Digraphia: the Case of Chinese' in K. Bolton and H. Kwok (eds.), *Sociolinguistics Today: International Perspectives.* London: Routledge, 207-217.

Chi, A. 2003. *An Empirical Study of the Efficacy of Integrating the Teaching of Dictionary Use into a Tertiary English Curriculum in Hong Kong.* Hong Kong: Language Centre, Hong Kong University of Science and Technology.

Chin, W.K. 1997. 'From Dialect to Grapholect: Written Cantonese from a Folkloristic Viewpoint.' *Hong Kong Journal of Applied Linguistics* 2(2): 77-91.

Ching, F. 2005. 'Make every Hongkonger Feel at Home.' *South China Morning Post*, 22 March 2005.

Chow, I.C. 2005. 'Automating the Import of Lexical Data into a Relational Network' in S. Hwang, B. Sullivan and A. Lommel (eds.), *LACUS Forum XXXII: Networks.* Houston: LACUS, 59-66.

Chow, I.C. and Webster, J.J. 2006. 'Populating FrameNet with Chinese Verbs – Mapping Bilingual Ontological WordNet with FrameNet.' *International Conference on Computer Processing of Oriental Languages (ICCPOL) 2006. Lecture Notes of Computer Science* (LNCS), Vol. 4285, 165-172.

Chow, I.C. and Webster, J.J. 2007. 'Integration of Linguistic Resources for Verb Classification: FrameNet Frame, WordNet Verb and SUMO.' *Conference on Intelligent Text Processing and Computational Linguistics CICLing 2007. Lecture Notes of Computer Science* (LNCS), Vol. 4394, 1-11.

Chow, I.C. and Wong, T.K. 2006. 'Axiomatizing Relational Network for Knowledge Engineering: Exploring WordNet and FrameNet' in *Proceedings of the 2006 Institute of Electrical and Electronics Engineers (IEEE) International Conference on Information Reuse and Integration (IEEE IRI 2006).* Hawaii, "US", 262-267.

Chromá, M. 2004. *Legal Translation and the Dictionary* (Lexicographica Series Maior 122). Tübingen: Max Niemeyer Verlag.

Church, K.W. and Hanks, P. 1989. 'Word Association Norms, Mutual Information and Lexicography' in *Proceedings of the 27th Annual Meeting of the Association for Computational Linguistics.* Vancouver, 76-83.

Clyne, M. 1987. 'Cultural Differences in the Organisation of Academic Texts.' *Journal of Pragmatics* 11(2): 211-241.

Connor, U. and Mauranen, A. 1999. 'Linguistic Analysis of Grant Proposals: European Union Research Grants.' *English for Specific Purposes* 18(1): 47-62.

Cook, G. 1992. *The Discourse of Advertising*. London: Routledge.
Coulson, S. 1997. *Semantic Leaps: Frame-Shifting and Conceptual Blending*. Ph.D. dissertation, University of California, San Diego.
Cowie. A.P. 1989. 'The Language of Examples in English Learners' Dictionaries' in G. James (ed.), *Lexicographers and their Works*. Exeter: University of Exeter Press, 55-65.
Cowie, A.P. 1995. 'The Learners' Dictionary in a Changing Cultural Perspective' in B.B. Kachru and H. Kahane (eds.), *Cultures, Ideologies and the Dictionary* (Lexicographica Series Major 64). Tübingen: Max Niemeyer Verlag, 283-295.
Cowie, A.P. 1998. *Phraseology: Theory, Analysis, and Applications*. Oxford: Oxford University Press.
Cowie, A.P. 1999. *English Dictionaries for Foreign Learners: a History*. Oxford: Clarendon Press.
Cowie, A.P. 2004. 'Lexiculture and the EFL Dictionary.' *Kernerman Dictionary News* 12: 6-8.
Crystal, D. 1995/2003 (2e). *The Cambridge Encyclopedia of the English Language*. Cambridge: Cambridge University Press.
Crystal, D. 2001. *Language and the Internet*. Cambridge: Cambridge University Press.
Crystal, D. 2003. 'The Ideal Dictionary, Lexicographer and User' in R.R.K. Hartmann, 319-327.
Crystal, D. 2004. 'English Word Classes' in B. Aarts, et al. 191-211. [originally published as 'English' in *Lingua* 17 (1967): 24-56].
Dale, I.R.H. 1980. 'Diagraphia' *International Journal of the Sociology of Language* 26: 5-13.
Damaso, J. and Cotter, C. 2007. 'UrbanDictionary.com.' *English Today* 23(2): 19-26.
Daudé J., Padró L. and Rigau G. 2000. 'Mapping WordNets Using Structural Information' in *Proceedings of the Association for Computation Linguistics 2000*. Hong Kong, 504-511.
Daudé J., Padró L. and Rigau G. 2001. 'A Complete WN1.5 to WN1.6 Mapping' in *Proceedings of the North American Chapter of the Association for Computational Linguistics (NAACL) Workshop 'WordNet and Other Lexical Resources: Applications, Extensions and Customizations,'* Pittsburg, USA. http://www.lsi.upc.es/~nlp/papers/naacl01-dpr.ps.gz/.
DeFrancis, J. 1984. 'Digraphia.' *Word* 35: 59-66.
De Cock, S. 2002. 'Pragmatic Prefabs in Learners' Dictionaries' in A. Braasch and C. Povlsen (eds.), *Proceedings of the Tenth EURALEX International Congress, EURALEX 2002, Copenhagen, Denmark, August 13-17 2002*. Copenhagen: Center for Sprogteknologi, Vol. II, 471-481.
De Schryver, G.M. 2003. 'Lexicographers' Dreams in the Electronic-Dictionary Age.' *International Journal of Lexicography* 16(2): 143-199.
Deterding, D. and Poedjosoedarmo, G. 2000. 'To what Extent can the

Ethnic Group of Young Singaporeans be Identified from their Speech?' in A. Brown, D. Deterding and E.L. Low (eds.), *The English language in Singapore: Research on Pronunciation*. Singapore: Singapore Association for Applied Linguistics, 1-9.

Dörnyei, Z. 2003. *Questionnaires in Second Language Research: Construction, administration, and Processing*. Mahwah, NJ: Lawrence Erlbaum Associates.

Drysdale, P. 1987. 'The Role of Examples in a Learner's Dictionary' in A. Cowie (ed.), *The Dictionary and the Language Learner. Papers from the EURALEX Seminar at the University of Leeds, 1-3 April 1985*. Tübingen: Max Niemeyer Verlag, 213-23.

Education and Manpower Bureau. 2004. *Progress Report on the Education Reform 3 December 2004*. http://www.emb.gov.hk/FileManager/EN/Content_689/progress%20eng.pdf/.

Erbaugh, M.S. 1995. 'Southern Chinese Dialects as a Medium for Reconciliation with Greater China.' *Language in Society* 24: 79-94.

Fauconnier, G. 1985. *Mental Spaces: Aspect of Meaning Construction in Natural Language*. Cambridge, MA: MIT Press.

Fauconnier. G. 1998. 'Mental Spaces, Language Modalities, and Conceptual Integration' in M. Tomesello (ed.), *The New Psychology of Language: Cognitive and Functional Approaches to Language Structure* (Vol. 1). Lawrence Erlbaum, 251-280.

Fauconnier, G. and Turner, M. 1998. 'Conceptual Integration Networks.' *Cognitive Science* 22: 133-187.

Feast, V. 2002. 'The Impact of IELTS Scores on Performance at University.' *International Education Journal* 3(4): 70-85.

Fellbaum, C. (ed.) 1998. *WordNet: An Electronic Lexical Database*. Cambridge, Mass: MIT Press.

Fillmore, C.J. 1968. 'The Case for Case' in E. Bach and R.T. Harms (eds.), *Universals in Linguistic Theory*. New York: Holt, Rinehart and Winston, 1-88.

Fillmore, C.J., Johnson, C. R. and Petruck, M.R.L. 2003. 'Background to FrameNet.' *International Journal of Lexicography* 16: 235-250.

Fitzgerald, S. 2000. 'Re(de)fining Dictionaries: From Paper to Pixel' in D. Gibbs and K.-L. Krause (eds.), *Cyberlines: Languages and cultures of the Internet*. Sydney: James Nicholas, 45-58.

FrameNet. http://framenet.icsi.berkeley.edu/.

Frawley, W., Hill, K.C. and Munro, P. 2002. 'Making a Dictionary: Ten Issues' in W. Frawley, K. Hill, and P. Munro (eds.), *Making Dictionaries: Preserving Indigenous Languages of the Americas*. Berkeley: University of California Press, 1-24.

Giegerich, H. 2004. 'Compound or Phrase? English Noun-plus-noun Constructions and the Stress Criterion.' *English Language and Linguistics* 8(1): 1-24.

Goatly, A. 2000. *Critical Reading and Writing.* London: Routledge.
Gong, W. 2005. 'English in Computer-Mediated Environments: a Neglected Dimension in Large English Corpus Compilation' in *Corpus Linguistics 2005.* Birmingham University, UK. http://www.corpus.bham.ac.uk/PCLC/Wengao.pdf/.
González-Jover, A.G. 2006. 'Meaning and Anisomorphism in Modern Lexicography,' in L. Marie-Claude (ed.), *Processing of Terms in Specialized Dictionaries.* Homme, 215-234.
Grabe, W. and Kaplan, R. 1996. *Theory and Practice of Writing.* London: Longman.
Graddol, D. 2006. *English Next: Why Global English May Mean the End of 'English as a Foreign Language.'* Plymouth: Latimer Trend and Company.
Greenbaum, S. and Nelson, G. 2002. *An Introduction to English Grammar* (2e). Harlow: Longman/Pearson Education.
Greenbaum, S. and Quirk, R. 1990. *A Student's Grammar of the English Language.* Harlow: Longman.
Grefenstette, G. 1992. 'Sextant: Exploring Unexplored. Contexts for Semantic Extraction from Syntactic Analysis' in *Proceedings of the Association for Computational Linguistics (ACL).* Newark, USA: the Association for Computational Linguistics, 324-326.
Grabe, W. and Kaplan, R. 1996. *Theory and Practice of Writing.* London: Longman.
Guangdong Education Bureau. 2002. *Basic Rules for Chinese Language and Orthography.* Guangzhou: Jinan University Press.
Gupta, A.F. 1994. *The Step-Tongue: Children's English in Singapore.* Clevedon: Multilingual Matters.
Haas, M. 1962. 'What Belongs in the Bilingual Dictionary?' in Householder and Saporta, 45-50.
Halliday, M.A.K. and Matthiessen, C.M.I.M. 1999. *Construing Experience through Meaning.* New York: Continuum.
Halliday, M.A.K. and Matthiessen, C.M.I.M. 2004. *An Introduction to Functional Grammar* (3e). London: Arnold.
Hanks, P. 1994. Linguistic Norms and Pragmatic Exploitations, or Why Lexicographers need Prototype Theory and Vice Versa' in F. Kiefer, G. Kiss, and J. Pajzs (eds.), *Papers in Computational Lexicography: CompLex '94. Research Institute for Linguistics.* Budapest: Hungarian Academy of Sciences, 89-113.
Hanks, P. 2003. 'Definitions and Explanations' in R.K.K. Hartmann, 191-206.
Harrison, G. and So, L. 1996. 'The Background to Language Change in Hong Kong.' *Current Issues in Language and Society* 3(2): 114-123.
Hartmann, R.R.K. (ed.) 1979. *Dictionaries and Their Users, Papers from the 1978 BAAL Seminar on Lexicography. Exeter Linguistic Studies* 1(4). Exeter: University of Exeter Press.

Hartmann, R.R.K. 1982. 'Das zweisprachige Wörterbuch im Fremdsprachenerwerb' in H. Wiegand (ed.), *Studien zur neuhochdeutschen Lexikographie Vol. II (Germanistische Linguistik 3-6/80)*. Hildesheim: G. Olms. 73-86 [reprinted in English translation as Chapter 13 in Hartmann 2007, 109-117].
Hartmann, R.R.K. (ed.) 1983. *Lexicography: Principles and Practice.* London: Academic Press.
Hartmann R.R.K. (ed.) 1984. *LEXeter '83 Proceedings: Papers from the International Conference on Lexicography at Exeter, 9-12 September 1983.* Tübingen: Max Niemeyer Verlag.
Hartmann, R.R.K. 1987. 'Four Perspectives on Dictionary Use: A Critical View of Research Methods' in A.P. Cowie (ed.), *The Dictionary and the Language Learner: Papers from the EURALEX Seminar at the University of Leeds. 1-3 April 1985* (Lexicographica Series Maior 17). Tübingen: Max Niemeyer Verlag, 11-28.
Hartmann, R.R.K. (ed.) 1999. *Dictionaries in Language Learning. Recommendations, National Reports and Thematic Reports from the TNP Sub-Project 9: Dictionaries.* Berlin: Freie Universität. www.fu-berlin.de/elc/TNPproducts/SP9dossier.doc/.
Hartmann, R.R.K. 2001. *Teaching and Researching Lexicography* (Applied Linguistics in Action Series). Harlow: Longman/Pearson Education.
Hartmann, R.R.K. (ed.) 2003. *Lexicography: Critical Concepts* [3 volumes]. London: Routledge/Taylor & Francis.
Hartmann, R.R.K. 2004. '*Lexicography and Translation*' in Chan, 7-21.
Hartmann, R.R.K. 2005a. 'Pure or Hybrid? The Development of Mixed Dictionary Genres' in *Facta Universitatis*. Series Linguistics and Literature (Niš) 3(2): 193-208.
Hartmann, R.R.K. 2005b. 'Interlingual References: On the Mutual Relations between Lexicography and Translation.' *The Hong Kong Linguist* 25: 43-52.
Hartmann, R.R.K. 2006. 'Desiderata in Lexicography: Looking Back at Some Problems, and Forward to Solutions' in G. Sica (ed.) *Open Problems in Linguistics and Lexicography.* Monza/Milano: Polimetrica. 155-161.
Hartmann, R.R.K. 2007. *Interlingual Lexicography. Selected Essays on Translation Equivalence, Contrastive Linguistics and the Bilingual Dictionary* (Lexicographica Series Maior 133). Tübingen: Max Niemeyer Verlag.
Hartmann, R.R.K. and James, G. 1998. *Dictionary of Lexicography* [see DoL – 'Dictionaries and other reference works'].
Hatherall, G. 1984. 'Studying Dictionary Use: Some Findings and Proposals' in R.R.K. Hartmann, 183-189.
Hayakawa, I. 2001. *Methods of Plagiarism. A History of English-Japanese Lexicography.* Tokyo: Jiyusha.
Heuberger, R. 2000. *Monolingual Dictionaries for Foreign Learners of*

English: A Contrastive Evaluation of the State-of-the-Art Reference Works in Book Form and on CD-ROM (Austrian Studies in English 87). Vienna: Braumüller.
Ho, A.L. 2007. '3 JCs to offer *A-level English*' in *The Straits Times* (Singapore), 30 August 2007.
Householder, F. and Saporta, S. (eds.) 1962. *Problems in Lexicography* (Publications of Indiana University Research Centre in Anthropology, Folklore, and Linguistics 21). Bloomington: Indiana University Press.
Howarth, P. 1996. *Phraseology in English Academic Writing: some Implications for Language Learning and Dictionary Making.* Tübingen: Max Niemeyer Verlag.
Huang, D.F. 2003. *Taiwanese University English Majors' Beliefs about English Dictionaries and their Dictionary Strategy Use.* Ph.D dissertation, University of Texas at Austin.
Huang, D.F. 2007. 'Instruction of Online Dictionary Skills and Strategies.' Keynote Speech and Paper Presented at the 2007 Conference on English Teaching, Air Force Institute of Technology. Gangshan, Taiwan, 1-17.
Huang, J. 1994. 'Chinese and Western Metalexicography' in James 1994, 228-238 [reprinted. as Chapter 67 in Hartmann 2003, Vol. III: 391-404].
Huddleston, R. and Pullum, G.K. 2005. *A Student's Introduction to English Grammar.* Cambridge: Cambridge University Press.
Hulstijn, J.H., Hollander, M. and Greidanus, T. 1996. 'Incidental Vocabulary Learning by Advanced Foreign Language Students: the Influence of Marginal Glosses, Dictionary Use, and Reoccurrence of Unknown Words.' *The Modern Language Journal* 80(3): 327-339.
Hulstijn, J.H. and Atkins, B.T.S. 1998. 'Empirical Research on Dictionary Use in Foreign-Language Learning: Survey and Discussion' in B.T.S. Atkins, 7-19.
Hupka, W. 1989. *Wort und Bild. Die Illustrationen in Wörterbüchern und Enzyklopädien* (Lexicographica Series Maior 22). Tübingen: Max Niemeyer Verlag [Chapter 8 reprinted in English translation as Chapter 66 in Hartmann 2003, Vol. III: 363-390].
Iannucci, J.E. 1957. 'Meaning Discrimination in Bilingual Dictionaries: A New Lexicographical Technique.' *Modern Language Journal* 41: 272-281.
Iannucci, J.E. 1962. 'Meaning Discrimination in Bilingual Dictionaries' in Householder and Saporta, 201-216 [reprinted as Chapter 10 in Hartmann 2003, Vol. II: 217-229].
Iannucci, J.E. 1976. 'Subcategories in Bilingual Dictionaries' in J.D. Anderson and R.J. Steiner (eds.), *Lexicography as a Science and as an Art.* Louisville, Kentucky: University of Louisville, 1-6.
Ide, N. and Véronis, J. (eds.) 1998. Special Issue on Word Sense Disambiguation: The State of the Art. *Computational Linguistics* 24(1): 1-40.
Izard, C.E. 1977. *Human Emotions.* New York: Plenum Press.

Izard, C.E. 1991. *The Psychology of Emotions*. New York: Plenum Press.
Izumi, E., Uchimoto, K. and Isahara, H. (eds.) 2004. *Nihonjin 1200-nin no Eigo Speaking Corpus* (*A NICT Japanese Learner English Corpus: An Introduction*). Tokyo: ALC Press.
Jackson, H. 2002. *Lexicography: an Introduction*. London: Routledge.
Jain M.P. 1981. 'On Meaning in the Foreign Learners' Dictionary.' *Applied Linguistics* 1981(II): 274-286.
James, G. (ed.) 1994. *Meeting Points in Language Studies. A Festschrift for Ma Tailai. Working Papers*. Hong Kong: Hong Kong University of Science and Technology, Language Centre.
Kent, D. 2001. 'Korean University Freshmen's Use and Perceptions regarding Dictionaries'. *Korea TESOL Journal* 4(1): 73-92.
Kifer, M., Lausen, G. and Wu, J. 1995. 'Logical Foundations of Object-Oriented and Frame-Based Languages'. *Journal of The Association of Computing Machinery (JACM)* 42: 741-843.
Kilgarriff, A. 1997a. 'I Don't Believe in Word Senses.' *Computers and the Humanities* 31: 91-113.
Kilgarriff, A. 1997b. 'What is Word Sense Disambiguation Good For?' in *Proceedings of the Natural Language Processing Pacific Rim Symposium (NLPRS 97)*. Phuket, Thailand, 209-214.
Kilgarriff, A. and Palmer, M. (eds.) 2000. 'Introduction to the Special Issue on SENSEVAL.' *Computers and the Humanities* 34 (1-2): 1-13.
Kilgarriff, A. and Tugwell, D. 2001. 'WASP-Bench: an MT Lexicographers' Workstation Supporting State-of-the-art Lexical Disambiguation' in *Proceedings of the MT Summit VIII*. Santiago de Compostela, Spain: 187-190.
Kilgarriff, A. and Rundell, M. 2002. 'Lexical Profiling Software and its Lexicographic Applications – a Case Study' in A. Braasch and C. Povlsen (eds.), *Proceedings of the Tenth EURALEX International Congress, EURALEX 2002*. Copenhagen: Centre for Sprogteknologi, 807-818.
Kilgarriff, A., Koeling, R., Tugwell, D. and Evans, R. 2003. 'An Evaluation of a Lexicographer's Workbench: Building Lexicons for Machine Translation' in *Proceedings of the European Association for Machine Translation Workshop on MT Tools*. Budapest, 211-214
Kilgarriff, A., Rychly, P., Smrz, P. and Tugwell, D. 2004. 'The Sketch Engine' in G. Williams and S. Vessier (eds.), *Proceedings of the Eleventh EURALEX International Congress, Lorient, July 6-10, 2004*. Lorient: Université de Bretagne Sud, Faculté des Lettres et des Sciences Humaines, 105-116.
Kipfer, B.A. 1987. 'Dictionaries and the Intermediate Student: Communicative Needs and the Development of User Reference Skills' in A.P. Cowie (ed.), *The Dictionary and the Language Learner*. London: Longman, 44-54.
Kirby, J.R. 1988. 'Style, Strategy, and Skill in Reading' in R.R. Schmeck (ed.), *Learning Strategies and Learning Styles*. New York: Plenum Press, 229-271.

Knight, S. 1994. 'Dictionary Use while Reading: the Effects on Comprehension and Vocabulary Acquisition for Students of Different Verbal Abilities.' *The Modern Language Journal* 78(3): 285-299.
Knowles, G. and Zuraidah, M.D. 2003. 'Tagging a Corpus of Malay Texts, and Coping with Syntactic Drift' in D. Archer, P. Rayson, A. Wilson and T. McEnery (eds.), *Proceedings of the Corpus Linguistics 2003 Conference.* UCREL Technical Paper No. 16. Lancaster University: UCREL, 422-428.
Knowles, G. and Zuraidah, M.D. 2004. 'The Notion of a Lemma: Headwords, Roots and Lexical Sets.' *International Journal of Corpus Linguistics* 9: 69-81
Knowles, G and Zuraidah, M.D. 2006. *Word Class in Malay: a Corpus-based Approach.* Kuala Lumpur: Dewan Bahasa dan Pustaka.
Kobayashi, C. 2004. 'Pocket Electronic or Printed Electronic Dictionaries?' Paper presented at the National Conference JALT 2004, Nara, Japan, 19-22 November 2004.
Kouraogo, P. 1993. 'Language Learning Strategies in Input-poor Environments.' *System* 21(2): 165-173.
Kress, G. and van Leeuwen, T. 1996. *Reading Image: the Grammar of Visual Design.* London: Routledge.
Kromann. http://www.oxfordreference.com/.
Lai, S.F. and Huang, D.F. 2006. 'The Role of English Dictionary Use in Taiwanese Universities of Technology Students' Reading Tasks' in *Proceedings of the 2005 International Conference on Applied Linguistics.* Tainan, Taiwan, 23-35.
Lakoff, G. and Johnson, M. 1999. *Philosophy in the Flesh: The Embodied Mind and its Challenge to Western Thought.* New York: Basic Books.
Lamb, S.M. 1999. *Pathways of the Brain: The Neurocognitive Basis of Language.* John Benjamins.
Lamb, S.M. (ed.) 2002. *Language and Brain: Neurocognitive Linguistics.* http://www.ruf.rice.ed.u/~lngbrain/.
Lamb, S.M. and Webster J.J. 2004. *Language and Reality.* London: Continuum Books.
Landau, S.I. 1984/2001. *Dictionaries: the Art and Craft of Lexicography.* New York: C. Scribner's Sons (1e); Cambridge: Cambridge University Press (2e).
Lau, A.C. 1995. *Written Representation of Oral Features in Cantonese Chinese.* Ph.Ed dissertation, Columbia University, Teachers College.
Lau, C.K. 1995. 'Language of the Future.' *South China Morning Post,* 18 September 1995.
Laufer, B. and Hill, M. 2000. 'What Lexical Information do L2 Learners Select in a CALL Dictionary and how does it Affect Word Retention?' *Language Learning and Technology* 3(2): 58-76.
Lee, D. 2001. 'Defining Core Vocabulary and Tracking its Distribution Across Spoken and Written Genres: Evidence of a Gradience of Variation from the

British National Corpus.' *Journal of English Linguistics* 29(3): 250-278.
Leech, G., Deuchar, M. and Hoogenraad, R. 2006. *English Grammar for Today: a New Introduction.* (2e). Basingstoke: Palgrave Macmillan.
Lemmens, M. 1996. 'La Grammaire dans les Dictionnaires Bilingues' in H. Béjoint and P. Thoiron (eds.), *Les Dictionnaires Bilingues.* Louvain-la-Neuve, Belgium: Duculot, 71-102.
Lethbridge, H. 1976. *Hong Kong: Stability and Change.* Hong Kong: Oxford University Press.
Lew, R. 2002. 'Questionnaires in Dictionary Use Research: a reexamination' in A. Braasch and C. Povlsen (eds.), *Proceedings of the Tenth EURALEX International Congress, EURALEX 2002.* Copenhagen: Centre for Sprogteknologi, 759-763.
Lewis, M.B. 1947. *Teach Yourself Malay.* London: English Universities Press.
Li, D.C.S. 1999. 'The Functions and Status of English in Hong Kong: a Post-1997 Update.' *English World-Wide* 20(1): 67-110.
Li, D.C.S. 2000. 'Phonetic Borrowing: Key to the Vitality of Written Cantonese in Hong Kong.' *Written Language and Literacy* 3(2): 199-233.
Li, L. 2005. 'The Growing Prosperity of On-line Dictionaries.' *English Today* 21(3): 16-21.
Li, M. 2006. *Language Situation in China: 2006.* Beijing: The Commercial Press.
Li, M.F.M. 1997. *Attitudes toward Written Cantonese and Mixed Codes in Written Language in Hong Kong.* M.Ed thesis, University of Hong Kong, Faculty of Education.
Lim, G. 2001. 'Till Divorce do Us Part: the Case of Singaporean and Malaysian English,' in V. B. Y. Ooi (ed.), *Evolving Identities: the English Language in Singapore and Malaysia.* Singapore: Times Academic Press, 125-139.
Lim, L. 2000. 'Ethnic Group Differences Aligned? Intonation Patterns of Chinese, Indian and Malay Singaporean English' in A. Brown, D. Deterding and E.L. Low (eds.), *The English Language in Singapore: Research on Pronunciation.* Singapore: Singapore Association for Applied Linguistics, 10-21.
Lin, D. 1998. 'A Dependency-based Method for Evaluating Broad-Coverage Parsers.' *Journal of Natural Language Engineering.* 4(2): 97-114.
Low, E.L. and Brown, A. 2005. *English in Singapore: an Introduction.* Singapore: McGraw Hill.
Lü, Y. and Zhou, M. 2004. 'Collocation Translation Acquisition Using Monolingual Corpora' in *Proceedings of the Association for Computational Linguistics (ACL).* Barcelona, Spain, 167-174.
Luna, P. 2004. 'Not Just a Pretty Face: The Contribution of Typography to Lexicography' in G. Williams and S. Vessier (eds.), *Proceedings of the Eleventh EURALEX International Congress, Lorient, July 6-10, 2004.*

Lorient: Université de Bretagne Sud, Faculté des Lettres et des Sciences Humaines, Vol. III: 847-857.

MacConchie, R.W. 1997. *Lexicography and Physicke: The Record of Sixteenth-Century English Medical Terminology*. Oxford: Oxford University Press.

Maedche, A.D. 2002. *Ontology Learning for the Semantic Web*. Kluwer Academic Publishers. London.

Magnini, B., Strapparava, C., Pezzulo, G. and Gliozzo, A. 2001. 'Using Domain Information for Word Sense Disambiguation' in *Proceedings of SENSEVAL-2*: 111-114.

Mahmood, H. 1995. *Pembentukan Tatabahasa Melayu Mengiku Proses Hukum Morfologi dan Sintaksis*. Petaling Jaya: UIA.

Marello, C. 1989. *Dizionari Bilingui con Schede sui Dizionari Italiani per Francese, Inglese, Spagnolo, Tedesco* (Fenomeni Linguistici 6). Bologna: Zanichelli [Chapter 1 reprinted. in English translation as Chapter 44 in Hartmann 2003, Vol. II: 325-342].

Matthews, P.H. (ed.) 2007. *Oxford Reference*. http://www.oxfordreference.com/views/ENTRY.html?subview-Mainandentry-t36.e1718/.

McArthur, T. 1998a. *The English Languages*. Cambridge: Cambridge University Press.

McArthur, T. 1998b. 'What then IS Reference Science?' in T. McArthur, *Living Words. Language, Lexicography, and the Knowledge Revolution*. Exeter: University of Exeter Press, 215-222 [reprinted as Chapter 69 in Hartmann 2003, Vol. III: 422-428].

McCarthy, D., Koeling, R., Weeds, J. and Carroll, J. 2004. 'Finding Predominant Senses in Untagged Text' in *Proceedings of the Association for Computational Linguistics (ACL)*. Barcelona, Spain, 280-287.

McCracken, J. and Kilgarriff, A. 2003. 'Oxford Dictionary of English – Current Developments' in *Proceedings of the European Association for Computational Linguistics (EACL), Budapest*. ACL Anthology reference E03-1046.

McCreary, D.R. and Dolezal, F.T. 1999. 'A Study of Dictionary Use by ESL Students in an American University.' *International Journal of Lexicography* 12(2): 107-145.

Metz, C. 1974. *Film Language: A Semiotics of the Cinema*, M. Taylor (trans.). New York: Oxford University Press.

Michael, I. 1970. *English Grammatical Categories and the Tradition to 1800*. Cambridge: Cambridge University Press.

Ministry of Education, Singapore. 2004a. 'Speech by Mr Tharman Shanmugaratnam, Acting Minister for Education, at the launch of "Popcorn," Prize Presentation Ceremony for the "Make Your Own Newspaper" Competition and the Chinese Language Teachers Forum on Saturday 21 Feb 2004 at 9.30 am at Orchard Hotel.' http://www.moe.gov.sg/med.ia/speeches/2004/sp20040221.htm/.

Ministry of Education, Singapore. 2004b. 'Opening Speech by Tharman Shanmugaratnam, Minister for Education, at Parliamentary Debate on Report of the Chinese Language Curriculum and Pedagogy Review Committee on 24 November 2004.' http://www.moe.gov.sg/med.ia/speeches/2004/sp20041124_print.htm/.
Mok, K.L.C. 1998. *The Sociolinguistics of Written Chinese in Local Comic Book Subculture: Stigmatized. Language Varieties in Hong Kong.* M.Phil thesis, University of Hong Kong, Faculty of Arts (English).
Murata, M., Osaki, S. and Kokawa, T. 2007. 'Kokoseiyo Denshijiho oyobi Eigojujitsugata no Daigakusei Ippan Shakaijinyo Denshijisho ni tsuite no Hikakukenkyu' [A Comparative Study of Hand-held Electronic Dictionaries for High School Students and for University Students and Adults with Advanced English Contents]. *Wayo Joshi Daigaku Kiyo [Wayo Women's University Journal]*, 47: 71-92.
Naiman, N., Frohlich, M., Stern, H.H. and Todesco, A. 1978. *The Good Language Learner.* Toronto: Ontario Institute for Studies in Education.
Nakamura, T. and Tono, Y. 2003. 'Lexical Profiling Using the Shogakukan Language Toolbox' in M. Murata, S. Yamada and Y. Tono (eds.), *Dictionaries and Language Learning: How can Dictionaries Help Human and Machine Learning?* (Proceedings of the third ASIALEX Conference). Tokyo: Meikai University, 170-176.
National Curriculum Online. http://www.nc.uk.net/.
Nesi, H. 1998. 'Defining a Shoehorn: the Success of Learners' Dictionary Entries for Concrete Nouns' in B.T.S. Atkins, 159-178.
Nesi, H. 1999. 'The Specification of Dictionary Reference Skills in Higher Education' in Hartmann, 53-67 [Thematic Report 3, reprinted as Chapter 20 in Hartmann 2003. Vol. I: 370-393].
Nesi, H. and Haill, R. 2002. 'A Study of Dictionary Use by International Students at a British University.' *International Journal of Lexicography* 15(4): 277-305.
Niles, I. and Pease, A. 2003 'Linking Lexicons and Ontologies: Mapping WordNet to the Suggested Upper Merged Ontology' in *Proceedings of the IEEE International Conference on Information and Knowledge Engineering*, 412-416.
Norman G. 2002. 'Description and Prescription in Dictionaries of Scientific Terms.' *International Journal of Lexicography* 15(4): 259-276.
Notohara, A. 1987. 'The Results of the Dictionary Using Skills Test (I).' The 13th Zenkoku Eigo Kyoiku Gakkai in Okayama.
Oakley, T. 1998. 'Conceptual Blending, Narrative Discourse, and Rhetoric.' *Cognitive Linguistics* 9: 321-360.
Oltramari, A. 2006. 'Frame-Guided. Exploration of WordNet' in *Proceedings of the Fifth International Conference on Language Resources and Evaluation.* Singapore: LREC.
O'Malley, J.M., Chamot, A.U., Stewner-Manzanares, G., Kupper,

L. and Russo, R.P. 1985. 'Learning Strategies Used by Beginning and Intermediate ESL Students.' *Language Learning* 35: 21-46.
O'Malley, J.M. and Chamot, A.U. 1990. *Learning Strategies in Second Language Acquisition*. Cambridge: Cambridge University Press.
Ooi, V.B.Y. 1998. *Computer Corpus Lexicography*. Edinburgh: Edinburgh University Press.
Osaki, S., Ochiai, N., Iso, T., and Aizawa, K. 2003. 'Electronic Dictionary vs. Paper Dictionary: Accessing appropriate Meaning, Reading Comprehension and Retention' in M. Murata, S. Yamada and Y. Tono (eds), *Dictionaries and Language Learning: How can Dictionaries Help Human and Machine Learning?* (Proceedings of the third ASIALEX Conference). Tokyo: Meikai University, 205-212.
Osselton, N.E. 1983. 'On the History of Dictionaries: the History of English-language Dictionaries,' in R.R.K. Hartmann 13-21.
Oxford, R.L. 1990. *Language Learning Strategies: What Every Teacher Should Know*. New York: Newbury House.
Packard, J.L. 2000. *The Morphology of Chinese: a Linguistic and Cognitive Approach*. Cambridge: Cambridge University Press.
Pedersen, V.H. 1988. *Essays on Translation*. Copenhagen: Nyt Nordisk Forlag Arnold Busck.
Picken, J. 1999. 'State of the Ad: the Role of Advertisements in EFL Teaching.' *ELT Journal* 53(4): 249-255.
Piotrowski, T. 1989. 'Monolingual and Bilingual Dictionaries: Fundamental Differences' in M. Tickoo (ed.), *Learners' Dictionaries: State of the Art* (Anthology Series 23). Singapore: SEAMEO Regional Language Centre, 72-83.
Poon, A. 2004. 'Language Policy of Hong Kong: Its Impact on Language Education and Language Use in Post-handover Hong Kong.' *Journal of Taiwan Normal University* 49(1): 53-74.
Pruvost, J. 2004. 'Some Lexicographic Concepts Stemming from a French Training in Lexicology.' *Kernerman Dictionary News* 12. http://kdictionaries.com/kdn/kdn12-2.html/.
Qian, Z. 1998. *Guan Zhui Bian [Limited Views: Essays on Ideas and Letters]* (selected and translated by Ronald Egan). Massachusetts: Harvard University Asia Centre.
Quirk, R. 1991. 'Foreword' in *Longman Dictionary of the English Language*. Harlow, Essex: Longman.
Quirk, R., Greenbaum, S., Leech, G. and Svartvik, J. 1985. *A Comprehensive Grammar of the English Language*. London: Longman.
Ramli, H.K. 1993. *The Language of Television Advertisements in Malay and English*. MA thesis, University of Malaya, Faculty of Languages and Linguistics.
Reif, J.A. 1987. 'The Development of a Dictionary Concept: an English Learner's Dictionary and an Exotic Alphabet' in A. Cowie (ed.), *The*

Dictionary and the Language Learner, Papers from the EURALEX Seminar at the University of Leeds, 1-3 April 1985. Tübingen: Max Niemeyer Verlag, 146-158.
Robinson, R. 1954. *Definition*. Oxford: Clarendon Press.
Rosso, P., Masulli, F. and Buscaldi, D. 2003. 'Word Sense Disambiguation Combining Conceptual Distance, Frequency and Gloss' in *Proceedings of Natural Language Processing and Knowledge Engnieering 2003 (NLPKE 2003)*. http://www.icl.pku.ed.u.cn/WebData_http-dir-listable/Proceedings/NL-PKE2003/pdf/A05-01.pdf/.
Rubin, J. 1975. 'What the "Good Language Learner" can Teach Us.' *TESOL Quarterly* 9: 41-51.
Rundell, M. 2002. 'Good Old-fashioned Lexicography: Human Judgment and the Limits of Automation' in M.H. Corréard (ed.), *Lexicography and Natural Language Processing: A Festschrift in Honour of B.T.S. Atkins*. Grenoble: EURALEX, 139-155.
San Vicente, F. (ed.) 2006. *Lessicografia Bilingue e Traduzione* (Lexicography Worldwide). Monza/Milano: Polimetrica.
Santangelo, P. 2003. *Sentimental Education in Chinese History: an Interdisciplinary Textual Research on Ming and Qing Sources*. Leiden: Brill.
Sarris, A. 2004. 'Notes on the *Auteur* Theory in 1962' in P. Simpson, K. J. Shepherdson and A. Utterson (eds.), *Film Theory: Critical Concepts in Media and Cultural Studies*, Vol. 2. London: Routledge, 21-33.
Saw, S.H. 1999. *The Population of Singapore*. Singapore: Institute of Southeast Asian Studies.
SCOLAR. 2003. *Action Plan to Raise Language Standards in Hong Kong*. Hong Kong: SCOLAR, Education and Manpower Bureau.
Schmeck, R.R. 1988. 'An Introduction to Strategies and Styles of Learning' in R.R. Schmeck (ed.), *Learning Strategies and Learning Styles*. New York: Plenum Press, 3-18.
Schneider, E.W. 2007. *Postcolonial English: Varieties Around the World*. Cambridge: Cambridge University Press.
Scholfield, P. 1997. 'Vocabulary Reference Works in Foreign Language Learning' in N. Schmitt and M. McCarthy (eds.), *Vocabulary: Description, Acquisition and Pedagogy*. Cambridge: Cambridge University Press, 279-302.
Schűtze, H. 1998. 'Automatic Word Sense Discrimination.' *Computational Linguistics* 24(1): 97-124.
Scollon, R. and Scollon, S.W. 1998. 'Literate Design in the Discourses of Revolution, Reform, and Transition.' *Written Language and Literacy* 1: 1-39.
SENSEVAL-2. 2001. http://www.senseval.org/.
SENSEVAL-3 2003. http://www.senseval.org/.
SENSEVAL-3 2004. http://www.senseval.org/.

SENSEVAL-4 / SEMEVAL-1. 2007. http://www.senseval.org/.
Shi, L. and Mihalcea, R. 2005. 'Putting Pieces Together: Combining FrameNet, VerbNet and WordNet for Robust Semantic Parsing.' *Conference on Intelligent Text Processing and Computational Linguistics CICLing '2005. Lecture Notes of Computer Science LNCS,* Vol. 3406: 100-111.
Sinclair, J. 1985. 'Lexicographic Evidence' in R. Ilson (ed.), *Dictionaries, Lexicography and Language Learning.* Oxford: The British Council and Pergamon Press, 81-94.
Sinclair, J. 1996. 'The Empty Lexicon.' *International Journal of Corpus Linguistics* 1(1): 99-120.
Singapore Department of Statistics. 2007. *Population Trends (Singapore).* http://www.singstat.gov.sg/pubn/popn/population2007.pdf/.
Snell-Hornby, M. 1986. 'The Bilingual Dictionary – Victim of its own tradition?' in R.R.K. Hartmann (ed.), *The History of Lexicography.* Amsterdam: John Benjamins, 207-218.
Snow, D. 1993. 'Chinese Dialect as Written Language: the Cases of Taiwanese and Cantonese.' *Journal of Asian Pacific Communication* 4(1): 15-30.
Snow, D. 1994. 'A Short History of Published Cantonese: what is a Dialect Literature?' *Journal of Asian Pacific Communication* 4(3): 127-148.
So, D. 1996. 'Language Policy' in P. Dickson and A. Cumming (eds.), *National Profiles of Language Education in 25 Countries.* Berkshire, England: National Foundation for Educational Research.
Sowa, J. F. 2000. *Knowledge Representation: Logical, Philosophical and Computational Foundations.* Pacific Grove, CA: Brooks/Cole.
Steiner, R. 1984. 'Guidelines for Reviewers of Bilingual Dictionaries.' *Dictionaries* 6: 166-181.
Stern, H.H. 1975. 'What can we Learn from the Good Language Learner?' *Canadian Modern Language Review* 31: 304-318.
Summers, D. 1988. 'The Role of Dictionaries in Language Learning' in M. Carter and M. McCarthy (eds.), *Vocabulary and Language Learning.* London: Longman, 111-125.
Summers, D. 1996. 'Computer Lexicography: the Importance of Representativeness in Relation to Frequency' in J. Thomas and M.H. Short (eds.), *Using Corpora for Language Research.* Harow: Addison Wesley Longman, 260-266.
Svensén. B. 1993/2004. *Practical Lexicography: Principles and Methods of Dictionary-Making.* Oxford: Oxford University Press [Swedish 2e 2004. Stockholm: Norstedts Akademiska Förlag].
Teubert, W. 2000. 'Starting with Trauer: Approaches to Multilingual Lexical Semantics' in F. Kiefer, G. Kiss and J. Pajzs (eds.), *Papers in Computational Lexicography, Complex '99.* Budapest: Linguistics Institute, Hungarian Academy of Sciences, 153-170.
Teubert, W. and Cermakova, A. 2004. 'Directions in Corpus Linguistics' in M.A.K. Halliday, W. Teubert, C. Yallop and A. Cermakova (eds.),

Lexicology and Corpus Linguistics: an Introduction. London: Continuum, 113-166.
Thomas, J. 1995. *Meaning in Interaction: an Introduction to Pragmatics*. Essex: Pearson Education.
Thumb, J. 2004. *Dictionary Look-up Strategies and the Bilingualised Learner's Dictionary* (Lexicographica Series Maior 117). Tübingen: Max Niemeyer Verlag.
Tomaszczyk, J. 1983. 'On Bilingual Dictionaries: The Case for Bilingual Dictionaries for Foreign Language Learners' in Hartmann, 41-51.
Tono, Y. 1984. *On the Dictionary User's Reference Skills*. B.Ed Dissertation, Tokyo Gakugei University.
Tono, Y. 1986. 'A Scientific Approach Toward Lexicography: the User Perspective.' *LEO* 15: 37-54.
Tono, Y. 1988. 'Assessment of the EFL Learners' Dictionary Using Skills.' *JACET Bulletin* 19: 103-126.
Tono, Y. 1989. 'Can a Dictionary Help One Read Better?' in G. James, 192-200.
Tono, Y. 1992. 'The Effect of Menus on EFL Learners' Look-up Processes.' *LEXIKOS* 2 (AFRILEX SERIES 2): 229-253.
Tono, Y. 2001. *Research on Dictionary Use in the Context of Foreign Language Learning. Focus on Reading Comprehension* (Lexicographica Series Maior 106). Tübingen: Max Niemeyer Verlag [Chapter 4 reprinted as Chapter 21 in Hartmann 2003, Vol. I: 394-412].
Tono, Y. 2004. 'Multiple Comparisons of IL, L1 and TL Corpora: the Case of L2 Acquisition of Verb Subcategorization Patterns by Japanese Learners of English' in G. Aston, S. Bernardini, and D. Stewart (eds.), *Corpora and Language Learners*. Amsterdam: John Benjamins, 45-66.
Tono, Y. 2006. 'English Bilingual Lexicography in Japan: Meeting Serious Challenges' in S. Ishikawa et al. (eds.), *English Lexicography in Japan* (JACET Anthology). Tokyo: Taishukan, 18-25.
Tono, Y. 2007. *Chukosei 1-man-nin no Eigo Corpus: JEFLL Corpus* (JEFLL Corpus: A corpus of 10,000 secondary school students' English compositions). Tokyo: Shogakukan.
Tono, Y., Kaneko, T., Isahara, H., Saiga, T. and Izumi, E. 2002. 'The Standard Speaking Test Corpus.' *Studies in Lexicography* 11(2): 7-18.
Tsang, S. (ed.) 1995. *A Documentary History of Hong Kong: Government and Politics*. Hong Kong: Hong Kong University Press.
Tseng, D. 2005. *The 2005-06 Policy Address*. http://www.policyaddress.gov.hk/05-06/.
Tung, C.H. 2005. 'Foreword' in the programme for the *Ballet Nacional de España*, 33rd Hong Kong Arts Festival, Hong Kong.
Turner, M. 1996. 'Conceptual Blending and Counterfactual Argument in the Social and Behavioral Sciences' in P. Tetlock and A. Belkin (eds.), *Counterfactual Thought Experiments in World Politics*. Princeton

University Press, 291-295.
Turner, M. and Fauconnier, G. 1995. 'Conceptual Integration and Formal Expression.' *Journal of Metaphor and Symbolic Activity* 10(3): 183-204.
Tylor, E.B. 1871. *Primitive Culture: Researches into the Development of Mythology, Philosophy, Religion, Art, and Custom*. New York: Brentano's.
van Sterkenburg, P. 2003. *A Practical Guide to Lexicography*. Amsterdam: John Benjamins.
Verschueren, J. 1999. *Understanding Pragmatics*. Beijing: Foreign Language Teaching and Research Press and Edward Arnold.
Web Concordancer. http://www.ed.ict.com.hk/concordance/.
Webster, J.J. and Chow, I.C. 2005. 'Mapping WordNet to a Relational Network' in *Proceedings of the Institute of Electrical and Electronics Engineers (IEEE) Natural Language Processing and Knowledge Engineering 2005* (IEEE NLP-KE'05). Wu Han, 718-722.
Wellenkamp. J.C. 1988. 'Notions of Grief and Catharsis among the Toraja.' *American Ethnologist* 15(3): 486-500.
Wierzbicka, A. 1999. *Emotions Across Languages and Cultures: Diversity and Universals*. Cambridge: Cambridge University Press.
Wiseman, N. and Feng, Y. 1998. 'Compilers' Preface' in *A Practical Dictionary of Chinese Medicine* (2e). Brookline, Mass: Paradigm Publications, iv–x.
Wong, H.L.S. 2006. *The Integration of Yue Dialect Words into Modern Written Chinese*. Master of Arts thesis, University of Hong Kong, Faculty of Arts (Linguistics).
Wordbank. *Collins COBUILD* CD-ROM. Glasgow: HarperCollins/Lingea, 2002.
World Factbook, The. https://www.cia.gov/library/publications/the-world-factbook/index.html/.
WordNet 3.0. Princeton University. http://wordnet.princeton.edu/.
Wu, F.H. 2003. *A Study of Written Cantonese and Hong Kong Culture: the Development of Cantonese Dialect Literature Before and After the Change of Sovereignty*. MA thesis, University of Hong Kong, Faculty of Arts (Linguistics).
Yamada, S. 2006. 'Students' Evaluation and Use of Web-based EFL Dictionaries' in M. Murata, S. Ishikawa, and Y. Tono (eds.), *English Lexicography in Japan*. Taishukan, 311-324.
Yamada, S. 2007. 'Gakushu Ei-ei Jiten no Shomondai' [Problems of EFL Dictionaries] in *Proceedings of the 36th Conference of the Japan Society of English Usage and Style*, June 16-17. Tokai University Fukuoka Junior College.
Yarowsky, D. 1993. 'One Sense per Collocation' in *Proceedings of the Advanced Research Project Agency (ARPA Human Language Technology Workshop 1993)*. San Francisco: Morgan Kaufmann, 266-271.
Yarowsky, D. 1995. 'Unsupervised Word Sense Disambiguation Rivaling

Supervised Methods' in *Proceedings of the Association for Computational Linguistics (ACL) 1995*. 189-196.

Ye, Z. 2001. 'An Inquiry into "Sadness" in Chinese' in J. Harkins and A. Wierzbicka (eds.), *Emotions in Crosslinguistic Perspective*. Berlin/New York: Mouton de Gruyter, 359-404.

Yip, P. 2000. *The Chinese Lexicon: a Comprehensive Survey*. London/New York: Routledge.

Yong, H. and Peng, J. 2007. *Bilingual Lexicography from a Communicative Perspective*. Amsterdam: John Benjamins.

Zgusta, L. 1971. *Manual of Lexicography*. The Hague/Paris: Mouton.

Zgusta, L. 1984.'Review of Studien zur Neuhochdeutschen Lexikographie Vols. I-IV H. Wiegand (ed.), (in *Germanistische Linguistik* 1979-1983)' in *Dictionaries* 6: 268-275.

Zhang, Y. 2004. 'An Empirical Study of Electronic Dictionaries and Translation Software' in Chan, 89-105.

INDEX

adjectives 42-46, 62, 92, 108, 144, 162, 168, 173, 175-179
adverbs 43-44, 108, 168, 173, 179
advertising 69-85
BBI Dictionary 184-188
bilingual dictionaries (see **dictionary: bilingual**)
blogs 213, 215-216
British National Corpus (BNC) 112-114, 175, 179, 186-188, 215, 243
Cambridge Advanced Learner's Dictionary 87-90, 93, 95, 99-100, 104, 109-110, 121, 139, 163
Cambridge International Dictionary of English 106, 193
Cantonese Chinese 19, 78-86, 117-127, 199
CD-ROM (dictionaries) 87-88, 92, 94, 97-98, 139-147, 193
Chambers Dictionary 215-216
Chinese (language) 9, 11-12, 17, 18, 20-21, 51, 68, 78, 121, 215-216
Chinese learner 25, 27, 30, 34, 36, 189-190
Chinese Learner English Corpus (CLEC) 184, 189
cognition and cognitive strategies 27, 151-157, 232
coinages: (see **neologisms**)
Collins COBUILD English Dictionary 34, 51-52, 105-107, 142, 162-164, 174, 178, 181, 185, 193, 240
Collins English Dictionary 123, 215-216
collocation 31, 33, 36, 41, 88, 92, 99, 104, 110, 112, 130, 142, 144-145, 163-167, 179, 183-191, 220, 240-248
combinatory dictionary 184, 187, 191
compilation of dictionaries (see **dictionary: compilation**)
computers and the dictionary (see **dictionary: IT**)
conceptual blending 14
corpus 13, 21, 35-36, 39-40, 42, 53-54, 66, 69, 75-76, 78, 80, 83, 105-115, 124, 141, 147, 175, 184, 208, 211, 215, 217-218, 239-249
Corpus of Asian Magazine Advertising 69-85
cross-referencing 144
dialect
    Cantonese 119-120, 199
    Chinese 16, 78, 80
    Hokkien 199
    Hong Kong 11
    Taiwan 11
dictionary
bilingual 14, 23, 25-28, 30, 32-37, 58, 97, 112, 134, 139-140, 145, 161-170,

177-178, 181, 194, 203-210
compilation 11, 23, 25, 122, 124, 213, 201, 207, 214, 217-222, 240
corpus-based (see **corpus**)
& corpus (see **linking dictionary and corpus**)
criticism 204-205, 208
ecology 213-223
examples 123-126, 143, 146, 183-191
history 204-205, 208, 210
& idioms (see **idiom**)
IT 9, 17, 63, 87, 115, 124, 141, 208, 213, 213-215, 218-219
learner 25, 26, 28, 30, 33, 34, 35-36, 87, 91, 105, 107, 109, 112, 115, 123, 139, 140, 157, 161-168, 173-181, 183-191, 193
& multimodality 249-258
paper/print 87, 93, 135, 141-144, 166, 219-223
problems 11, 26, 87, 93, 96, 249
research 12-14, 26, 31, 105-108, 113, 120-121, 130, 141, 149, 157, 161, 163, 168, 194, 203-204, 208, 210-211
structure 123, 207, 209, 245
survey 11, 29, 34, 90, 130-131, 137, 162
traditional 105, 141, 145, 194-195, 201
typology 183, 204-208, 214, 219-223
use 35, 89, 94, 96-97, 106-107, 130, 132, 139, 149-150, 153, 156-158, 162, 168, 170, 204, 208

English
    as a Native/first Language (ENL) 9, 36, 51, 121, 149, 166, 193-195, 197-198
    as a Foreign Language (EFL) 87, 95-97, 99, 107, 109, 112-113, 119, 149-150, 154-157, 189, 190-191, 195
    as a Second Language (ESL) 119, 149, 161, 162, 163, 168, 195, 198
ethnic(ity) 69, 71, 196-198
examples in dictionaries (see **dictionary: examples**)
flashback 253-255
Frame Logic 226-228
frequencies, word 20-21, 53, 100, 108, 121, 124, 142, 175, 184, 186, 188, 190-193, 218
grammar 39, 43, 48, 88, 93, 108-109, 135, 142, 147, 161-162, 168, 173-174, 180, 193, 199, 207, 225-226, 240
Hokkien Chinese 199
idiom 27, 31, 37, 57, 62-63, 73, 88, 97, 104, 122, 126, 135, 178, 181, 184-185, 190, 193, 205, 207, 250
interlingual lexicography (see **lexicography: interlingual**)
International Corpus of English (ICE) 215
International English Language Testing System (IELTS) 161-162
Internet 9, 17, 23, 63, 87, 145, 213-219, 222-223 (also see **dictionary: IT**)

Japanese (language) 75-76, 89, 91, 95, 111-112, 130, 131, 134, 142, 163, 177, 205-206, 213
Japanese EFL Learner Corpus (JEFLL) 107, 110, 112-115
Japanese learner 107, 110-111
Kamus Dewan 48
katakana pronunciation 142 (see **pronunciation**)
Kenkyusha's Luminous English-Japanese Dictionary 175, 178, 179, 180, 181
Lamb's Relational Network Theory 225
learner (see **dictionary: learner**)
L2 learner 30, 36, 105, 107-109, 112-113, 115
lemma/lexeme 39, 40, 43-46, 61-62, 173-174, 180, 184, 226-227, 229, 230, 234, 236, 240, 245
lexical entry (see **lemma/lexeme**)
lexicography
    Asian 69-70, 78, 107
    'bottom-up' 222 (also see **corpus**)
    cyber 222 (also see **dictionary: IT**)
    ELT 107, 121
    interlingual 203-211
    L2 107 (also see **L2 learner**)
    Malay 48
    meta 204-205
    narrative 251
    pedagogical 37, 105, 113, 115
lexicon 11, 39, 41, 44, 51, 58, 61-62, 67, 70-71, 200, 208, 218, 239, 247, 250, 258
lexis 42, 113, 121, 213-217, 225
linking dictionary and corpus 240
Longman Dictionary of Contemporary English 28-29, 31-37, 88-89, 91-99, 101, 103, 106, 109, 113, 142, 163, 174-179, 181, 185
look-up strategies 150-152
Malay (language) 39-49, 74, 76, 84, 196-198, 213
Malaysian English 199
MALEX project 39
memory strategies (see **cognition and cognitive strategies**)
metalexicography (see **lexicography: meta**)
metaphor(s) 15-16, 71, 74, 218
Monitor Corpus of Chinese Language Resources 21
monolingual dictionaries 140
monolingual learners' dictionary (see **dictionary: learner**)
morphology 15, 20, 23, 39-40, 43, 45, 62, 110, 174-176
multilingual 71, 73, 76, 198, 203, 206, 240
multimedia 251, 257
multimodal dictionary (see **dictionary: multimodal**)

native English speaker (see **English: as a Native/First Language**)
neologisms 9-23, 215-219, 223
Netspeak 213-214
New Oxford Dictionary of English 51-52, 206
NICT JLE Corpus 113
nouns 10, 22, 40-46, 95, 108, 110, 112, 124, 162, 165, 168, 173, 175, 176, 177, 213
ontology 46-47, 225-226, 229, 232
Oxford Advanced Learner's Dictionary of Current English 27-29, 32-36, 87-93, 95-99, 100-106, 121-123, 140, 162, 164, 174-175, 178-179, 181, 185, 193, 205
Oxford English Dictionary 194, 245, 253-257
parallel corpus 35, 59, 64
part(s) of speech 28, 36, 39-42, 48, 88, 90-91, 94, 95, 96, 99, 101, 104, 123-124, 126, 162, 173, 184, 213
pedagogy (see **dictionary: learner**)
phonology (sound patterning) 21, 84, 126, 167, 168, 178, 245
point-of-view shot 255-257
pragmatics 25-37, 162, 177
pronunciation 18, 21, 22, 79, 80, 88-89, 93-100, 104, 119, 120-121, 126-127, 142, 146, 161-169, 198, 207, 210, 220
register 26, 130, 161, 165, 167, 200, 207, 241
relational network 225-238
representativeness 217-218, 223
second language learner (see **L2 learner**)
semantic information 15, 19, 21-22, 25-26, 30, 36, 46, 48, 51-53, 62-63, 67, 75, 79-80, 124, 174, 176-177, 183-184, 207, 225-226, 229, 232-237
SEMCOR Corpus 239-248
Singapore(an) English 195, 198-201
Singaporean learner 194, 201
Singlish 197-198
Sketch Engine, the 106, 113-114, 186, 243, 247
syntax 39, 41-42 (also see **grammar**)
Systemic Functional Linguistics (SFL) 74, 231-238
Times-Chambers Essential English Dictionary 196, 201
translation 14, 19-21, 26-29, 31, 33, 37, 95, 111, 125, 140, 145, 149, 153, 157-158, 161, 203-204, 206-211, 250
typology of dictionaries (see **dictionary: typology**)
User-Friendliness Principle 191
verbs 10, 37, 40, 43-46, 88, 97, 108, 122, 144, 162, 168, 174-175, 232, 246
voice-over narration 254-255
Web, the 10, 11, 16, 17, 20, 87-89, 92-94, 222, 225, 236
word class (see **part of speech**)
word combinations 183-191 (also see **collocation**)

Word Sense Disambiguation (WSD) 239-240, 244-246
word sketch 241-244, 248
WordNet 52, 55-57, 124, 229-230, 232, 239-240
Xiandai Hanyu Cidian 59-60, 62, 215, 216

Editors and Contributors

Ian Castor **CHOW** teaches computational linguistics, Internet publishing, web content management, language and ideology, and Systemic Functional Linguistics. His research interests include ontology and linguistic resources interoperation, computational lexicography, Web mining, knowledge engineering and representation.

Wengao **GONG** has taught at the School of Foreign Languages of Yangtze University and also studied at the National University of Singapore. His research interests include computer-mediated communication, lexicography, and second language acquisition.

Reinhard Rudolf Karl **HARTMANN** specialises in dictionary criticism, dictionary history (tracing their varying traditions), dictionary typology (classifying their different genres), dictionary use, contrastive linguistics, translation, and bilingual lexicography. He has been involved in the founding of various associations of lexicography and helped pioneer the founding of the *International Journal of Lexicography* and *Lexicographica Series Maior*.

Azirah **HASHIM**'s research interests include English in Malaysia and in the region, academic and professional discourse, and language and the law. Projects that she is currently involved in include International Commercial Arbitration Practices: A Discourse Analytical Study, Electronic English in Malaysia, and Spoken Language and Social Activities.

Da-Fu **HUANG** teaches English, linguistics, and German. His research includes foreign language learning strategies, research methodologies, dictionary education, and translation.

Adam **KILGARRIFF** is Director of Lexical Computing Ltd., which has developed the Sketch Engine, a leading tool for corpus research. His scientific interests lie at the intersection of computational linguistics, corpus linguistics, and dictionary-making.

Gerry **KNOWLES** has developed the MALEX system, which is a corpus-based approach to the study of Malay, and is currently working on techniques to extract information on spoken Malay from speech wave forms. His research interests include phonetics and corpus linguistics.

Jacqueline **LAM** is an educational consultant and, until, 2007, taught English in the Language Centre of the Hong Kong University of Science and Technology. She collaborates with Lan Li and Tom McArthur on a set of biliterate and trilingual dictionaries of Putonghua, Cantonese, and English.

Lan **LI** has been teaching English at university level for over 20 years. She is engaged in a number of research projects relating to language corpora and lexicography. Her publications cover bilingual lexicography, English for Specific Purposes, sociolinguistics and application of corpus linguistics.

Saihong **LI**'s research and teaching interests include corpus linguistics, cognitive linguistics, lexicography, and language teaching. She has worked with K Dictionaries as chief editor of a Chinese learner's dictionary core and translator from English to Chinese.

Tom **McARTHUR** is founder editor of *The Oxford Companion to the English Language* (1992; Abridged 1996; Concise 1998) and of the quarterly journal *English Today: The International Review of the English Language* (Cambridge University Press, 1984–2007). He has published some 20 books on language, language teaching, lexicography, communication, yoga and Indian philosophy.

Julia **MILLER** has taught English to students in the UK, France, Portugal, and Australia. Her research interests include loanword studies, the English article system, English prepositions and pedagogical lexicography.

Zuraidah **MOHD DON** has research interests in ELT, pragmatics, corpus linguistics and prosody. Her current research includes a project on speech synthesis and recognition, the Malay Lexicon (MALEX), the Malaysian Corpus of Learner English (MACLE), the Corpus of Spoken English (COMEL), and the relations between language, power and ideology.

Andrew **MOODY** teaches sociolinguistics and varieties of English. His research interests include English in Asian pop culture and the development of World Englishes in Asia. His articles have appeared in, amongst others, *World Englishes*, *Asian Englishes* and *American Speech*.

Sadayuki **NAKANE** teaches English Linguistics and Philology. Among his many publications and roles, he has contributed as an editorial collaborator and emendator to the publication of the fourth edition of *Taishukan's GENIUS English-Japanese Dictionary*.

Vincent B.Y. **OOI** teaches and researches the theory and practice of the lexicon, computer-mediated communication and the Internet, corpus-based language studies, and varieties of English (especially Singaporean and Malaysian English). He has published with, among others, Oxford University Press, John Benjamins, Rodopi, and Continuum.

Shinya **OZAWA** has published research articles on the topic of teachers' beliefs on teaching in the language classroom, the reading and writing process, and literacy teaching methodology. His recent research interests also include the development of language learners' pragmatic competence.

Anne **PAKIR** teaches sociolinguistics and applied linguistics, and her current active research interests include language policy, language planning, World Englishes, English in Southeast Asia, and Baba (Peranakan) Malay. She serves on several editorial boards.

Jim **RONALD** has taken part in the COBUILD project and, among other interests, studied L2 vocabulary acquisition through dictionary use. L2 dictionary use remains a major research interest, together with learner independence and teacher development.

Monika **SZIRMAI** has taught English for more than 20 years in Hungary and in Japan. She has also taught French, Russian and Hungarian. Her research interests include corpus linguistics, CALL, lexicography, and translation studies.

Ismail **TALIB**'s areas of concern include narrative, stylistics, systemic linguistics, postcolonial theory, and postcolonial literatures and Singapore literature in English. His current active research interests involve narratology, Singaporean literature in English, the history of postcolonial literatures, and the relation between the English language and postcolonial literatures.

Peter K.W. **TAN** has wide-ranging teaching and research interests in pragmatics, discourse analysis, conversation analysis, language ideology and power, intertextuality, and generic approaches to texts. He is also particularly interested in the history and development of English (especially in relation to English in Singapore and Malaysia), onomastics and its interaction with language in dramatic texts and general stylistics.

Yukio **TONO** serves on a few editorial boards related to lexicography and corpora. His research interests include corpus linguistics, lexicography, L2 vocabulary acquisition, and language teaching. He has designed a well-known English conversation programme for the NHK television network in Japan, and has appeared on screen.

Jonathan **WEBSTER** has research interests in text linguistics, computational lexicography, and example-based machine translation. He is, among others, the general editor of the Equinox journal *Linguistics and the Human Sciences*, and co-chief editor of the two-volume *Continuing Discourse on Language: A Functional Perspective*.

Hai **XU** teaches Chinese linguistics and lexicography. His research interests include pedagogical lexicography, corpus linguistics, and cognitive linguistics.

Shigeru **YAMADA** has contributed to a number of dictionary projects, including *Kenkyusha New English-Japanese Dictionary* and the *Luminous Japanese-English Dictionary*. He serves actively on the boards of the Asian Association for Lexicography and Japan Association for College English Teachers Society of English Lexicography.

Ruihua **ZHANG**'s areas of specialisation include corpus linguistics, parallel corpora, and contrastive studies. She has published studies on contrastive-semantic and corpus-based perspectives on *xin* (heart) and *qing* (emotion/feeling).

Yihua **ZHANG**'s research interests include lexicography, semantics and translation. His research particularly involves the integration of cognitive linguistics and cyber-linguistics theories into lexicographical research, computational lexicography, and the multilingual dictionary generation system.